AUDITING AND CORPORATE GOVERNANCE

EXCLUSIVE PARTNER

Paradox
PUBLICATIONS GUIDE HOUSE
+91 8848074612 \ +91 7907367147

AUDITING AND CORPORATE GOVERNANCE

Dr. Umesh U

INDIA | UNITED KINGDOM | SWEDEN

AUDITING AND CORPORATE GOVERNANCE

by: Dr. Umesh U

■

RED'SHINE PUBLICATION PVT. LTD.
Headquarters (India): 88-90 REDMAC, Navamuvada,
Lunawada, India-389 230
Contact: +91 76988 26988
Registration no. GJ31D0000034

In Association with,
RED'MAC INTERNATIONAL PRESS & MEDIA. INC
India | Sweden | UK

■

■

ISBN: 978-81-960634-2-9
ISBN-10: 81-96063-42-3
DIP: 18.10.8196063423
DOI: 10.25215/8196063423
Price: ₹ 500
January, 2023 (First Edition)

■

The views expressed by the authors in their articles, reviews etc. in this book are their own. The Editor, Publisher and owner are not responsible for them. All disputes concerning the publication shall be settled in the court at Lunawada.

■

www.redshine.co.in | info@redshine.in
Printed in India | Title ID: 8196063423

PREFACE

The field of auditing and corporate governance has become increasingly important in recent years, as organizations and investors alike place a greater emphasis on transparency and accountability. The global financial crisis of 2008 served as a stark reminder of the consequences of poor corporate governance and inadequate oversight, and has led to a renewed focus on these issues.

Auditing, in particular, plays a critical role in promoting transparency and accountability in organizations. It provides assurance that financial statements are accurate and reliable, and that an organization's financial position and performance are being reported in a fair and honest manner. This, in turn, helps to build trust and confidence among investors, creditors, and other stakeholders.

Corporate governance, on the other hand, refers to the systems and processes that organizations use to govern their operations and ensure that they are being run in the best interests of shareholders and other stakeholders. This includes the roles and responsibilities of the board of directors, the management team, and other key players, as well as the policies and procedures that are in place to govern decision-making, risk management, and other key areas.

This book provides a comprehensive overview of the key concepts and practices related to auditing and corporate governance. It covers a wide range of topics, including financial reporting, internal controls, risk management, and the role of auditors and other stakeholders in ensuring that organizations are operating in a transparent and accountable manner.

The book begins by discussing the basics of financial reporting, including the different types of financial statements and the key accounting principles that underlie them. It then goes on to explore the importance of internal controls, which are systems and processes that organizations put in place to ensure that financial statements are accurate and reliable. The book also covers the role of auditors in providing assurance on the integrity of financial statements, and the standards and regulations that govern their work. The book also delves into the topic of corporate governance, including the role of the board of directors, the management team, and other key players in ensuring that organizations are being run in the best interests of shareholders and other stakeholders. It covers the policies and procedures that organizations put in place to govern decision-making, risk management, and other key areas, as well as the various codes of conduct and standards that are in place to promote ethical behaviour and good governance. Throughout the book, real-world examples and case studies are used to illustrate key concepts and practices, and practical advice is provided for those looking to build a career in accounting, finance, or management. The book also includes review questions and exercises to help readers test their understanding of the material.

In conclusion, this book is an essential guide for anyone interested in understanding and navigating the complex world of auditing and corporate governance. It is aimed at students and professionals who are interested in gaining a deeper understanding of these critical areas, and will be an invaluable resource for anyone looking to build a career in accounting, finance, or management. With its clear explanations, real-world examples, and practical advice, this book is an ideal tool for anyone looking to gain a deeper understanding of these critical areas and the role they play in ensuring that organizations are operating in a transparent and accountable manner.

- Dr. Umesh U

SYLLABUS

MODULE NO.	CONTENTS
1	**INTRODUCTION TO AUDITING:** • Meaning • Objects • Basic Principles and Techniques • Auditing and investigation • Classification of Audit • Management Audit • Proprietary audit • Performance audit • Tax audit • Social Audit • Environmental Audit • Audit Planning • Qualities of an auditor • Advantages and Limitations of audit.
2	**AUDIT PROCEDURES:** • Vouching: Definition, Features • Examining Vouchers • Vouching of cashbook • Vouching of trading transactions • Verification and valuation of assets and liabilities: Meaning, Definition and objects • Vouching v/s verification • Verification and valuation of different assets and liabilities.
3	**INTERNAL CONTROL:** • Internal Check • Internal Audit: Definitions, Necessity • Difference between internal check and internal control • Fundamental principles of internal check • Difference between Internal Checks and Internal

MODULE NO.	CONTENTS
	Audit • Special areas of audit: Tax audit and Management audit • Recent Trends in Auditing • Relevant Auditing and Assurance Standards (AASs) • Rights, duties and liabilities of Auditor • Audit committee • Auditor's report: Contents and Types • Auditor's Certificate.
4	**CONCEPTUAL FRAMEWORK OF CORPORATE GOVERNANCE:** • Corporate Governance: Meaning, Theories • Models and benefits of Corporate Governance • Board Committee's and their Functions • Insider Trading • Rating Agencies • Green Governance/E-Governance • Clause 49 of Listing Agreement • Class Action • Whistle Blowing • Shareholders Activism.
5	**MAJOR CORPORATE GOVERNANCE FAILURES:** • BCCI (UK) • Maxwell Communication (UK) • Enron (USA) • Satyam Computer Services Ltd. • TATA Finance • Kingfisher Airlines • Common Governance Problems Noticed in various Corporate Failures • Codes and Standards on Corporate Governance.

CONTENTS

MODULE - 1
INTRODUCTION TO AUDITING

Auditing – Meaning

The term "audit" refers to the process of verifying the accuracy of a company's financial statements and related accounting data. It's a methodical process where the entity's financial health is examined in detail. An "Auditor" is someone who volunteers to take charge of the inspection.

As part of this procedure, we examine whether or not our company is generating a profit. The corporation, its investors, the government, its creditors, its shareholders, and anybody else with an interest in the business should take the auditing process seriously. To make crucial business choices, they heavily depend on audit findings.

The essence of auditing may be summed up like this.

Definition of Auditing:

"Auditing is an examination of accounting records undertaken with a view to establishment whether they correctly and completely reflect the transactions to which they purport to relate."

-L.R.Dicksee

"Auditing is concerned with the verification of accounting data determining the accuracy and reliability of accounting statements and reports."

- R.K. Mautz

"Auditing is the systematic examination of financial statements, records and related operations to determine adherence to generally accepted accounting principles, management policies and stated requirement."

-R.E.Schlosser

To verify that all divisions are adhering to a standard method of recording transactions, an audit involves a thorough examination of all relevant books of account and a physical inventory count. It is done so that investors may have faith in the company's financial statements.

Both staff and department heads are qualified to conduct internal audits, but a company or an independent auditor must be hired to conduct external audits. The purpose of having the books of accounts audited and verified by an outside organization is to guarantee that no fraudulent activity or misrepresentation has occurred.

All publicly listed firms must have their books audited by a third party before they can release their quarterly results to the public.

In order to conduct an audit, what experience and training are required? Chartered accountants from the ICAI will do an impartial audit of any Indian organisation. Certified Public Accountants in the US have established guidelines (Certified Public Accountants).

As far as I can tell, there are four stages to an audit. First, the auditor and the client must agree on the scope of the audit and other conditions of engagement in a signed document.

The second step was to get everything ready for the audit, including a schedule and a list of entities that would be reviewed.

Where does the auditor's authority lie inside the organization? Due to the complexity of the audit, it might take anything from a day to a week to complete.

The findings of an auditor's review of a company's books and inspection of its principal financial statements are often documented in a report or otherwise created systematically.

The last and most critical part of an audit is analyzing the results. Throughout the report, the auditor's findings are laid out in full.

Assurance Concepts and Practices

Planning, candor, confidentiality, audit evidence, internal control system, expertise, competency, other people's labor, working documents, and legal frameworks are the foundations of auditing.

State of the Audit

The meaning of "auditing" has been clarified. The process begins with a review of the company's financial records and continues with a count of the available stock. The auditor then bases his judgment on his findings and evaluation of the company's financial records and issucs a report detailing his findings and recommendations.

Financial statements are produced in accordance with generally accepted accounting principles (GAAP), all regulatory obligations are met, and records are presented correctly, with all relevant information being reported.

Audits' Pros and Cons
Benefits of Auditing
1.   The most significant benefit of auditing is the confidence it provides to owners, investors, etc., about the truthfulness of their financial accounts.

2. Errors and fraudulent entries in the books of accounts are uncovered during the auditing process. Such mistakes are avoided because their authors are afraid of being caught.
3. During an external audit, the accounts are examined in great detail and a second opinion is provided to management on the company's financial health.
4. Because of the rigorous scrutiny, staff members are more likely to be truthful and take their responsibilities seriously while compiling reports.
5. When audited, financial statements gain trustworthiness.

Disadvantages of Auditing
1. Since auditing entails such a thorough evaluation of documents, it inevitably results in more expense for the business.
2. The audit reports serve as proof for adjusting the profit distribution accounts significantly.
3. The adjustments are targeted, and they annoy the workers.
4. As corporate laws are subject to change, audit outcomes are also subject to change.
5. Companies may get away with fraud since the audit report is accredited, and auditors will be compelled to commit crimes as a result.
6. Most small businesses do not see the need for an audit and instead do business as usual.
7. There is no assurance that the auditing report will be accurate since it is reliant on the customers' input.

In response to the need for auditing advice for integrated management systems, ISO released ISO 19011: 2002 in October 2002.

It provides thorough standards for assessing quality and/or environmental management systems. The hope is that by adopting this document, businesses will be able to save time, money, and effort by doing things like:

- Ensuring that everyone is on the same page on the goals of the quality or environmental audit.
- Making sure audit reports are properly formatted and include all necessary data.
- Reaching consensus on the desired outcomes of specific audits within the larger audit program.
- Using relevant criteria to assess the abilities of audit team members.
- Consolidating environmental and quality checks to cut down on unnecessary work.

The purpose of these principles is to help businesses streamline their auditing processes, regardless of the motivation for the audit itself (certification, internal review, contract compliance, etc.).

Therefore, it is quite beneficial to learn as much as possible about auditing.

Four essential decision/support tools for effective quality and environmental audit planning, execution, and assessment have recently been consolidated into a single standard.

- An elucidation of the foundational concepts behind management-system auditing.
- Auditor assessment and qualification standards.
- Direction for the administration of auditing initiatives.
- Instructions for doing either an internal or external audit.

The foundation of the standard is a collection of principles that may be used by anybody involved in an audit to improve the quality of their work. It is flexible enough to be used for auditing any kind of management system, since its emphasis is on the fundamental procedures of audit management.

Audits are highly valued as a management tool for ensuring that an organization's quality and/or environmental policy is being followed according to the guidelines set out in the International Standards (ISO) 9000 and ISO 14000 series. External certification/registration, as well as review and monitoring of the supply chain, are two examples of conformity assessment operations that rely heavily on audits.

This International Standard offers advice for overseeing audit programs, performing internal or external audits of quality and/or environmental management systems, and assessing auditors' abilities and performance. It is written with a wide audience in mind, including auditors, organizations implementing quality and/or environmental management systems, organizations conducting audits of quality and/or environmental management systems due to contractual obligations, and organizations certifying or training auditors, certifying or registering management systems, accrediting auditors, or standardizing conformity assessment.

This International Standard's recommendations are meant to be adaptable. Different organizations, with different sizes, types, and levels of complexity, and with different audit goals and scopes will have to employ these standards in different ways, as discussed throughout the article. The boxed language throughout this International Standard provides further instruction or examples on key issues. To some extent, this is meant to encourage the adoption of this International Standard by smaller businesses.

Auditing standards are outlined in Clause 4. These guiding concepts prepare the user for clauses 5, 6, and 7 and help them understand the fundamental nature of auditing.

The challenges of allocating responsibilities for managing audit programs, setting the audit program goals, coordinating auditing operations, and providing appropriate audit team resources are all addressed in Clause 5 of the provided guidelines on managing audit programs.

Choosing audit teams and performing audits of quality and/or environmental management systems are covered in Clause 6.

The evaluation of auditors and the competencies they need to have are outlined in Clause 7.

The user of this International Standard may choose to perform quality management system audits independently of environmental management system audits in cases when both systems are deployed simultaneously.

The auditing of quality and/or environmental management systems is the primary focus of this International Standard; however, the user may choose to modify or expand the information offered herein to apply to audits of other management systems.

The sole thing this International Standard does is provide users some pointers on how to go about creating their own audit-related criteria.

The recommendations in this International Standard may also be helpful to anybody else who has an interest in ensuring that products and services comply with applicable standards, rules, and regulations.

Clause 1- The scope of this Standard

This International Standard details auditing's foundations, how to run an audit program, how to check for quality and environmental management system compliance, and how to assess an auditor's skill set. It may be used by any business that needs to administer an audit program or perform quality and/or environmental management system audits, either internally or externally.

Clause 2: Standard Cnformances

ISO 19011: 2002 makes reference to the following two standards, both of which deal primarily with the foundations and vocabulary of the terms and words used in this standard.

Term definitions and introduction to ISO 9000:2000.

Words and phrases for environmental management; ISO 14050:2002.

Clause 3-Terms and definitions

In this part of the specification, fourteen different words are specified. You may find them in the "Key Words" section down below. However, the definition of audit as stated in the standard is reprinted here to explain the many kinds of audits.

An organization's self-declaration of compliance may be based on the results of an internal audit, also known as a first-party audit, which is done by or on behalf of the organization for management review and other internal reasons. A clear sign of independence, especially in smaller organizations, is the absence of any accountability for the auditing process.

As a side note, 2nd and 3rd party audits are also examples of external audits. An organization's clients or other stakeholders may commission a second party to undertake an audit on their behalf. An external, independent auditing organization, such one that provides registration or certification of conformance with the standards of ISO 9001 or ISO 14001.

Note 3: A combined audit is the phrase used when both a quality management system and an environmental management system are being evaluated.

Note 4: A "joint audit" occurs when two or more auditing firms work together to conduct a single audit.

Basic Principles and Techniques of Auditing

The auditing process is defined by the adherence to a set of guiding principles. This makes the audit a dependable and useful instrument for bolstering management's policies and controls, through which the business may get insight into how to boost its efficiency and productivity. The ability of independent auditors to arrive at consistent findings under identical conditions depends on the consistency with which audits are conducted, and this in turn depends on adherence to these principles. It is important for auditors to keep in mind the following guidelines.

a)   Professionalism rests, first and foremost, on a person's ethical behaviour. Integrity, secrecy, and discretion are also crucial in auditing.

b)   Honest and accurate reporting is required for a fair presentation. The audit operations are correctly reflected in the audit findings, audit conclusions, and audit reports. The report details the major challenges the audit team faced, as well as any outstanding differences of opinion between the audit team and the auditee.

Applying one's own skill, knowledge, and judgment in an auditing capacity constitutes

c) Due professional care: Due diligence is performed by auditors because of the gravity of the responsibility they have been entrusted with by their audit clients and other parties having a stake in the audit. Possessing the appropriate skill set is crucial. The audit itself serves as a basis for further principles since it is by definition objective and methodical.

d) Independence: The foundation upon which the audit's objectivity and fairness rest. It is not possible for an auditor to be biased or conflicted with an audit since they are objective third parties. To guarantee that audit findings and conclusions are founded only on audit data, auditors have an unbiased mindset throughout the audit.

e) Evidence-based approach is the reasonable way for arriving at trustworthy and repeatable audit results. The results of an audit may be checked. Given that an audit is undertaken in a limited amount of time and with limited resources, it is based on subsets of the available data. The reliability of audit findings is directly proportional to how well sampling is done. The remainder of this International Standard is built on the aforementioned ideas.

Managing an Audit Program

Depending on the size, kind, and complexity of the organization being audited, an audit program may consist of a single audit or many audits. These audits might be conducted for a wide range of reasons, and they could even include a combined or joint audit. (For more explanation, see Notes 3 and 4 to the Audit Definition in Section 3.1.

All the work that goes into figuring out what kinds of audits need to be done, how many of them, and how to get the resources needed to do them well and on schedule is also part of an audit program.

A company might have many auditing programs. Administrative control over the audit program should be delegated by the company's upper management.

Those in charge of the audit program must do two things:

a) set up the program and make sure it's being followed, monitored, reviewed, and improved; and

b) figure out what resources will be needed and make sure they're available.

Aims and Scope of the Auditing Program
A. The Reason for Conducting an Audit

In order to guide the preparation and execution of audits, it is important to define the goals of the audit program. Considerations like
a)   Management priorities,
b)   Commercial intentions,
c)   Management system requirements,
d)   Statutory, regulatory, and contractual requirements,
e)   The requirement to evaluate suppliers,
f)   Customer requirements,
g)   The requirements of other interested parties, and
h)   Risks to the organization can all inform these goals.

B. The Scope of an Auditing Initiative

The size, kind, and complexity of the organization being audited, as well as the following, will all play a role in determining the depth of the audit program to be implemented.
a)   the frequency of audits;
b)   the scope, objective, and duration of each audit;
c)   the number, importance, complexity, similarity, and locations of the activities to be audited;
d)   standards, statutory, regulatory, contractual requirements, and other audit criteria;
e)   the need for accreditation or registration/certification;
f)   the results of previous audits or the findings of a previous audit program review;
g)   Any language, cultural, or linguistic barriers.

Responsibility, Infrastructure, and Practices for Auditing a Program
Responsibilities of an Auditing Program

Someone or a group of people should be tasked with overseeing an audit program, and they should have a basic familiarity with auditing concepts like independence, objectivity, and due process. They need to know how to manage people and have a firm grasp on the commercial and technical aspects of the processes being audited. Those in charge of the audit program should:
a)   Determine the program's goals and scope,
b)   Designate roles and duties and provide necessary resources,
c)   Oversee the program's execution,
d)   Keep detailed records of all audit activities, and
e)   Assess its performance over time.

Program Resource Audit

The following factors should be taken into account when determining the audit program's resources:

a) The budget for developing, implementing, managing, and bettering audit activities;
b) Audit techniques;
c) Processes to achieve and maintain auditor competence and to improve auditor performance;
d) The availability of auditors and technical experts with competence appropriate to the particular audit program objectives;
e) The scope of the audit program; and f) the audit program's goals.

Methods for Auditing a Program

The following should be included in the audit program's procedures:

Planning and scheduling audits; ensuring the competence of auditors and audit team leaders; selecting appropriate audit teams and assigning roles and responsibilities; conducting audits; conducting audit follow-up, if necessary; keeping audit program records; monitoring the performance and effectiveness of the audit program; reporting to upper management on the overall achievements of the audit program.

All of the aforementioned steps may be accomplished with a single operation for smaller businesses.

Evaluation of Program Procedures

The following are some concerns that should be addressed in an auditing plan:

The Audit Committee is responsible for:

a) Disseminating the audit plan to those who need to know about it;
b) Coordinating and scheduling audits and other activities related to the audit plan;
c) Putting in place and maintaining a system to assess the performance of the auditors and their commitment to ongoing professional development in accordance with Sections 7.6 and 7.5;
d) Ensuring the selection of audit teams; e) supplying audit teams with the resources they need;

The Auditing Procedure Records

Evidence of the audit program's execution requires the keeping of records, such as those describing:

There are three types of audit documentation: a) records pertaining to individual audits, including audit plans, audit reports, non-conformity reports, corrective and preventive action reports, and audit follow-up reports, if applicable; b) results of audit program review; and c) records pertaining to audit personnel, including auditor competence and performance evaluation, audit team selection, and maintenance and improvement of competence. It's important to keep records and make sure they're secure.

Checking and Reviewing Auditing Procedures

Audit program implementation should be tracked and evaluated at regular intervals to see whether goals have been attained and where changes can be made to further enhance the program. Those in charge need to be informed of the findings. It's important to employ performance indicators to keep an eye on things like:

- the audit teams' capacity to carry out the audit plan;
- compliance with audit programs and schedules; and
- comments from audit clients, auditees, and auditors.

Examples of things to think about when reviewing an audit program include:

a)   trends and results from monitoring;
b)   adherence to procedures;
c)   changing needs and expectations of interested parties;
d)   audit program records;
e)   alternative or new auditing practices; and
f)   consistency in performance across audit teams in similar situations.

The audit program may be strengthened by implementing the findings of evaluations of the program.

Clause 6: Proceedings of the audit

This section provides instructions for organizing and carrying out audits as part of a larger program. The figure below gives a summary of common auditing procedures. The applicability of this rule is conditional upon the kind and breadth of the audit being performed and the planned use of the audit's findings.

Auditing and investigation

If you need to evaluate a company's financials for anything particular, you may conduct an investigation, which is a kind of examination or inquiry. The primary purpose of any examination of a company's finances is to gather evidence of wrongdoing. Rather than attempting to confirm the veracity of the claims, the inquiry will focus on gaining a better understanding of what really occurred.

A thorough investigation will include such steps as searching, observing, questioning, inspecting, etc. The inquiry may be thought of as a specialized type of auditing designed to serve a single objective. Experts perform an investigation in the same way they would an audit: in accordance with the organization's established norms. However, investigations inside a company are uncommon, not required, and so have no set time frame.

An inquiry, as contrast to an audit, is initiated by either an individual inside the business or the organization itself. An investigator is hired by the party seeking information about the firm, and the investigation is carried out in accordance with a certain scope and objective.

An outsider who is interested in joining the company or buying its stock might also commission an inquiry on their own behalf.

Investigation-related statutes

The Companies Act of 2013 establishes guidelines for corporate investigations. The Central government has the authority to designate any individual as an inspector for investigation under Section 210 of the Act, and these inspectors are responsible for carrying out the legal investigations that take place.

Under Section 211, the Central Government may establish an agency known as the Serious Fraud Investigation Office (SFIO) and appoint as many inspectors as necessary to undertake inquiries into allegations of fraud.

The investigative process and its requisite authorities

The method for the inquiry is outlined in Section 217 of the Companies Act. Once an inspector has been designated, he is free to begin looking into whatever preexisting conditions or arrangements are pertinent to the inquiry. Paragraph (Section 216)

The inspector has the authority to demand the retention and presentation of any and all records he deems relevant to the company's financial operations. In accordance with Section 217 of the Act, all company employees and officers are required to cooperate fully with the inquiry and give any help that may be reasonably required.

According to Sections 219 and 220 of the Act, the inspector is also authorized to undertake searches, seizures, and inquiries, including those involving affiliated businesses.

Finally, when an investigation is complete, the inspector must submit a final report to the federal government as well as periodic updates detailing the inquiry's progress. An investigation report may be used as evidence in court, and anybody found guilty of a crime on the basis of the report can be brought to justice. ([Paragraphs 223 and 224])

Auditing and investigating are two different processes.

Audits and investigations have some same ground in terms of their underlying principles, but there are significant differences between the two. Here are some of the main distinctions between audits and investigations:

An audit is a check of a company's financial records. A financial investigation, on the other hand, is a focused inquiry of a company's finances.

There is a distinction between audits and investigations in terms of their objectives. Audits are carried out to verify the veracity of records and detect any discrepancies. An investigation might be conducted for a variety of reasons, but it's usually meant to discover what went wrong.

Auditors conduct these inspections frequently because it is in their nature to do so and because it is required of all businesses. No one is required to submit to these probes; they are done only on rare occasions and for unique reasons.

The scope of an audit includes a review of all of a business's financial documents and statements. However, investigations only include reviewing documents that are directly related to the inquiry's goals and objectives.

Since the audits are comprehensive in nature, they may be considered to have a broad scope since they examine every aspect of the business. However, investigations are restricted in that they can only go so far into a subject and only examine things that are directly connected to the issue at hand.

The purpose of an audit is to determine the company's actual financial health (profit and loss, cash flow, investment rates, etc.) and market worth. The scope of the examination is limited to what is necessary to accomplish the stated goal, and has nothing to do with the company's actual financial health.

Audits are only performed by certified public accountants who have been licensed in accordance with the Chartered Accountants Act of 1949. Inspectors undertake the investigations; they need not be Chartered Accountants, but may be anybody from the public or the government.

Due to the fact that audits are often performed for a single fiscal year, the time frame for which they are done is also known. The length of time an inquiry takes might be longer or shorter than one fiscal year depending on the circumstances.

The auditor goes into the process with an open mind and no preconceived notions about what they may uncover. However, inquiries are often launched because of a preconceived assumption or the mere suspicion that a lapse or mistake has occurred.

Proof An audit does not collect absolute or undeniable proof. Instead, it relies only on the collection of compelling evidence, therefore it is not fool-proof. An investigative report may be used as evidence in a legal proceeding because it contains facts and figures that cannot be reasonably disputed.

BASIS	AUDITING	INVESTIGATION
Meaning	Examination of the financial records of a company for verification	Enquiry of the financial activities of a company for a special purpose
Objectives	Check accuracy and find errors	Find the cause of errors
Nature	Mandatory routine	Only for special purposes, occasionally
Subject matter	Examination of all the financial records of a company	Examination of only relevant records
Scope	Wide coverage of records	Narrow coverage of records
True position	Ascertains the true financial position of the company	Does not give the true financial position of the company
Conducting Authority	Only by Chartered Accountants	Any inspector appointed
Period	One financial year	No fixed period
Predetermined findings	Conducted without any predetermined findings	Based on some preconceived notion
Evidence	Gathers only persuasive evidence	Gathers conclusive evidence
Guiding Standards	Guided by standards set by the Institute of Chartered Accountants	No set of standards

The Institute of Chartered Accountants of England and Wales (ICAEW) standards should be used as a baseline for any audit. There is no framework directing the research in any way.

Classification of Audit

Accounting Audit Types

In accordance with the Business Structure 1. Statutory Audit: A statutory audit is an examination of a company's or government's financial statements and records that is mandated by law. A statutory audit is an examination of a company's financial records, such as its bank accounts, accounting entries, and transactions, to ascertain whether or not they fairly and accurately reflect the company's financial status.

Private enterprises, from sole proprietorships to multinational conglomerates listed on public stock exchanges, are audited independently of the government. Companies' goals are diverse since it is up to the proprietors to decide how to spend their income, often for pure capitalist exploitation.

First, an audit of the company's finances is required by law in India (the Companies Act) and will vary depending on who owns the company. To conduct an audit of a company's books, you need to be a chartered accountant. For the first time, the Firms Act of 1913 made it law that all publicly traded companies must have their financial records audited annually by a certified public accountant. Changes affecting the appointment, responsibilities, qualification, authority, and liabilities of a qualified auditor may be found in both the Companies Act of 1956 and the Companies Act of 2013.

It's possible that trust beneficiaries won't be privy to or even aware of the trust's financial records, which makes it important for the trustees to conduct an annual audit. The trust's property and affairs are entrusted to the trustees, who are charged with their care and management. The trust's financial records are kept in accordance with the trust agreement's stipulations. Beneficiaries get a share of the trust's revenue. Increased opportunities for financial wrongdoing are created. Both the trust deed and the Public Trust Act require an independent auditor to review the trust's financial records annually. The trust's audited financial statements provide an accurate and complete picture of the organization's financial standing.

Co-Operative Societies are formed under the Co-Operative Societies Act, 1912. Co-Operative Societies are subject to an annual audit of their financial records. It has rules and procedures for running these societies. A few of the states have embraced it as-is, while others have made modifications. The Co-operative Society's auditor has to be well-versed on the law that the organization is governed by. He must also review the society's bylaws to ensure that any changes that have been made to them over time have been properly recorded with the

Registrar's Office. The Co-operative Societies are excluded from the scope of the Companies Act. The accounts of the society must be audited annually by the Registrar of Co-operative Societies, or by a person authorized by him.

Audits of government agencies are included here, as are reviews of individual government agencies and departments. The Government of India has a specialized division devoted to accounting and auditing called the Accounts and Audit Department. The Comptroller and Auditor General of India is in charge of this office. Only government agencies are served by this division. A private company is not within the scope of audit for this division. It operates in accordance with all applicable laws and regulations.

When a proprietor has cause for proprietary worry, he or she may choose to have an audit performed on the business's books. The sole proprietor is responsible for determining the kind and extent of any audits conducted. The auditing process will be determined by the terms of the contract between the auditor and the business owner.

For clarity and peace of mind, partnerships conduct annual audits of their financial records. Financial accounts may be audited if the partners agree to do so in the partnership's deed. All of the partners vote to designate an auditor. The partners might change the joint agreement to alter the auditor's rights, obligations, and liabilities.

Audit of Individuals: If a person's sales, gross receipts, turnover, etc., exceed the stipulated limit, then that person is obliged to have their books of account audited by a Chartered Accountant, as well as acquire and present a Tax Audit Report under the Income Tax Act (1961).

Depending on When the Audit Was Performed

Interim Audit —

An audit performed between two yearly audits is called an interim audit. It might need a whole year's worth of accounting records being reviewed. This is sometimes done so that the board of directors may issue a dividend payment during the interim period. The objective might also be related to working with quarterly sales numbers.

The second kind of audit is the Continuous Audit, which is performed often yet consistently throughout the year. A continuous audit is a thorough review of all transactions performed by the auditor on a regular basis (every week, every two weeks, or once a month) during the whole trading period.

Third, a Final Audit is an audit that takes place following the end of the fiscal year. It is generally accepted that an audit that does not begin until after the end of the financial period and continues until completion is a final audit.

An audit of a company's balance sheet involves verifying its assets, liabilities, reserves and surplus, provisions, and profit and loss statement. In the context of this audit, the standard operating procedure involves going in the other direction. In order to verify an item, first it must be found in the balance sheet, and only then can the actual record be discovered.

Following Audit's Purposes and Criteria

One kind of audit is called a "management audit," and its purpose is to analyze a company's performance by carefully analyzing its management's choices and actions. The purpose of a management audit is to evaluate the effectiveness of the Company's management in directing and controlling its operations. This is done by looking at the management team's oversight of the business from multiple angles, including their goals, policies, procedures, structure, and controls. An audit of management looks at how an organization is run from the top down, including how resources are allocated and used, how plans are made both short-term and long-term, and what can be done to better the working conditions of employees.

Second, an internal audit means that the company's own employees are checking the books. The purpose of an internal audit is to provide a preventative and helpful service to management by evaluating the organization's accounting, financial, and other activities. This kind of control operates through gauging and assessing the efficacy of other forms of regulation. Accounting and finance are its primary focus, while it may also be appropriate to address issues of an operational nature.

As for the third definition, "Cost Audit" refers to the process of confirming that all cost accounts have been maintained accurately and that all cost accounting strategies have been followed. The purpose of a cost audit is to confirm the accuracy of the costing system, methods, and accounts, and to guarantee that the goals of cost accounting are being met.

Auditing the company's compliance with the Companies Act and other applicable legislation is the focus of the fourth kind of secretarial audit. Included in the secretarial audit report is a determination of

a) whether or not the books have been kept in accordance with the Companies Act of 2013.

b) Whether or not the requisite permissions were received from the central Government, the Company law board, or other authorities.

Lastly, the competent auditor who is independent of the company does the audit. It is the responsibility of the independent auditor to determine whether the financial statements are an accurate reflection of the company's financial health and performance. The primary purpose is to protect the interests of owners, stockholders, and those who aren't involved in the day-to-day business decisions.

Sixth, an audit of your tax paperwork is crucial in today's world to make sure you're not missing any money. The majority of a tax audit is spent looking at things like receipts, bills, bank statements, and investments. The concept of a tax audit was created in the modern era. As a result, auditing has advanced by one additional stage. Auditing tax paperwork guarantees their veracity and authenticity.

Management Audit

The purpose of a management audit is to evaluate the performance of the company's management to predetermined goals and benchmarks. This review may be conducted at any level of management.

Management audit, as defined by **L. R. Howard**, is "an inquiry of company from the highest level downward to discover if solid management prevails throughout, therefore permitting the most effective interaction with outside world and smooth operation of internal organization."

According to **Taylor and Perry**, "management auditing is a technique for assessing the efficacy of management across an organization," which "involves the investigation of a business by an independent body from the highest executive level downward, to ascertain whether sound management prevails through and to report as to its efficiency or otherwise with recommendations to ensure its effectiveness where such is not the case."

Management Audit's Field of Study

Management audit is broader than financial audit since it assesses not only the financial audit but the whole company. It is a system for measuring the efficacy of management at all levels. This means that the primary focus of management audit is on:

Audit the Management's Efficacy

The purpose of a management audit is to assess and rate the effectiveness of the organization's management at every level.

Management Principles and Policy Adoption and Implementation The goals of a management audit are to determine whether the management's defined principles and policies have been effectively executed.

Determine Distinctions: It finds inconsistencies in productivity compared to the norms established by management.

Investigate the Causes of Dissimilarities: An audit of the management system looks at why the organization hasn't been able to reach its goals.

Recommend Improvement Suggestions: It offers advice on how to enhance operations across a wide range of functional areas, including manufacturing, retail, wholesale, banking, human resources, and management.

Management Audit Aims

An audit of management's effectiveness and efficiency in carrying out its policies is known as a "management audit." As a result, it is a comprehensive review of the whole management structure, not just the books. There are goals of a management audit. Here, we'll go through these:

Effectiveness Verification

The purpose of a management audit is to evaluate the effectiveness of management and the policies that underpin it.

Provides Valuable Advice and Means to Improve Efficiencies Management audit draws attention to inefficiencies in all facets of management and provides helpful suggestions and ways to do so.

Management audits look at the efficacy of plans and policies by analyzing and assessing them to see whether they've been carried out correctly.

Profitability is boosted since management is provided with suggestions for improving the company's use of available resources.

Coordination is aided by the findings of a management audit, which may reveal hidden connections between tasks, assess who should take on what roles, and provide helpful advice on how to better coordinate the work of different departments.

Offers Excellent Advise The management auditor offers valuable advice to the top management on various policies and future courses of action by scanning the management efficiency and discovering the weak areas of different levels of management.

Management Audit and Its Significance

The benefits of a management audit for a business are several. A management audit is necessary to assess the efficacy of management at all levels of a growing firm. Below, we'll talk about the benefits and significance of management auditing:

The purpose of a management audit is to assess how well the company's management is carrying out its responsibilities and whether or not it is meeting the standards it has established for itself.

Examining the Programs, Policies, and Procedures: A management audit may shed light on the degree to which management's plans, policies, and processes have been put into action in order to achieve the organization's objectives.

Resources for Revising Strategies, Policies, and Procedures: Management audits allow for the modification and revision of firm strategies, rules, and processes to better suit the organization.

Decision-Making Tools: An audit of the management system evaluates the reliability with which key choices can be made and suggests ways in which weaknesses may be fixed.

Helps Get Loan: Lenders of large sums of money are interested in learning about a company's management and profitability. The results of a management audit will serve as a useful guide.

Helps Get Support: The government is interested in learning how effective and efficient an organization's management is before providing any kind of subsidy to that organization. The results of a management audit might be useful here.

Profitability is boosted since management is provided with suggestions for improving the company's use of available resources.

Management Audit's Weaknesses

1. The management audit is an examination conducted by and for the management. The management team is responsible for choosing the auditors. These auditors may be competent, but they might not.

2. The management auditors have extensive knowledge of the company and its workers. Personal details must not be ignored in audits of this kind. It's possible that some people may use this audit to even the score with others, while others will use it to help forward their own agendas.

3. They are more prone to accept the information at face value and not do thorough follow-up research.

4. The duration, operation, and breadth of such audits may be constrained by time and money restrictions.

5. The management audit team that has been chosen may not behave or seem like a team. The whole purpose of the audit

might be compromised by conflicting interests, attitudes, and inclinations.

Proprietary audit

Definition of Propriety Audit: "Audit concerning the decisions of the executives, with emphasis on public interest, financial discipline, basically to get audit satisfaction that such decisions are within the frame-work of sanction, authority, rule, procedure, and law made by a competent body," with the goal of "advising the executives either in preventing or reducing losses and increasing productivity or improving performance by timely reporting."

There is no way to lay down hard and fast regulations for auditing procedures to ensure they are conducted properly. Over and beyond the legality of the spending, a proper audit would also look at whether or not it was wise, faithful, and cost-effective. In addition to verifying that a necessary expenditure has been approved by the right people, it should look into why that expense was made and how much it was worth.

During the propriety audit, auditors should always make sure the following canons of financial propriety are followed:

a)   At first glance, the cost must not exceed what is reasonable given the circumstances. Every public servant has a duty to be as careful with taxpayer dollars as they would be with their own cash.

b)   It is inappropriate for a person in a position of responsibility to use his or her ability to approve expenditures in order to issue a directive that would benefit him or her in any way.

c)   Money from the government shouldn't go to a select few, unless these conditions are met:

d)   A little quantity of money is being spent, or

e)   Legal action or arbitration might be taken to recover the money,

The money was spent because it was the right thing to do according to generally accepted norms or practices.

Allowances (including travel allowances) should be controlled so that they do not provide an unearned financial benefit to their receivers.

In addition to examining individual transactions to look for signs of unlawful spending, an auditor undertaking a propriety audit should check to see whether the transactions approved are sufficient to meet all of the financial obligations arising from the numerous projects funded.

The following are some of the main areas an audit should look at to determine whether or not the impact of financial duties is enough or improper:

1. If the technical estimates or detailed program and cost schedules are being drafted and followed, and if they are not, whether there are sufficient explanations for the overruns, delays, etc., or whether they are the result of inefficient handling, wastes, etc., or incorrect preparation of the original estimates.

2. The second question is whether or not the overall cost of the plans has increased due to major delays that might have been prevented.

3. How much money was wasted, and whether this was due to a lack of coordination or other factors.

4. Have there been any consistent losses?

5. How do the outcomes and costs stack up against those of other areas or other public initiatives that used comparable schemes?

The extent to which the physical goals have been accomplished within the allotted or predicted time frame.

How close we are to achieving our long-term goals as a result of this investment.

These constraints are inherent to every propriety audit:

First, while making a call:

As the auditor reviews the CEO's every move in a propriety audit, the executive is less likely to act quickly and courageously. It slows down development and stunts creativity.

To follow the rules:

There is a tendency for the executives to become too conformist. It's not a guarantee that we'll hit our marks.

Punctuality:

The audit and report will be of little service if they are delayed. After suffering losses, submitting a report on a contract that is not lucrative will be pointless.

The following types of organizations are now reaping the advantages of a proper audit:

i. Corporations owned by the government, including those run by the federal and state governments. In addition to the required statutory audit, the Comptroller and Auditor General of India may follow his own set of principles and instructions to do a propriety audit with a focus on improving efficiency and saving money.

ii. Companies open to the public. According to the requirements of Section 227 of the Companies Act of 1956, a chartered accountant in practice within the meaning of the Chartered Accountants Act, 1949 also has some power to undertake such propriety audit in a restricted sense.

Instances when the Central Government has issued directives mandating a Cost Audit under Section 233B of the Companies Act, 1956, and where the company is required to keep detailed cost accounting records. An audit may be conducted, and a report covering all the relevant points can be submitted, by any Cost Accountant in practice within the terms of the Cost and Works Accountants Act, 1959.

The Comptroller and Auditor General of India oversees the propriety audit for government-owned businesses, with his Resident Audit Parties performing the bulk of the work through continuous audits, test audits, and audits performed by statutory auditors in accordance with his instructions and guidelines. This audit may be considered pretty effective.

For most limited liability businesses, the stockholders are dispersed geographically. They don't really have any influence or say in how the firm is run. Company policy is determined by the Board of Directors. Stockholders must have faith that their money is being handled responsibly.

A statutory auditor's duty under the Manufacturing And Other Companies (Auditors') Report Order, 1988 is to report on his findings from any investigations he conducts into the company's finances that are intended to prevent specified types of fraud perpetrated by those in charge. While these clauses certainly address some aspects of propriety, they do not provide complete protection. The audit is inadequate in this regard.

It is recommended that particular laws be developed to offer sufficient parameters for a propriety audit in this sort of organizations to promote the growth of a healthy corporate sector.

Any business that wants to maximize its efficiency, economy, etc., may have a propriety audit performed on it, regardless of its legal structure. Before accepting or instituting such an audit, however, the company should do a cost-benefit analysis to guarantee it is worthwhile.

Requirements for Propriety and Elements of Propriety in Reporting under Indian Company Law:

Propriety obligations and components of reporting are addressed under Sections 227 and 233B of the Companies Act, 1956.

The Auditor must inquire into the following matters about propriety in accordance with Section 227 (1-A) of the Act:

a)   Whether the Company's loans and advances based on security have been adequately secured and whether the conditions on which they were arranged are not adverse to the interests of the Company and its members.

b)   Whether the company's transactions that are only reflected in the books are really in the company's best interests.

c)   Whether or not a significant portion of the firm's assets, including shares, debentures, and other instruments, have been sold at a price lower than at which they were obtained, if the company is not an investment company within the meaning of Section 372 or a banking company.

d)   Whether or not the business's loans and advances have been classified as deposits (d).

e)   If one's own money has been taken out of their earnings.

If the company's records indicate that any shares were issued in exchange for cash, but no cash was actually exchanged for those shares, then the company's books and records are inaccurate and deceptive.

The auditor is obliged to inquire in all of the aforementioned situations, but is only obligated to report if he receives an adverse response. Obviously, his investigations should be crafted to prevent common forms of wrongdoing by firm executives. The ethics of the business are the basis for his audit.

In addition, the auditor must file a report in accordance with the Company Law's Manufacturing and Other Companies (Auditors' Report) Order, 1988, which addresses several aspects of appropriateness. When things seem bad, he turns in his report.

Section 227 (4-A), which deals with reporting propriety, mandates that the auditor state whether or not the following situations are favourable in his report:

The first question should be, "Does the firm make timely deposits of the Provident Fund dues with the proper authority?" The Company is bound by law, societal norms, and good business practice to make timely deposits of the provident fund contributions with the relevant government agency. Workers would be harmed and treated unfairly if this commitment was not met on time or in a regular fashion. Disclosure of such misconduct is unquestionably founded on ethics. The auditor's report should be more precise regarding the magnitude of the irregularity by drawing a direct line between the length of the delay and the amount of provident fund dues.

To what extent the prices paid to subsidiaries and other parties in whom the Directors have an interest are appropriate in comparison to the rates charged by other suppliers for stores, raw materials, or components with a value exceeding ten thousand rupees for each kind.

The goal is to prevent employees from misusing business resources for their own gain.

Thirdly, we look at "whether the procedures taken by the Company for recovery of the principal amount handed out as loans or advances in the type of loans and the collection of interest, if any thereon, are fair and regular." Some workers may be gaining advantages at the expense of the company as a whole. A report by the auditor on such improper behaviour must therefore be based on propriety.

The rate of interest and the terms and circumstances of any loans taken out by the company, whether secured or unsecured, from businesses or other parties according to Sections 301 and 370 (1) (c) of the Act, and whether such loans are prima facie harmful to the interests of the company. The auditor is responsible for making an objective determination of reasonableness based on factors such as the degree of urgency, the availability of alternative financing, the interest rates in effect, the value of the securities pledged, and any other relevant factors.

The Cost Auditor's report, which addresses the following issues, is lawful under Section 233B of the Companies Act.

a)   Things that seem fundamentally incorrect or illogical to him,
b)   Cases in which careless or wasteful use of business cash has occurred.
c)   Circumstances whereby manufacturing costs, etc., might have been reduced by taking preventative measures that were not taken.

Performance audit

What is a Performance Audit?

An organization's performance may be evaluated objectively via a performance audit. This kind of audit is used to check whether or not certain departments or activities are effectively carrying out their duties. Since the majority of government organizations get federal financing, performance audits are often connected with them.

Typically conducted by government bodies, a performance audit is an impartial examination of how an organization functions.

The purpose of these reviews is to assess the efficacy of the aforementioned initiatives and to recommend necessary adjustments.

The United States Government Accountability Office establishes auditing requirements (GAO)

An audit of performance may include a wide range of issues, from operational excellence to adherence to regulations.

Appreciating the Value of Performance Audits

A performance audit is an examination of a government program's efficiency and effectiveness with the intent of making changes in order to improve those metrics. Generally Accepted Government Auditing Standards (GAGAS) define a "program" as anything related to or operated by a government agency.

Audits are conducted according to criteria established by the United States Government Accountability Office (GAO), and its primary purpose is to provide unbiased information that may be utilized to save costs and enhance operations.

Different audits may have different goals. Efficient use of resources, a well-designed plan, and adherence to laws and regulations are all things that might fall under this category. The purpose of an audit might range from identifying potential areas of fraud to identifying inefficient procedures that are preventing a program from reaching its goals.

The Need for a Performance Review

The GAO establishes requirements for the performance audit in three categories: overall, on the ground, and in writing.

Fundamental Principles

Professional judgment, quality control (QC), and auditor and audit process competency are all examples of topics that fall under the umbrella of "general standards." The auditor must be objective, competent, and subject to internal quality controls in order to meet general criteria.

Standards in the Field

Field standards pertain to the processes of preparation, evaluation data collection, and documentation. This section will describe the goals, why they are important, and how they will be attained.

Norms for Reporting

Guidelines for reporting focus on the accuracy and clarity of the report's presentation of its findings. These describe the audit report's structure and specify the recipients and channels for the report's dissemination.

Rewards of Conducting Performance Audits

The results of a performance audit are reported to the relevant authorities after they have been compiled. The results will be used to make any necessary adjustments to existing procedures that will facilitate the accomplishment of the set objectives. A performance audit is conducted after an audit has been completed to see whether any of the recommendations made by the auditor have been adopted and if the company is better off as a result.

To ensure that public funds are being used properly, performance audits are essential. Through performance audits, public agencies are held accountable for meeting the objective criteria set for them in carrying out the duties they have been given by law.

To ensure public services and programs are run efficiently, legally, and within budget, audit reports are reviewed by appointed and elected authorities at the highest levels. Results should be made public so that voters may make informed judgments about how to use their tax funds.

Compliance Audits

The corporate world also uses performance audits, which have many of the same objectives.

A performance audit is a kind of audit used in the investment industry where an independent accounting company checks to see whether a manager's reported performance data are accurate. Global Investment Performance Standards are the CFA Institute's defined performance criteria (GIPS). Even though they aren't required, they assist make sure all investment information is out in the open.

Tax audit

The purpose of a tax audit is to check that a taxpayer's books are in order and comply with the requirements of the Income Tax Act 1961. The Indian government now requires all taxpayers to submit to random audits.

The yearly gross turnover or revenues must be audited for tax purposes if they surpass a certain threshold under the Income Tax Act of 1961. A tax audit as described by Section 44AB of the Income Tax Act, 1961 is carried out by a Chartered Accountant.

Those listed in Section 44AB as "applicable for tax audit" are subject to audit.

The company's annual gross revenue exceeds 10 crore.

According to Section 44AB of the Income Tax Act, an assessee must submit to an audit if his or her yearly gross turnover is more than Rs. 1 crore.

Professional Annual Gross Income > 50 Laces

This process is available to Assessees whose annual gross income from their occupation is more than fifty million rupees.

Tax Audit Goals

The following are some of the main goals of the tax audit:

1. The tax auditor may then attest to the accuracy of the books of account.
2. Tax auditors are required to disclose any anomalies or irregularities they find after conducting a thorough examination of the books of account.
3. The major objective of this audit is to compile a report that satisfies the criteria set out by forms 3CA, 3CB, and 3CD. All of the foregoing forms must be filed, but an audit of the taxpayer's books and records is also necessary to guarantee that the latter correctly reflect the former's income and allowable deductions.
4. It is costly and time-consuming to conduct a yearly audit. Due to provisions in the Income Tax Act, an audit of a taxpayer's books is required of all those who are deemed to be "qualified Assessees." Tax Audit is performed in India by a tax consultant (Chartered Accountant).
5. It has the potential to boost a company's bottom line.
6. An audit lends trustworthiness to a report that is sent to stakeholders including workers, consumers, suppliers, investors, and tax authorities.
7. The Audit ensures investors that the financial statements are a true and fair reflection of the company's financial situation.

Tax Audit Varieties

The many forms of tax audits are described here.

1. The taxpayer's place of business is visited in a field audit. The auditor will require the records, and the taxpayer will have to furnish them.
2. In-House Audit

   The IRS Audit is conducted at the IRS Headquarters. The tax payer must have the necessary paperwork on hand. The taxpayer will get a letter from the IRS Office outlining the required paperwork.

3.   Evaluating Auditing Procedures Via Correspondence
        In this case, the IRS writes a letter to the taxpayer, asking for the missing papers or anything else that would shed light on the tax returns. The sole need for the taxpayer is to submit in the necessary paperwork.
4.   Accounts That May Be Subject to a Tax Exam
        Individual/Proprietorship
        Essential documents needed for a tax audit of a hindu undivided family business, partnership firm, association of person, or local authority

Required Tax Audit Documents
Required Tax Audit Report Documents

Assessor's Street and City Documentation proving the payment of indirect taxes, such as the assessee's Permanent Account Number (PAN) or Aadhaar card.

Assessee is a person for income tax purposes according to Section 2(31) of the Income Tax Act of 1961

Section 44ab, applicability to the prior year and the assessment year

Business characteristics and any resulting alterations

If the Assessee filed Form 10-IB/IC/ID and elected the tax and reporting provisions of Sections 115BA/115BAA/115BAB, then:

Information Required from Books of Accounts for a Partnership or AOP Under Section 44AA

Whether or whether there is a profit or gain on the P&L (as determined by the presumption scheme of Sections 44AD, 44ADA, 44AE, 44AF, 44B, 44BB, 44BBA, 44BBB, Chapter XII-G, First Schedule, or any other applicable law).

Previous year's accounting approach and any adjustments made

Is there a need to make a change to the profit and loss account to meet ICDs U/s 145 requirements? (2)

Formula for determining the value of stocks at year's end

The specifics of the underlying capital asset that was exchanged for shares, if any

Acquiring Capital

Specifics of Decay

Amount allowable under ITA 1961 sections 32,33, and 35

The sum paid or received by workers.

Total amount that was charged to the P&L.

Total interest due under Section 23 of the Micro, Small, and Medium-Sized Enterprises Act of 2006

Any amount disbursed to individuals under Section 40A 2 (b)

Taxable income

Considered a Gain

Profit subject to taxation Amount referred to in Section 43 B

Accompanying the Assessee's certificate stating the identical Sum mentioned u/s 43B should be the specifics of the loan or deposit amount.

An accelerated loss or depreciation.

Profit-sharing tax

Financial synopsis for taxes

Revenue to Expenses Ratio

Important Tax Audit Documents Management Representation Letter Appointment Letter for Scope Determination

A complete list of all associated parties and all business dealings

An unfavorable weight distribution

Receipts and Balance Sheets Authorized by the Owners

Legal Requirements

Estimation of Liabilities (including Potential Future Liabilities)

A Few Remarks on the Business World

Estimated Depreciation Report

Documentation of capitalization of revenue expenditures and acquisition of assets

Nature of Unusual Items and Their Disclosing

Verification of a Bank Balance

The Bank Statements

Balance verification with major miscellaneous debtors and creditors

Quantitative statement of input and outflow of funds for the whole year and inventory valuation

Disclosure of accounting procedures and notes to the accounts

Retail and Wholesale Invoice Examples

Ratio analysis

Auditing a company's taxes is a routine operation.

The process of an auditing tax returns consists of the following steps:

Election of a Tax Auditor

Step one is to hire a tax auditor. The auditor may be the company's own Certified Public Accountant or an Internal Revenue Service employee.

Process of Filing the Form and Supplying the Auditor with the Required Materials

The next thing to do is to send the necessary paperwork to the tax auditor together with the completed form.

Auditor Verification of Records

After the taxpayer has completed the required paperwork, the auditor will double check all of the crucial information and documentation. If the auditor needs further information regarding the taxpayer's transaction, they may request it.

The Audit Report Preparation Process

The auditor then compiles all of the evidence into an audit report. The audit report is evidence that the taxpayer has followed all tax regulations.

Program of Assumptive Taxation Per Section 44AD of the Criminal Code

Companies with yearly sales below Rs 2 crore are eligible for this program.

Books of Accounts need not be kept as per Section 44AD.

It is predicted that your net income will be 8% of your total revenue.

Payments are received in full through digital means.

The percentage of sales used to determine net income ranges between 6% and 8%.

If the Assessee elects presumptive taxation under section 44AD, he must continue to be audited in accordance with the same provisions for the next five fiscal years.

To take advantage of these programs, you must submit Form ITR 4.

Section 44ADA's Presumptive Taxation Scheme

This plan is geared at occupations with an annual gross income of less than Rs 50 lakhs.

In accordance with Section 44ADA, it is not required that accounting records be kept.

When calculating a taxpayer's net profit, half of their total revenue is used as a benchmark.

If a taxpayer chooses Presumptive Taxation under Provision 44ADA, the taxpayer must continue to audit under that same section for the following five fiscal years.

Advice on Surviving a Tax Audit

Any endeavor pursued for monetary gain is considered to be selfish. Profits should only be made in a moral and ethical manner. To have a successful Tax Audit, try doing the following:

The Income Tax Act of 1961 makes it a requirement that businesses keep accounting records.

Chapter IV requires the determination of gain or profit.

Possibility of deducting losses against taxable income

Be sure to include your taxable income and any deductions you were able to take in your tax return.

When conducting a tax audit, what exactly does "Turnover" include?

The Turnover during a fiscal year includes duty drawbacks received after export sales.

If excise tax is included in turnover, it should be debited in the profit and loss statement. Similarly, interest revenue gained by moneylenders or foreign exchange income acquired by an exporter are considered to be a part of turnover in a fiscal year or Advance received and lost from consumers.

When doing a tax audit, what doesn't count toward Turnover?

Moves involving the Purchase or Sale of Physical Assets

Investment gains realized via asset sales

Income from Renting Out a House or Storefront

Money received as interest or refund of costs.

In the long run, it benefits the company's reputation.

A Tax Audit's Constituents

Form 3CA or 3CB, whichever is applicable, is the report format used by the tax auditor, and it is presented in this case where:

In the event that a company owner or professional is already required to submit to an audit of his or her financial records by virtue of another legislation, he or she must submit Form No. 3CA.

If you own a company or practice a profession and are not required to submit to an audit of your financial records under any other legislation, you should file Form No. 3CB.

The Date of Audit for Tax Purposes

Any person or people who are required to file an income tax return under Section 44AB must have their books audited and acquire the audit results no later than September 30 of the tax year in question.

Costs associated with submitting a Tax Audit Report late or not at all

The following penalty applies to any taxpayer who fails to complete the audit:

0.5% of Rs 1,500,000 in sales, turnover, or gross revenues

In what ways does Corpbiz facilitate its client's success during tax audits?

Corpbiz's qualified and seasoned business consultants will help you through the full Tax Audit process. Corpbiz offers a variety of tax audit services to aid its clients.

Good examination of the regulations and financials, answering any of your questions concerning the audit.

Taking the necessary steps in documenting a project and analyzing reports and financial figures.

Conducting a thorough study of the company's business practices and tax filings to ensure compliance with all regulations.

Makes certain that the audit services are valued as a long-term investment.

Social Audit

Depending on who you ask, the word "social audit" might mean a few different things. For most people, this is the single most important factor in determining whether or not a corporation is doing its part to contribute to society. In the eyes of specialists, however, it is a methodical analysis of a company's contribution to the overall well-being of society.

There are several contexts when social auditing becomes necessary. The company sacrifices social and environmental well-being for the sake of increasing profits for its stockholders. Their prices are not reflective of the true cost since many of them do not factor in the societal costs of such negative ramifications. Companies are doing it more often because of intense competition. However, if society's greater interests are to be protected, social good must be taken into account.

Like any person, the firm has responsibilities to act in a socially responsible manner. It can't turn its back on moral principles or disregard real-world constraints. Managers should answer to more than just shareholders for their actions. Nowadays, businesses should aim to maximize their resources for the greater good of society. Profit may still be important, but it shouldn't be the primary driving force. The corporation must realize it has a duty to act in the public interest and advance the common good.

Businesses have a social responsibility to spread the wealth created by economic expansion. In addition, the goodwill and excellent image established over the years thanks to the company's social care proves to be a benefit for them in the long term, particularly amid environmental difficulty.

Purpose and Aims

Traditional economic and technical values are seen as sub-systems inside the wider social system in an effort to facilitate social audit. Generally speaking, the scope of a social audit will include the following:

i.   Ethical Problems: They provide a framework for thinking about what's good and wrong in every particular circumstance. Unethical behavior is the finest way to illustrate ethical principles. Price discrimination, unfair commercial practices, consumer deception, idea theft, and breach of contract in the workplace are just a few instances.

ii.   Equal treatment in the workplace and a fair justice system inside the business are two more important social issues that are analyzed in a social audit. Organizational hiring choices should be based on merit and competence, not on artificial quotas based on factors like color, religion, or gender.

iii.   People want more out of life than just a safe, healthy, and humane workplace. iii) Work-Life Balance. Employees would like a more responsible workplace that offers opportunities for professional development, autonomy, and a fair compensation structure. Considering the difficult circumstances to which today's workers are often subjected, there is also an increasing need for employee support programs.

iv.   Consumerism: Businesses should prioritize their customers since they are the reason for their existence. It is the primary responsibility of businesses to meet the demands of their customers by providing them with the necessities they need at a reasonable price, in a timely manner, and with a satisfactory level of quality. However, many Indian items are unsafe, and customers end up paying for the misdeeds of corrupt and dishonest business organizations.

v.   Environmental Protection: In response to the increasing water, air, and environmental pollution caused by a wide range of enterprises, there has been a growing public outcry demanding "environmental protection" at any cost.

RESPONSIBILITY AND CSR IN BUSINESS

The public's rising expectation that businesses not only announce CSR pledges but also create systems to manage, execute, and rigorously review and report on progress related to those promises is one of the most important recent developments in the subject of CSR. The term "corporate accountability" refers to the structures put in place by a firm to provide the guidelines, metrics, and procedures necessary to oversee all of its endeavors. Companies are now held not just responsible for their own performance but also for that of their business partners and other players throughout the company's value chain, an expectation that has grown significantly in recent years. Effective processes for improving accountability usually enable a firm to be inclusive, responsive, and involved with its stakeholders, but the mechanisms a company employs to show accountability are various and need to alter and expand as a company matures.

Companies are now being held more and more accountable for their actions in non-financial sectors of society, such as corporate ethics, diversity, marketplace behavior, governance, human rights, and workers' rights, in addition to the more conventional areas of financial and environmental performance.

In many parts of the world, social issues are now ascendant, and these qualitative, complex issues are likely to be the ones against which companies find it hardest to measure and verify performance. This interest in the interrelationships between issues will also increase the complexity of the corporate accountability debate.

Management systems that are both efficient and transparent may aid businesses in creating environments where employees actively promote and reap the benefits of corporate social responsibility (CSR). To that end, several businesses are strengthening board-level responsibility for CSR performance. As a result, the board's composition may shift, its approach to social and environmental concerns may alter, and the board's ability to meet its obligations to shareholders and other stakeholders may improve. Some businesses have even gone so far as to establish a new management role whose only duty is to monitor the company's CSR initiatives from top to bottom. Finally, many businesses are making efforts to incorporate CSR performance accountability into their long-term planning as well as their day-to-day decision-making by, for example, reevaluating their product and service design processes and revising their methods of recruiting, retaining, and rewarding employees.

Today, calls for greater corporate responsibility come from all corners of society. This is seen by the growing popularity of market indexes focused on sustainability as well as by consumer pressure for product certification and labeling. This call for more corporate responsibility stems from the belief that businesses may and should be more open with their operations and results in terms of social responsibility, environmental impact, and bottom line growth. Recent occurrences have contributed to the loss of confidence granted to corporations, which has led to these heightened expectations. Companies are under increasing pressure from their stakeholders to provide information about the effects of their activities, initiate conversations with those stakeholders, and address the issues that arise during such conversations. Companies in positions of leadership are also thoroughly exploring the worth of different sorts of assurance that might back up their reporting efforts with the goal of bolstering the veracity of the information given.

Spread of Guidelines for Environmental and Social Reporting: A number of groups and efforts are working to provide uniform guidelines for reporting on social and environmental impacts, so that interested parties may more readily compare businesses' results across locations, industries, and national boundaries. In this regard, the Global Reporting Initiative (GRI) stands out as the preeminent worldwide reporting standard for voluntary adoption by organizations reporting on the economic, environmental, and social dimensions of their operations, goods, and services. Companies, NGOs, accountancy organizations, business associations, and other stakeholders from all over the world actively participate in the ongoing development of the GRI's reporting guidelines through the Coalition for Environmentally Responsible Economies (CEREs), which is convened by the UN Environment Programme in partnership with CEREs. The Ethos Institute for Social Responsibility in Brazil, for instance, has established a set of indicators to assist businesses in incorporating CSR into their management processes and monitoring their development, providing an example of a more localized norm. As of the end of 2001, Ethos has received reports from 71 Brazilian businesses detailing their performance across 35 variables related to values and transparency, workplace, environment, suppliers, consumers/customers, community, government and society, and other business activities.

SOCIAL AUDIT METHODS

There are many different kinds of social audits, some of which are described here.

1. *Observation of Social Procedures Audit*

It seeks to evaluate the efficiency of the organization's efforts, particularly those that are focused on achieving broader societal goals. In this scenario, executives at large corporations strive to take a hard look at their processes. There are four phases to the procedure:

i. Determine what prompted the company to launch a social auditing initiative; i

ii. Detail the program's desired outcomes; and

iii. Explain how the company intends to achieve those outcomes.

iv. Compare the actual results to the intended outcomes via a qualitative assessment of the two

2.   *Auditing the social impact of your company's finances*

The traditional financial data is shown with social activity data in these financial statements. Management consultants About Associates suggested include both social assets and social obligations, liabilities, and equity in the traditional balance sheet format. Social benefits, social expenses, and net social income from corporate activities should all be shown in the income statement.

A number of people have voiced concerns that this strategy might lead to more complexity and difficulty in grasping the subject at hand.

3.   *Audit of Macro and Micro Social Indicators*

In order to conduct this kind of audit, the company's performance on several social indicators (micro indicators) must be weighed against the broader, more general trends in those indicators. Health, safety, education, affordable housing, reduced risk of accidents and pollution, etc., are all examples of societal expectations that fall under the umbrella of macro social issues. Company performance on the issues tracked by macro social indicators may be evaluated using micro social indicators.

The lack of trustworthy macrosocial indicators is a major flaw of this method. Does the availability of more health clinics for starting a family suggest improved healthcare? Further, it is not simple to describe whether the company's particular acts have genuinely enhanced the quality of life of a community; such actions may eventually be branded as unimportant, minor, and sometimes useless. This method is useful for every business because it provides a reasonable foundation for assessing the positive impact it has on society.

4.   *Evaluation of Social Performance*

The social performance of socially responsive corporations is routinely measured, evaluated, and ranked by a wide variety of interest groups in industrialized nations. These organizations include churches, colleges, mutual funds, and consumer advocates. Companies that make proactive social initiatives and gain public goodwill are identified via regular opinion polling.

5.   *Societal Evaluation in Part*

In this example, the corporation commits to measuring one facet of its social performance (such as the environment, energy, or human resources) because it either places a high priority on that facet or because that's where its social efforts are currently focused:

Companies in industrialized nations not only comply with legislation, but also aggressively research ways to recycle trash into valuable goods, thanks to the rigors of environmental auditing. A report detailing the unit's approach to addressing critical environmental challenges is compiled by an internal committee. In order to verify compliance with air/water pollution measures, hazardous waste discharge, and safety laws, an external auditor will typically reexamine this report.

Audits of energy production, use, and conservation are conducted with the purpose of reducing strain on finite energy supplies.

Personnel Resource Accounting (HRA) Human resource accounting is predicated on the idea that people are valuable assets and need to be treated as such in financial statements. Using traditional systems of bookkeeping, profits are understated since investments in people are treated as operational expenditures. When calculating costs and income, companies often overlook the present worth of their human capital, leading to an inaccurate representation of the company's financial health.

6.   *In-Depth Inspection*

It seeks to quantify, validate, and assess the organization's overall performance, including its CSR initiatives. It places more emphasis on managerial structures than on incidental details. Its goal is to assess the reliability of procedures and data used to make business judgments.

Challenges of Social Auditing

There are a lot of obstacles to a successful social audit, and its scope is unclear. It might be confusing to determine which tasks should be included as "social" and which should be ignored if we list everything a company does in a certain time period, like an accounting year. After all, most business operations may have social significance in one way or another. To prevent this, we must place significant constraints on the'scope of social audit,' which means focusing solely on activities with demonstrable social benefit. It's not always easy or correct to turn the needs of different stakeholders (workers, consumers, shareholders, the public, the government, etc.) into "social rhetoric." The 'setting of yardsticks' for assessing the cost and success of activities presented in the social audit is another significant challenge, as previously mentioned.

TRANSPARENCY AND REPORTING: IMPORTANT NEW DEVELOPMENTS

The Expansion of CSR Practices in Major Corporations: Because of CSR's rising profile, businesses are being held to a higher standard of accountability with regards to their governance, labor practices, employee relations, environmental regulations, and community outreach. Companies are facing rising demand from a wide variety of stakeholder groups for data-driven, granular reporting on these issues. They want businesses to examine their operations more closely and be transparent about both their successes and failures in resolving these concerns.

Increasing Calls for Discretion: Companies are under pressure from a variety of stakeholders, including government regulators, financial analysts, employees, nonprofit advocacy organizations, labor unions, community organizations, and the media, to disclose more data about their CSR performance goals, decision-making processes, and outcomes. Stakeholders' worries that businesses won't hold themselves responsible for their CSR pledges without public disclosure motivate these requests. For instance, the "Publish What You Pay" coalition of non-profits is pushing for regulations to be put in place that would force publicly traded resource companies to disclose data on their total payments to governments, royalties, and other public sector entities in all countries where they do business.

Increase in Environmental Impact Reporting: Thousands of businesses provide reports on parts of CSR performance like the environment or charity, but only around 500 issue full reports on their social and environmental actions and consequences, a significant rise from the seven reports produced in 1990. While the number of reports being published is growing, the standards by which they are written are becoming stricter as their authors aim for uniformity and relevancy on par with those of yearly financial reports. For instance, Shell included its 2002 sustainability report under the same cover as the business's 2002 financial report, demonstrating the significance the corporation places on the document. However, there is much controversy concerning the connection between reporting and real changes in corporate behavior, despite the fact that many organizations find that full reporting may meet the information demands of many stakeholders. Stakeholders are now examining how the reporting process leads to changes in the company's policies and procedures, so it's clear that information sharing is crucial to fostering an accountable culture.

Increased Government Oversight Companies are under increasing pressure from regulators at all levels of government to improve the transparency of their operations by providing more and better information to the public. In general, European governments have been more vocal in lobbying for regulatory initiatives than the United States government has been. For instance, as of the start of 2003, all businesses listed on French stock exchanges were required by the recently updated French law known as the Nouvelles Regulations Economiques (NRE) to report to shareholders and stakeholders on a variety of social and environmental concerns. In addition to the United States, several countries have passed laws mandating that certain types of businesses report on their social and environmental impact.

There has been a rise in stakeholder activism, with more organizations than ever before interacting with businesses on a more personal level and use a broad variety of strategies, methods, and technology to get the attention of management on issues that are important to them. Many of these activists are also making an effort to inform policymakers, journalists, and the general public about businesses that are or are not meeting standards of accountability. Stakeholder groups are using a variety of strategies to get the firm to address their concerns, including public awareness campaigns, demonstrations, boycotts, and class action lawsuits. Conversely, stakeholders are rethinking conventional approaches in favor of more innovative methods that center on identifying shared ground with other organizations in order to form coalitions that go over traditional borders of location and topic. This gives them a much louder and larger platform from which to negotiate with businesses.

Individual and institutional shareholders alike have grown more active in recent years, calling for more corporate accountability. The demands of activist shareholders for more accountability have taken the form of resolutions calling for more information to be made public about a company's environmental and social impacts, more openness in board deliberations, and promises from the business that it will adhere to generally accepted norms in these areas. In order to appeal to a wider audience of shareholders, today's resolutions typically use more general language on adhering to the highest and best social and environmental standards appropriate to the company, rather than calling for the company's endorsement of specific standards like SA8000, the CEREs Principles, or the UN Global Compact. Shareholder advocates are also calling for mutual funds to disclose their proxy votes and the voting rules they use. For instance, shareholder activists have been instrumental in getting the U.S. Securities and Exchange Commission to mandate that mutual funds reveal how they vote on shareholder resolutions. As a means of communicating with management about matters of concern, the resolution process is still used by many corporations, and annual shareholder meetings are also still common. Yet, rather of waiting for the annual meeting, several corporations increasingly choose to engage with shareholder activists and institutional investors immediately. Some businesses have created jobs or whole departments whose only purpose is to address the social and environmental concerns of their stockholders.

The Development of Electronic Resources: Because of the Internet, businesses and people advocating for more corporate responsibility may now disseminate and receive information at an unprecedented scale, both factual and misleading. Since this type of communication is generally unpoliced, many businesses are realizing they need to keep a closer eye on it and participate more actively in it. Numerous businesses now utilize the web to provide proactive reports on their contributions to society and the environment. More and more businesses are taking use of the Internet as a platform for publishing news and other material that was originally written for print and is now available online, as well as for disseminating real-time, interactive data on how well they are doing. Companies may now gauge public reaction to their shared data because to the widespread availability of the Internet. Through direct engagement with activists and other stakeholders, several businesses are discovering that they may mitigate, if not entirely eradicate, the effects of negative, Internet-driven campaigns by vetting the material received by such groups. Concurrently, several NGOs, government agencies, and private businesses have launched online portals that give extensive data on corporate environmental performance, philanthropy, and other social consequences, often broken down on a facility-by-facility basis. The Internet is also increasingly being used to facilitate proxy voting, which may increase the power of activist institutions and individuals to rally other shareholders and affect corporate policy.

Corporate social responsibility (CSR) and accountability in general have recently received a great deal of attention and criticism from the business press and the general media. Articles on topics including board diversity and independence, CEO pay, board performance review processes, and business answers to shareholder complaints are appearing more often in a variety of periodicals. Companies' policies and practices on many CSR concerns have been scrutinized by the media and, in some circumstances, revised. For instance, the United States Supreme Court has agreed to hear a case against Nike in which the company is accused of falsifying commercial speech in defense of the working conditions at its supplier factories abroad, a case that has the potential to set a significant precedent in the area of corporate transparency. Nike has claimed it should be constitutionally protected in order to defend itself and demonstrate the human rights strides it has made in response to allegations that have surfaced against the firm over its international labor practices over the previous decade. Nearly 30 news organizations, including ABC, CBS, NBC, and top newspaper chains, as well as organized labor and groups like the American Civil Liberties Union, argued in court filings that if the case against Nike is upheld, reporters will not be able to get company executives to talk freely about product safety, racial discrimination, or environmental concerns about their industry.

Increasing Government Oversight: Companies are under pressure from regulators at all levels of government to improve the transparency of their operations and results reporting. Companies are confronting a rising body of law and regulation, especially in the field of environmental protection, that is intended to make them more accountable to the public.

The purpose of a social audit in business is to evaluate the extent to which a company is working to improve the social and environmental conditions in its local community and the wider world. In today's world, corporations are expected to spread the wealth they amass and contribute to the greater good. The term "corporate accountability" refers to the frameworks put in place by businesses to oversee their social responsibility initiatives. Today, there is a widespread need for more corporate responsibility, and many different kinds of social audit systems are being created to meet this need. As a result of a few major advancements made possible by the technological and informational revolution, the reach of such an audit inside businesses and shared with the public has been greatly expanded.

We have the biggest democratic nation in the world. A rising number of people want their governments to take more responsibility for the welfare of their citizens. The public is starting to speak out more for its right to know and have input into how its governments make decisions. The government and the legislature are on the lookout for new methods to assess performance in light of the public's growing role in decision making. Similarly, women are actively participating in all governmental functions. This circumstance calls for the implementation of the social and gender audit concept.

Additionally, "Social Audits" are being conducted by civil society groups to check the validity of corporations' and institutions' statements about their social performance. Organizations in the public and commercial sectors, as well as government agencies, are conducting "Gender Audits" to track the progress of the gender mainstreaming movement and identify any remaining gaps in the fight for gender parity. In this section, you will learn about social auditing, gender auditing, their respective concepts, features, stages, methodologies, and benefits. Students and employees in the developing sector would benefit greatly from learning more about social and gender auditing. It will aid them in making the government more open, accountable, and responsible to the people.

Government agencies may use social auditing to keep tabs on the internal and external effects of their business and social activities, as well as to better plan and manage such efforts.

Reasons Why Social Audit Is Necessary

- The welfare of the people is promoted and legitimized by the institutional/administrative system. Those living in a society may benefit from a better knowledge of the administrative system thanks to information gleaned through a social audit.

- When looking at the administrative system from the perspective of the people, a "Social Audit" is conducted.

- A social audit is an objective assessment of how well an organization is doing in terms of meeting its stated social objectives.

- It's a tool that helps businesses be more responsible members of society.

- The purpose of a social audit is to examine the operation of a public service in detail to determine whether or not it serves the public interest. It's a method for calculating and proving an organization's positive effects on people and the planet. It's a metric for gauging how well a company really pursues its stated mission and abides by its core principles.

- Through systematic and frequent monitoring based on the perspectives of its stakeholders, it offers an evaluation of the effect of an organization's nonfinancial aims.

Comparison of Social Auditing to Other Auditing

Many people wrongly believe that social auditing is just another kind of audit used to verify the veracity of monetary and statistical claims. The scope of a standard financial audit is limited to the examination of financial records by an external auditor in accordance with financial accounting principles; in contrast, the idea of Social Audit encompasses a far broader range of activities.

An organization's social performance on any given activity may be evaluated, comprehended, and enhanced via what is known as a "Social Audit." The method of social auditing is one that is developed in-house by the company in accordance with its own goals. The goal is to have everyone who has a stake in the outcome participate. It takes reliable measurements of social performance in order to report on progress and make adjustments when necessary.

Auditing of financial records in order to ensure their accuracy and legitimacy. In the same way, an audit of operations would check for things like efficiency in meeting goals and minimizing waste. Social Audit, on the other hand, takes into account community values and the equitable distribution of benefits among various social groups to assess how well a department or program is doing in terms of its declared core values. The creation of social wealth in the form of helpful networks and administration that is both responsible to and transparent with its stakeholders is bolstered by the additional information provided by a social audit. One of Social Audit's most notable impacts is the creation of social wealth. As a result, Social Audit improves both the state's and the public's faith in its authority.

In addition to traditional auditing methods, a social audit may provide light on how public agencies are seen by their constituents. Social audits are conducted at various governmental and non-governmental organizations. An organization's annual Social Audit document or report is the product of a continuous process that often spans a year.

Basic Concepts of Social Auditing

The primary goal of any Social Audit is to ensure that progress is being made toward the specified Social Goals. From global examples of Social Auditing, eight guiding concepts have emerged.

1. Multi-Perspective/Polyvocal: Seek to Include the Opinions of All Stakeholders (those who are Affected by or Involved with the Organization, Department, or Programme).
2. All-encompassing: Plans to report (eventually) on every facet of the company's operations and results.
3. It is participatory, meaning it seeks for and welcomes input from a wide range of interested parties.
4. It is bidirectional, meaning that stakeholders communicate and provide input on a number of different fronts.

5.   Ongoing: The goal is to create social accounts on a consistent basis, so that the idea and the practice become ingrained in the culture of the company and extend to all of its operations.

6.   Comparative: Allows for annual comparisons of the company's performance against relevant external standards or benchmarks, as well as allowing for comparisons to be conducted between companies doing similar work and reporting in a comparable method.

Verified, number seven, means that the social sums have been audited by a competent, impartial third party.

Assuring that the audited financial statements are made public to stakeholders and the general public is an important step in establishing trustworthiness and fostering openness in financial dealings.

Sociocultural, administrative, legal, and democratic contexts are the bedrock upon which Social Audit may be implemented. The goal of the Social Audit process is to increase the accountability of decision-makers, representatives, managers, and officials via increased public participation, transparency, and the free flow of information. Concepts of democracy and citizen engagement underpin the fundamental notions. There is great promise for Social Audit's implementation in Ievel to improve local government and make local authorities more open and accountable to the people they serve. The next diagram illustrates how Social Audit and common values work together.

What Social Audit Is and What It Does

To accurately evaluate the effect of government actions on people' social well-being, Social Auditing may be utilized as a tool to give crucial insights. It's useful for calculating the social returns and calculating the social costs of any program. In numerous states, citizens may keep tabs on how their favorite government agencies are doing thanks to a number of different ways. These methods, however, fail to fully account for the positive effects on society as a whole and the environment. Therefore, Social Audit may be used to offer particular inputs for the following by generating information on the social relevance, costs, and benefits of a programme/activity:

- To serve as a foundation for forming management strategy in a socially responsible and accountable manner and for developing strategies;
- To track the organization's social and ethical effect and performance.

Facilitate strategic management of institutions (including consideration of their impact on other institutions and the communities in which they operate) Inform the public, other organizations, and the general public about how their time and money are being spent; this relates to questions of accountability and ethics (such as in the case of ethical investment).

The Positive Effects of Social Auditing on Government Agencies
The advantages of doing a Social Audit include:

1. It improves the government's image by revealing important details on how various agencies and organizations are doing in terms of ethics and how the public views the services they deliver. Real or imagined, the social aspect of service delivery may have a significant impact on how the department and its employees are seen by the public. Government agencies nowadays are competing for public favor in an era of service benchmarking and rising public awareness of government offerings through citizens' charters. The legislative and executive branches may benefit from social auditing since it highlights areas for improvement and gives them a chance to take the initiative to find and implement solutions.

2. Social Auditing is a useful technique for managers to get insight into, and proactively address, stakeholder problems. Facilitating the interdependence between the government and the community, this technology gives crucial information on the interests, attitudes, and expectations of stakeholders.

3. Influences favorable changes in policy and practice within an organization Social auditing sets targeted objectives for enhancing an organization and shines a light on the steps taken to bring them to fruition. Employees who are responsible for making day-to-day decisions will be better able to take into account the needs and concerns of stakeholders if Social Audit is integrated into current management systems.

4. It improves transparency and accountability by requiring government agencies to provide only accurate and fair information. External verification is used in Social Auditing to ensure that the Social Audit is comprehensive. The department's efforts would be more convincing with an outside audit. Improvements in the department's performance over time in light of its goal, values, and objectives are the best proof of a Social Audit's veracity.

5. Helps reorient and refocus efforts in light of stakeholder needs and expectations. Social auditing has the potential to be an effective tool for guiding departments in this direction.

6.   Social Audit may provide departments or organizations more confidence to take action in social sectors that have been ignored or given less attention in the past.

Scales of Social Auditing

There are two ways to examine Social Audit. There is the level of civil society, which encompasses individuals and groups outside of formal institutions (government, private, and NGOs) (private, NGO, CBO, universities, schools, consumer organizations, SHGs, an individual etc.).

There is both internal and external competition at the organizational level. Social accounting and social bookkeeping are examples of internal components, whereas verification of social accounts by a third-party Social Auditor or audit panel is an example of an external component.

Data on community values, social benefits, social capital, and the quality of department/programming engagement with the public is gathered via an audit at the community/societal level. This lines up with findings from a social audit conducted throughout the enterprise or within a specific division. The analysis provides a basis for tailoring the program or its operations to meet the needs of the community or society. Community-based social audits also help strengthen civil society, promote equality, foster networking, and advocate for change.

During a social audit, stakeholders and the surrounding community are brought in for in-context interviews and records are kept. Methods include social accounting, stakeholder engagement, and interviews with department employees, non-governmental organization (NGO) representatives, program participants, and others who would be impacted by the department's initiatives. All of these tools are straightforward, so any division may do a Social Audit with only a little bit of familiarity with the kit.

It is from the organization's goals that everything else is derived, including the indicators of effect, the stakeholders, and the data gathering systems. The relevant agency or department keeps track of community information, records of stakeholder consultations, and social accounting records.

This social accounting should ideally be reviewed once a year by a panel of distinguished individuals with impeccable honesty and social commitment. This part of a Social Audit often entails an impartial investigation by means of extensive consultation with several members of the community and interested parties. The findings of the Social Audit may be released to the public. To further optimize societal benefits, these reports might be utilized by a wide range of stakeholders, including policymakers, to implement necessary adjustments.

Gender Audit

Social auditing includes a focus on gender equality. Unlike financial audits, this one focuses on product quality. The effectiveness and mutual reinforcement of the organization's gender mainstreaming activities and associated support structures are taken into account.

Attributes of a Gender Audit It creates a standard for gender fairness and equality.

It reveals serious voids and obstacles to implementing a gender-mainstreaming strategy.

Identifies strengths and weaknesses in promoting gender equality concerns Recommends solutions for closing gender gaps Suggests new approaches to old problems Good practices in achieving gender equality are documented, and the organization's collective ability to do so is bolstered

Supports internal buy-in for efforts to promote gender equality; Sharpens organizational learning on gender via processes that foster collaboration, disseminate data, and encourage introspection

The primary goals of a Gender Audit are to

1. Assess the degree to which policies have been institutionalized at the level of the organization, the work unit, and the individual, and 2) promote organizational learning on how to effectively implement gender mainstreaming in policies, programmes, and structures.
2. Develop an appreciation for how well gender mainstreaming has been absorbed and implemented by staff Members Evaluate how well gender mainstreaming has been implemented in terms of the creation and distribution of gender-responsive goods and services
3. Find and discuss organizational methods, practices, and mindsets that have contributed to advancing gender equality.
4. Determine how much money is being spent on gender activities and gender mainstreaming.
5. Check how gender is considered in HR policy.
6. Take a look at the gender ratios of upper and lower management.
7. Establish an organization's gender mainstreaming performance standards as a starting point for a sustained initiative.
8. Of using benchmarks to evaluate success in advancing gender parity in the workplace

9.   Track the development of gender mainstreaming action plans and suggest changes if necessary.
10.   Determine what might be done differently, and provide suggestions on how the action plan may be carried out more effectively.

Gender Audit with Participation

Development programs and organizations may evaluate their own policy implementation via a participatory gender audit. The primary goal of a participatory gender audit is for participants to gain insight into the following areas: what they are doing to advance gender equality and women's empowerment at work; how they are doing it; how it compares to the work of others; and how it can be enhanced and better situated within the context of their workplace.

The gist of this study is that it will inspire reform recommendations that put the new knowledge into practice. When compared to a traditional gender review, the participatory gender audit places more emphasis on introspective analysis. Employees, volunteers, and external partners such as funders are all regarded empirical experts who are competent and motivated to evaluate their own performance and that of their organization in regards to gender equality and women's empowerment.

Participatory Gender Audit as a Methodology

The participatory gender audit draws from four distinct schools of thought on gender and organizational transformation to form its approach.

Foundational Principle 1: A Developmental Perspective on Gender

Foundational Principle 2: Qualitative self-evaluation

Consideration of the Adult Learning Cycle

Lastly, a strategy based on organizational learning should be considered a cornerstone.

First Principle

A) Women's and Children's Empowerment in Development

Women and men, alike, are seen as powerful agents of change in gender and development frameworks. Gender roles are assumed to be uneven in most contexts. Patriarchal thought is the root cause of gender inequity. It is the institutions that govern our daily lives, structure our social relations, and create and maintain societies where unequal (power) relations are expressed in existing gender relations as well as through class, caste, religion, and ethnicity that must change if gender equality and women's empowerment are to become a reality.

In recent years, there has been a lot of focus on the organizational challenges of implementing new gender roles within the subject of gender and development (GAD).

Organizational problems including policy, strategy, actions, and structures and processes are investigated, as well as the culture of the company as a whole, during a gender audit. A participatory gender audit focuses on the following major organizational concerns:

- Mainstreaming gender equality and women's empowerment in the organization's strategy and activities;
- Existing gender expertise and investment in competence and capacity building;
- Information and knowledge management;
- Systems and instruments in the context in which the organization's programme is executed.
- The organizations selected as partners and how well they are informed about the company's stance on gender equality.

Achievement belief.

It is important to remember that the gender audit is not an examination of the audited organization's influence on the population or other organizations to whom it directs its efforts.

Subsequently,

B) The Organization as a Learning System

Individuals, groups, and the whole company are all responsible for learning and adapting in the context of a learning organization. Individuals, groups, larger organizations, and the whole world are all places where Watkins and Marsick say learning takes place in their learning organization model. Teams are seen as the intermediary layer between employees' discretionary efforts and the overarching goals of a business.

Level one: Individual learning is the process through which individuals within an organization gain new information and abilities.

Learning at the team level occurs when members contribute to one other's development of expertise and their ability to work together effectively.

Standard operating procedures, policies, cultures, work processes, and information systems that link remote workers together and preserve the company's collective memory all serve as repositories for lessons learned at the organizational level.

Evidence of this growth might be seen in fresh ideas for the company's future or in an increased understanding of its policies and procedures.

Learning at the global level entails considering the far-reaching consequences of one's actions, including how they could effect people's standard of living both within and outside of the organization.

The goals, vision, and mission of an organization are the driving forces behind its culture of learning. Real learning may take place and be connected at all levels, from people to teams to teams to the organizational level. Organizations will never be able to meet the many challenges posed by a dynamic and ever-evolving environment if their members and teams do not continue to learn.

In a Participatory Gender Audit, teams are given extra focus since they are seen as the connecting tissue between individual development and organizational growth.

The audit approach focuses on the person, the team, and the organization.

Third, the constructivist paradigm

C): Taking an introspective qualitative evaluation

The third tenet of the technique is a focus on knowing more than just the facts of a situation. This involves grasping both the hard and soft data of a scenario, as well as the possibilities for both objective and subjective analysis. The approach considers issues such, "What caused things to happen?"

Asking "Why are things this way?"

Why do we do the things we do? Where do the forces of change come from, and what are they?

The technique acknowledges and aims to highlight discrepancies between how we behave and how we imagine we act, as well as the significance of personal, team, and organizational reference points. When thinking about concerns of women's empowerment and racial equality, these factors seem to be particularly important.

The gender audit is problem-focused; it identifies issues when the actual state of affairs differs from the ideal state of affairs; in this example, when the actual state of gender mainstreaming and women's empowerment differs from the policy's stated goals. As the name suggests, problem-based education emphasizes gaining knowledge via experience.

Using this approach, we might also wonder whether we're on the correct track. Is the work we're doing efficient and effective? and even for larger concerns such, "Are we making the proper choice?" Is it the appropriate thing to attempt to accomplish what we are trying to do?

In a nutshell, an audit is an attempt to get insight into what is being done, why it is being done that way, whether it is the correct or best thing to do, and if and how it can be improved via a qualitative self-assessment.

D) The Adult Learning Cycle, the Fourth Pillar

Finally, the notion that adults learn best when the learning experience is based on actual experiences from their personal and professional life is the basis of the Participatory Gender Audit approach. Through introspection and analysis, they should be able to extrapolate from their own experiences and draw broader, more universal conclusions. Then, it may be used as a foundation for experimental ideas for change to be translated from other languages.

Gender audit procedures that encourage participation

Just now, we had a look at the procedures that make up the PGA methodology; these are the tools that may really be used to conduct a participatory gender audit. The participatory gender audit is a collection of techniques designed for use with collaborative groups of people—ideally, teams that already work closely together in the context of specific organizational initiatives. All of the approaches encourage self-evaluation by participants on their own performance in many facets of the program, project, team, and individual. Participants might feel that they've gained useful knowledge on women's empowerment and gender parity that they can implement in real-world settings thanks to the approaches.

There are a total of thirteen techniques outlined in the system. Audit participants, as well as the audit facilitation team, may examine how they individually, collectively, and institutionally address the organization's stated goal of advancing gender parity and women's empowerment.

- Having Real-World Impact
- Verifying the relevance of ideas in novel Thoughts and Reflections on Related Events
- The development of broad, overarching ideas.

Two of these techniques were developed with input from the audit facilitation team. The members of the audit facilitation team may examine and generalize data gathered with the use of these techniques (for example documents, key informants, workshops). They include a checklist of the gender issues facing the organization that should be covered in the gender audit, as well as a checklist of performance criteria that reflects the most up-to-date thinking on what constitutes good practice for businesses aiming to promote gender equality and women's empowerment.

These two tools address a wide range of concerns, such as the programme's or department's goals, strategies, activities, people, systems, structure, information and knowledge management, as well as its capacity development and competence management. Questions about how to implement the program in a way that is sensitive to both sexes are raised in regard to each of these organizational features. The substance of the organization's policy on gender equality informed the selection of indicators that may be used as benchmarks of excellent practice included in the key criteria checklist. Members of the audit facilitation team may evaluate the program in light of both industry-wide best practices and those unique to the auditing firm by using these two techniques.

Eleven more approaches are developed to encourage dialogue, introspection, and constructive action on gendered concerns in the delivery of programs and projects.

These techniques are most effective when utilized in workshop settings, with preexisting program or organization teams, and entail either individual or group interviews. Some of these techniques include:

1. Indicator of Quality
2. Test of understanding and comprehension
3. Considering the perspectives of relevant parties: a stakeholder analysis (Venn diagram)
4. Category of Projects and Programs
5. The culture of the organization
6. A Mind Map
7. Best management
8. many points of view on the success of transformation
9. SWOT analysis (strength, weakness, opportunities and Threat analysis)
10. Studying the study of learning
11. Interviews, either alone or in small groups

The majority of the techniques are revised versions of those already in use in workshops and training to foster collaboration, more self-awareness, deeper critical analysis, and a more open-minded worldview. A selection of approaches is made from the ensemble for each session. Some teams may employ five or six ways, while others will use just one or two, and this varies greatly based on the team's composition, purpose, and other factors.

Document from the PGA

The audit facilitation team takes notes during the PGA and analyzes the insights gained from the workshops. The audit concludes with a report that transmits the gained insights and expertise to those who had a hand in the investigation. This report incorporates the workshop attendees' suggestions. It is up to the program's leadership to develop a strategy that takes into account the audit's suggestions. It will play a crucial role in setting goals for the year.

Environmental Audit

The need of a sound legal framework for the smooth running of any enterprise or government agency is well knowledge. The government is responsible for creating the legal framework, which consists of laws, acts, and regulations. If a person or company is found to have violated this legal framework, for instance, they might face severe fines. As an added downside, those who flout the law may face social stigma and condemnation. On March 23, 2013, in the Tamil Nadu industrial town of Tuticorin, locals awoke to symptoms like eye and throat irritation and difficulty breathing. Although initial investigations pointed to a problem with residential LPG cylinders, it was ultimately determined that very high emissions of air pollutants from adjacent industries were to blame. A large number of persons rapidly developed respiratory issues, including difficulty breathing, nausea, and vomiting, within a few of hours. In a state of fear, people flock to neighboring medical professionals. The matter was reported to government authorities, and after monitoring the air quality, the Tamil Nadu Pollution Control Board (TNPCB) discovered the emission of poisonous gas from the facility, with levels of sulphur dioxide found to be much beyond the safe acceptable range. After some time, the TNPCB issued a warning to shut the plant until the air quality reached acceptable levels and the emission control devices were repaired.

So, let's have a look at another another example of China's proactive and preventative approach to problems. Numerous large steel mills in China halted or decreased production in early November 2017; many more cement facilities in northern China are preparing to shut down before Christmas. The purpose of these actions is to reduce wintertime particle air pollution by 15% year-over-year during the next five months, as part of a preventative action plan. The bad air quality in

Beijing and the neighboring industrial regions has risen to "extremely harmful" levels, prompting calls for rapid action to reduce emissions.

The lessons learned from these two occurrences highlight the importance of environmental management to the long-term success of any organization. Environmental stewardship may be simply defined as the practice of paying close enough attention to the waste and materials utilized in a production to take into account methods to reduce wastes and emissions, reuse by-products, conserve energy, and work at peak performance at all times. Excellent environmental sense is increasingly generally recognized as good commercial sense by a growing number of enterprises and corporate organizations. Their market share may grow thanks to environmental responsibility since more and more consumers and businesses are showing a preference for eco-friendly goods and services. Firms in the current economic climate need to demonstrate their commitment to environmental protection and long-term planning if they want to be seen as respectable players in society. An environmental audit is a management tool that ensures sustainable operations by promoting responsible behavior toward the environment.

THE MEANING OF ENVIRONMENTAL AUDITING

We learned the connection between an organization's actions and their effects on the surrounding environment via preliminary case studies. Companies have used a variety of environmental management techniques in an effort to reduce their negative effects on the environment. The acronym "EMS" stands for "Environmental Management System," and it is a complete procedure that includes many actions inside a company to accomplish environmental improvement and preservation. The success of an organization's environmental stewardship depends on the depth and breadth of its environmental policy. An environmental audit is a procedure for comparing an organization's environmental record with its stated environmental goals and policies. The policies and goals must be specified and written down. In reality, however, environmental audits performed for the first time are generally performed with less rigor than subsequent audits since adequate documentation is often lacking during the first phase. Auditing the environment's health helps shape new policies that better align with the global green economy.

First, let's talk about the audit that most people are probably already aware with, which is the financial audit. Auditing, in its broadest sense, is any action, such as an inspection or systematic examination, conducted on-site to verify that a process or quality system is operating as intended and in accordance with established standards. Auditing the environmental impacts of a project or program against predetermined benchmarks is a key part of environmental management.

A similar concept was developed by the International Chamber of Commerce (ICC) in 1989.

To help protect the environment, facilitate management control of practices, and assess compliance with company policies, which would include regulatory requirements and standards applicable, an environmental management system (EMS) is "a management tool comprising systematic, documented, periodic, and objective evaluation of how well environmental organisation, management, and equipment are performing."

The basic ideas are: Verification: audits assess conformity to legislation or other predetermined criteria.

Audits are systematic in the sense that they adhere to a predetermined methodology and schedule.

Audits are routinely performed at regular intervals.

The audit findings are given without any judgments or conclusions being added.

Notes are collected throughout the audit, and the results are documented afterwards.

Integration of audits into the management system as a "management tool" (such as a quality management system or environmental management system).

CHANGES IN ENVIRONMENTAL AUDITING

You may be pleased to learn that some private American companies began engaging in activities like environmental audits as early as the 1930s. Although it was not well known, in the 1930s, SC Johnson, a family-owned corporation, conducted social and ecological audits as part of internal management operations. At the same time, the US National Environmental Protection Act (NEPA) was enacted in 1969, elevating environmental concerns to a higher priority. A major turning point in international efforts to preserve the planet came on December 2, 1970, with the establishment of the Environmental Protection Agency (EPA).

Defense of the Environment. In turn, Silent Spring contributed to the establishment of USEPA (Box 1).

As an internal management tool to review and check the compliance of industrial operations with I local environmental laws and regulations ii) national environmental laws and regulations and iii) corporate policies, environmental auditing programs were developed independently by some industries in the early 1970s. Later in 1979, the US Environmental Protection Agency issued draft guidance to US regulators through the use of environmental "auditors" who would visit facilities, take samples, conduct studies, and report back to government authorities. Despite the report's eventual rejection, it served as a key catalyst for discussion on public policy and the private sector. As a consequence, environmental auditing emerged in the 1980s, and many companies used them to assess their obligations and document their compliance with regulations.

Subsidiary American businesses' efforts overseas had a significant impact on the global expansion of environmental auditing. Environmental auditing in the chemical and petrochemical industries was inspired by American operations in Europe and interactions with European companies, despite the fact that these industries already engaged in a similar kind of exercise to document the inherent environmental hazards of their businesses. Industry in the developed world adopted environmental auditing as a standard method of environmental management by the late 1980s, and this practice is now being adopted by both international and domestic corporations operating in the developing world. The term "Sustainable Development" (SD) was coined by the World Commission on Environment and Development (WCED) in 1987 (WCED 1987) in its report Our Common Future (also known as the Brundtland Report), which emphasized the importance of the industrial sector reducing its impact on the environment and natural resources.

Business owners in emerging markets also felt the effects of the term "sustainable development," which entered common parlance there not long after it had spread to the developed world. This means that environmental performance has emerged as a competitive advantage amid the many market situations. On the other hand, many multinational organizations are trying to get ISO 14001 certification with the introduction of the ISO 14000 series on Environmental Management Systems (EMS). An environmental audit is now a necessary step in developing a more responsible corporate environmental strategy and a successful environmental management system (EMS). This day and age, no company can afford to ignore environmental concerns while conducting business. Therefore, an environmental audit serves as a tool that informs and aids in management's control of the operation's environmental impacts.

The Environmental Movement, "Silent Spring," and the Writings of Rachel Carson

American scientist Rachel Louise Carson (May 27, 1907 – April 14, 1964) is remembered for her seminal work, Silent Spring. Carson worked as an aquatic scientist for the U.S. Bureau of Fisheries in the early part of her career before switching to nature writing full time in the 1950s. Carson, an avid birder, worried that chemical poisoning would lead to a steady decline in avian populations year after year, unless action was taken to reverse it. She showed how the widespread use of the synthetic pesticide DDT (dichlorodiphenyltrichloroethane) to kill mosquitoes and other insects was having a devastating effect on bird populations throughout the nation. After consuming DDT, birds reportedly laid eggs with thinner shells, which cracked prematurely in the nest, leading to significant population reductions, as recorded by Carson. The issue caused an 80% decline in bald eagle and other bird populations, including those of peregrine falcons and others. Carson thought the rising number of poisoned birds was due to the increased usage of synthetic pesticides. Despite strong pushback from the chemical industry, Silent Spring ultimately led to a countrywide ban on DDT and other pesticides. Along with that, it sparked a nationwide environmental movement that ultimately resulted in the establishment of the EPA in the United States. After her death, Jimmy Carter presented it to her family as a Presidential Medal of Freedom.

AUDIT TYPES AND SCOPE

In the past two paragraphs, we discussed how environmental audit developed into a useful instrument in environmental management. We will now learn about the various kinds of audits and their respective purviews. The primary factors in determining the kind of an environmental audit are the goals of the company and the nature of the activity being conducted. Environmental auditors are responsible for conducting thorough, well-documented investigations of businesses for the purpose of producing environmental audit reports. For instance, a compliance audit may tell you how far a business has gone over the safe limits set by the government if you want to know whether the toxins you emit into the environment are legal.

Audits of EMSs (Environmental Management Systems)

Successful EMS is dependent on EMS rules and procedure being carried out as intended. The purpose of an Environmental Management System (EMS) audit is to verify and assess the efficiency of an organization's EMS (ISO 14001). There are several facets of an EMS that go beyond just compliance that are investigated during an audit. By examining the site's policies, procedures, work instructions, guidelines, specifications, training requirements, and monitoring systems, an EMS audit may gauge the site's commitment to environmental responsibility. These workers cannot be expected to do a good job if they are not properly instructed and trained in EMS practices. As a result, verifying the existence, nonexistence, and efficiency of an EMS is the first step in any audit of a business's operations. In the end, an EMS audit may provide insights into policy, training requirements and procedures, implementation stage faults, and the need for extra technology and manpower.

Audits for Environmental Regulations

Audits of environmental compliance (or performance) tend to concentrate on whether or not a company is following the law and its own internal policies. The purpose of an environmental policy audit is to determine whether or not the policies, goals, laws, by-laws, ordinances, rules, and standards have been met. Additional numerical testing and more targeted inspections, for instance, on whether or not water and air permits and licenses are being adhered to, are common in such audits.

Conducting a Review of Environmental Impact Assessments

The purpose of an EIA audit is the same as that of a compliance audit: to guarantee that the recommended preventative and corrective actions outlined in the Environmental Impact Assessment have been carried out and that the organization is in full compliance with all applicable laws and regulations. Audits of this kind are commonplace in many nations for the purposes of quality control in EIAs and to lessen the burden of additional expenses and hassle in the event of an appeal.

Performing Audits of Environmental Responsibility

Audits conducted as part of environmental due diligence evaluate a site's or an operation's existing and prospective environmental liabilities. Pre-purchase inspections are often done before investing in a piece of real estate that has been or will be utilized for commercial or industrial purposes. Property acquisition due diligence audits are a standard aspect of a larger financial due diligence audit that analyzes several company risks.

Past dumping or burial of hazardous material may cause contaminants to contaminate groundwater, which can be uncovered via environmental due diligence audits. The landowner in such a situation may be held responsible for the expense of garbage removal. When buying a house, it's crucial to check for any hidden environmental obligations that can come with it.

Checkups of Waste Management Systems

When conducting an audit, waste specialists will look very closely at the facilities' waste management systems. Waste and emissions in the form of solids, liquids, and gases are all part of the border audit. Methods used, waste treatment techniques, system functionality, and final verification are just few of the areas that will be examined as part of the audit methodology. Site management may be hesitant to conduct comprehensive environmental audits, but a targeted waste audit may provide useful information for taking swift, cost-saving measures.

Conducting a trash audit may help a business become in better shape to deal with the garbage it produces on a daily basis in a way that is both effective and ethical. As a result of a waste audit, the company is able to improve its recycling practices and reduce its impact on the environment while still meeting regulatory requirements for the disposal of paper, plastic, and metal trash. Because of this, fewer harmful chemicals are released into the air and water, which in turn slows the rate at which the planet warms and helps preserve its natural resources.

Audits for EHS (Environmental, Health, and Safety)

The goals of an EHS audit are to determine the degree to which applicable regulations are being followed, to evaluate any associated risk, and to locate any obtainable avenues for process improvement. The results of an EHS audit may help a firm determine how best to capitalize on key opportunities, address problems, and proactively manage continuing risk at each location. As an added bonus, the on-site staff and the corporate EHS team received a more in-depth education during the informative follow-up visit.

In an attempt to cut down on expenses, interruption, and discomfort, many businesses have opted to integrate non-financial audits including health, safety, environment, and quality. In terms of benefits and drawbacks, this strategy is balanced. Some benefits include lower audit frequency and less potential for productivity losses at work. One potential drawback is that if many audits are combined, less attention will be paid to each particular part. To counteract this, auditors could need more time to complete their work, which might have a negative impact on productivity. If businesses could take advantage of the "added value" from audits—namely, the decreased waste, less risk, enhanced performance, and fewer incidents—the audits' potentially negative impact may be mitigated. These advantages are not always easy to put a price on, therefore audits continue to get a bad rap for being seen as a productivity drain.

When not in use, do you switch off the outside lights?

Do computers have any kind of inbuilt power saving features? If so, are they operational?

The question: "Are computers left on overnight?"

When not in use, do the screens go dark?

Asking, "Are photocopiers cost-effective?"

Is it common practice to leave photocopiers and printers running through the night and on weekends?

Can water coolers be kept on all the time?

Following an audit, an organization's energy costs may be reduced by instituting a set of recommended adjustments to operational procedures or energy-using equipment. First, data regarding the facility's operations and its electricity bill history must be gathered. By analyzing this information, the auditor may obtain a better feel for the facility's energy use and identify areas for potential savings. At last, an Energy Action Plan is developed, in which specific ECMs are chosen for execution, and the process of reducing energy use and costs may begin.

AUDIT STANDARDS
Planned Audit Preparation

It is impossible to conduct a successful audit without first carefully planning and organizing its logistics. The first order of business is to compile a list of who needs to be contacted and who should be contacted to answer audit inquiries. The next crucial step is to make a list of everything that will be needed to conduct a thorough audit (Figure 1). In order to demonstrate the audit's seriousness, it's a good idea to meet with senior management and talk about the audit's strategy and process. An guarantee from upper management will help confirm the dedication of employees and provide for a smoother audit.

Meeting before the Audit

Pre-audit meetings are crucial because they provide the first chance to meet the auditee and address any issues before the audit even begins. If you take the time to prepare ahead now, your audit will go off without a hitch. Information needed at this stage includes management structure, extent of the organization or activity being audited, legal status of the facility including permits and monitoring data, and specific information detailing activities carried out at the site. The audit protocol team is chosen, and the audit program is funded, as part of the pre-audit operations. In addition to reiterating the audit's objectives and discussing its logistics, this meeting is a great chance to bring everyone up to speed (e.g. access to key staff, photographs on site, site tour, access to documentation, etc.).

The following responsibilities are part of a pre-audit: Getting buy-in from upper management; Outlining the audit's goals, scope, and structure; Informing staff; Selecting an Audit Team; Ranking the Project's Priorities; Send out a questionnaire before the audit Collect the supplementary data

Another pre-audit meeting may be scheduled if needed to address any remaining questions, concerns, or ambiguities.

Location-Based Audit

It is vital for the audit team to meet with the organization's or activity's management in advance of beginning the audit to discuss the audit's goals, methodology, and timeline. At this meeting, we may also narrow the focus, give the auditors their individual tasks, and set hard timeframes. After the meeting, an initial site check should be conducted. The auditing crew will be briefed on the big picture of the company and its workings, allowing them to zero in on individual problem spots. The audit team may find new information during the site visit that was not previously known to be important to the audit. The bulk of the audit consists of asking questions based on the audit methodology, evaluating site documents (manuals, reports, monitoring data, work instructions, procedures, training schedules, etc.), and comparing the results to standards, policies, and action plans.

The following are examples of the sorts of tasks performed by the audit team during an on-site audit.

Reports will be generated to serve as an audit guide, and the simplest type of audit utilizes these reports to inform fill-in forms.

Protocols of the "check list" kind are often used since they provide exhaustive lists of all the topics that need to be discussed.

The auditor is expected to provide thorough answers to all of the questions on the list of questionnaires, which are utilized as part of the auditing process. An auditor often creates a uniform template for an audit's execution and report compilation.

Photographs - Photographs are used to corroborate results and showcase excellent practices; always get the site's management's OK and follow any rules for safety (e.g. use appropriate equipment in flammable zones etc).

The data and information gathered during the environmental audit will include, but not be limited to: the audit protocol, documentation provided by the owner of the organization or activity, auditor's notes and observation, sampling and monitoring results, photographs, plans, maps, diagrams, working papers, and other similar items. This data has to be carefully recorded so that it may be quickly retrieved when needed. To back up audit results and provide a foundation for verification is the primary goal of data collecting. The lead auditor is responsible for calling an exit meeting to collect final comments, explain major findings, highlight problem areas, and collect any other data that will be used in writing the audit report.

Activities Following an Audit

Together, the audit team's findings provide the basis for an initial audit report draft. The scope of the audit, the needs of the client, and the context of the audit will determine the structure, subject matter, and level of information in the audit report. If you want your reports to be easily understood by everyone in your company, you may make them as straightforward and accessible as possible. A simple audit report will have two sections: "Findings" and "Recommendations," with each finding corresponding to a question or section in the audit procedure. This preliminary report will be shared with the audit team and others who have a stake in the audit. The report is being checked for accuracy. Once the necessary changes have been made, the management will get the final audit report outlining the audit's findings and recommendations. Because of the importance of the data it provides for guiding future testing and analysis, it will also serve as a foundation for future audits. The periodic auditing schedule should be disclosed to the management and audit team to allow the efficiency of consecutive audits, since the results of environmental audits provide input to the process of continuous improvement. This highlights the importance of the audit's follow-up work, which includes evaluating the suggestions made and developing strategies for moving forward.

SAVER DOLLARS with An Environmental Audit

One of the major advantages of doing an environmental audit is the money saved. Throughout the course of the audit, we look for ways to save costs and make incremental changes. For instance, the three R's of trash management—reduce, recover, and reuse—open up novel avenues for garbage disposal and lead to significant cost savings when audited. Companies may incur additional costs while disposing of garbage in certain countries, especially if the waste in question is considered hazardous and must through additional processing steps before being sent to a landfill. Saving money on trash disposal costs is possible if a business can reduce the amount of garbage it generates. To reduce waste, it makes sense to use as few resources as possible. A lower raw material cost may result from using fewer raw materials, which might be achieved by switching to a more efficient technique. Companies nearly always have to pay for the water they use, so any method they can reduce that cost is a boon.

An audit of waste management procedures may help determine whether or not the by-products of one procedure can be recycled for use in a third. Water recycling, which may comprise treating/cleaning/cooling, may result in lower wastewater disposal costs for many water-intensive sectors. Sometimes, an audit of the problem area may reveal the necessity for a continuous improvement plan. An audit of waste production might lead to a waste reduction program, which can include a complete rethinking of goods or just some tweaks to how things are done. There is a financial upside for businesses who do frequent environmental audits to prove they are following environmental regulations. In India, businesses might face fines and even temporary shutdowns for not meeting environmental regulations. Therefore, massive financial losses may be averted with effective audit processes.

Marketing and the Company's Reputation

The public's perception of an organization rises when it demonstrates concern for the planet's natural resources and actively promotes environmental stewardship. Many individuals believe it is crucial for companies to adopt SDGs, and a recent survey found that 41% of enterprises said they plan to do so over the next five years. An environmental audit uncovers untapped opportunities to enhance environmental stewardship in accordance with international sustainability targets. Now more than ever, businesses understand the need of portraying a positive image in regards to environmental protection. Companies that project a "environmentally friendly image" may gain a competitive edge in the face of rising public knowledge of environmental concerns and subsequent customer demand. A new competing element has joined the market at a time when any positive PR is desirable due to the state of the economy. Environmental audits are an essential tool for businesses who take environmental responsibility seriously and are committed to improving their environmental management practices.

Costs of Environmental Damages and Insurance

Problems with the Environment

When a company conducts environmental audits on a regular basis, employees are more likely to understand their roles and how to best contribute to the company's environmental goals. Employees do become more environmentally conscious as a result of this training and start to feel uneasy about contributing to environmental degradation. More action is needed from governments and businesses to combat climate change, acid rain, and air and water pollution as public knowledge of these issues grows. Since there is such a significant public concern for the environment, many businesses are beginning to wonder whether their current methods are sustainable (and the market). A thorough environmental audit is really helpful here.

Audit Planning

Why Do We Need Audit Planning?

The auditor's approach for conducting the audit, including its purpose, duration, scope, and limiting factors, is described in detail in the audit plan.

To ensure that adequate relevant audit evidence is gathered, an engagement team must have a plan outlining the specific audit processes (such as risk assessment procedures) that will be carried out at certain times by specific individuals.

The Importance of Audit Preparation

1. Establishing an overarching audit strategy for the engagement and creating an audit plan, including specific risk assessment techniques and reactions to major misstatement risks, are essential parts of the audit planning process.
2. Rather than being a single, distinct step in the auditing process, planning is an ongoing, iterative procedure that may kick out soon after (or in conjunction with) the conclusion of the last audit. This will go on till the present audit is finished.
3. If the audit was conducted in accordance with widely recognized auditing methods, the existence of a well-documented plan and evidence of controls employed to ensure the work was completed as planned would be strong supporting evidence.
4. The purpose of audit controls is to guarantee that tasks are completed as planned.
5. The auditor maintains command over the audit's quality by properly overseeing his staff, coordinating the efforts of others, and recording all relevant audit activity.

6. The auditor has to create an audit plan that details the following, and then record it.
7. The intended processes for assessing risk, including their scope and frequency; The planned procedures for testing controls and substantive procedures, including their scope and frequency;
8. It is essential that all other audit processes be carried out as planned to ensure that the engagement is in line with PCAOB regulations.

The Importance of Planning and When to Do It

An audit of financial accounts might gain in numerous ways from adequate preparation.
1. Facilitating the auditor's ability to focus on what matters most throughout the audit.
2. Facilitating the auditor's ability to see and address issues before they become major obstacles.
3. Providing valuable assistance in planning, coordinating, and carrying out the audit engagement.
4. Helping choose team members for the engagement who have the skills and experience to handle the challenges that may come up will be a big help.
5. Supporting the management and evaluation of engagement team members' efforts.
6. Help coordinate the efforts of component auditors and subject matter experts as needed.
7. Communication between the client's management, personnel, and audit committee is essential for coordinating auditing efforts, both external and internal.

However, it is still the job of the external auditors to conduct any and all auditing processes.

Audit Preparation

Planning for an audit requires formulating a comprehensive approach to the investigation of issues including managerial honesty, mistakes, and wrongdoings. The auditor's audit strategy should be informed by a healthy dose of professional skepticism concerning such matters.

The auditor's familiarity with and understanding of the client, as well as the client's size and complexity, will affect the amount of preparation time needed before beginning an engagement.

An first audit, as may be anticipated, requires a lot more preparation than a routine audit.

Initial Interaction Procedures

At the outset of the audit, the auditor should carry out the following procedures:

Carry out actions related to the client's retention and the ongoing audit engagement,

Establish that the audit committee has a firm grasp on the conditions of the audit engagement and that the auditors have met independence and ethical criteria.

Organizing Future Events

The size and complexity of the organization, the auditor's familiarity with the company, and unexpected developments during the audit all play a role in determining the scope and depth of the preparation activities.

It is the responsibility of the auditor to determine if the following items are material to the financial statements and internal control over financial reporting of the firm, and if so, how they will influence the auditor's processes when designing the audit strategy and audit plan.

1. The auditor's familiarity with the company's internal control over financial reporting gained through previous auditing engagements;

2. Changes in financial reporting standards, economic circumstances, government regulations, and technology advances, all of which have an impact on the business sector in which the firm works;

3. Business-related issues, such as the company's structure, operations, and capitalization;

4. What, if any, recent changes there have been to the firm, its operations, or its internal control over financial reporting;

5. Initial assumptions made by the auditor on materiality, risk, and, in the case of integrated audits, other considerations relevant to the identification of significant deficiencies;

6. Issues with controls that have been reported to the audit committee or upper management;

7. Concerns that the corporation is aware of in the area of law or regulation;

8. The kind and breadth of evidence supporting the company's internal control over financial reporting effectiveness;

9. Initial assessments of the quality of internal financial reporting controls;

10. Details available to the public that bear on the assessment of the company's internal control over financial reporting and the avoidance of major misstatements in the financial statements;
11. As part of the acceptance and retention assessment, the auditor considers the candidate's familiarity with the company's risks; and
12. The relative difficulty of running the business.

Qualities of an auditor

A competent auditor will have the aforementioned understanding of financial concepts and audit methods, as well as the following personality traits and work experience. We'll talk about how having these traits makes you a better auditor.

One, familiarity with work, monetary jargon, accounting concepts, and the auditing procedure:

An audit can only be performed by someone who is familiar with the types of reports that a firm generates and has the background knowledge to interpret their meaning. An auditor's knowledge of what to look for and how to use the data gleaned from the reports is crucial.

Auditors need to be well-versed in things like ISO standards, accounting concepts, financial jargon, report structures, and auditing best practices. If you want to learn more about auditing, you can get a bachelor's, master's, ACCA, CPA, diploma, or other similar degree in accounting or finance, and you can also study a number of case studies on corporate audits to get some insight.

When performing an audit, an auditor has to be well-versed in not just tax law, but also the regulations governing the firm or industry being audited. Auditors benefit from having a basic understanding of technology and computer systems. Audits may be completed more quickly and with more precision if the auditor is familiar with the appropriate digital applications and tools. It's also worth noting that audit firms, including the "big five" audit firms throughout the globe, often have their own proprietary audit processing technology. Companies may use this tool to undertake audits systematically, ensuring they gather evidence for all relevant risks and processes.

In addition to the required academic credentials, an auditing career of any length is highly prized because of the practical experience it provides. Individuals who have evaluated reports in several situations of varying complexity have gained valuable experience with the audit process. Having greater experience means less time is wasted looking over reports for errors. As a result of their self-assurance in their abilities and expertise, experienced auditors are able to speed up the decision-making process. A key aspect of any job is getting along with others, therefore it's important that auditors have experience interacting with people and avoiding conflicts.

Along with the right education and work experience, a successful auditor also has to have the right personality traits.

The ability to pay close attention to detail is essential for a successful audit. A reliable auditor is thorough in their examination of financial documents. To ensure that no relevant data is overlooked, it is important to maintain a high level of vigilance and organization. In audits, every word matters, and every bit of data may serve as a performance indicator.

Accounting auditors are engaged in a similar anti-fraud mission to that of police. A good auditor is one who is forthright in their dealings and has a strong sense of fairness. They need to look at things dispassionately and not care who is in charge. A successful auditor is one who can persevere in the face of adversity and maintains their moral compass no matter what.

Effective communication is essential in every field, as it allows for the dissemination of ideas, thoughts, and suggestions with the least amount of backlash possible. An auditor's ability to present information clearly, concisely, and definitively is crucial.

Time management is crucial in every occupation or daily endeavor. Due to the massive amounts of data that need to be examined in a short period of time, efficient time management is essential for an auditor.

Patience: Auditing may be a difficult and lengthy procedure, so you'll need a lot of it. Auditors need to be detail-oriented and able to go through massive amounts of paperwork. An auditor's composure is crucial to the success of the audit. They need to be emotionally savvy so that they can work through the long hours alone and the pressure.

An auditor ought to be someone who takes the initiative to get things done. Auditors need access to all relevant information in order to analyze a company's performance. As a result, an auditor has to dig further than necessary.

Possessing the capacity for critical thought is a necessary trait for every auditor. In order to conduct a successful audit, people must suspend their preconceived notions and examine the issue objectively. They need to be able to see the larger picture and give sound logic.

The best auditors are naturally inquisitive people with a great eye for detail and an extraordinary capacity for observation. When people are curious in something, they tend to look into it thoroughly using various sources. Curious minds may help audits go more smoothly.

Putting up the time and effort required for an audit is essential. It's impossible for an auditor to give their complete attention to an audit unless they have a real passion for what they're doing. Finance and accounting are challenging areas that demand one's whole focus and energy. Those who are really invested in learning and the task will remain with it longer than those who aren't.

Skepticism from an Expert: Sometimes reports include fabricated data in the stories. The auditor's job is to double-check facts and verify data from trustworthy sources. Auditors need to probe all presented materials for discrepancies and keep an eye out for hints. An audit of any quality requires a healthy dose of skepticism. First, it's important to grasp just what it is that auditors perform.

What exactly does an auditor do?

An Audit is a series of steps used to determine whether or not a company's financial and other reports on operations are accurate and reliable in accordance with a predetermined standard. An audit's purpose is to reveal whether or not a corporation is being honest and fair in its practices and to root out any instances of corruption. Auditor refers to the individual or group tasked with doing an audit. An auditor is a professional who gathers and assesses information to provide a report on the veracity of an organization's claims that they follow a certain set of norms and guidelines. Auditors play a crucial role in ensuring that businesses operate ethically and reliably.

In a nutshell, these are the characteristics of a great auditor:

A company's financial records are reviewed by an auditor, who compares them to established guidelines and norms. The following characteristics are indicative of a competent auditor:

Knowledge of:
- Reports on the finances
- Guidelines for Accounting
- Legislation pertaining to technology and taxes Company procedures
- Professional norms
- A thorough examination of the auditing procedure
- Skills, qualifications, and personal qualities such as:
- Extremely careful and trustworthy
- Positive interactions based on clear and effective communication
- Planning and scheduling
- Patience
- Competence in Reading and Managing Emotions

- Taking the initiative
- Analytical pondering
- Curiosity
- Dedication and Cautiousness in the Workplace

Advantages and Limitations of audit

Pros and cons of auditing: An audit is an examination of a company's financial statements to see whether they follow the laws, accounting standards, and accounting principles of a certain jurisdiction. To rephrase, an audit is a procedure often used by institutions like corporations and governments to evaluate how well they are doing their jobs. Organizational or governmental policy will dictate the nature of the audit and its objectives. An audit may help you gain perspective and identify areas of improvement in your procedures. Delays, high expenses, lengthy hours, a lack of transparency, and a lack of ownership in the process are just some of the potential drawbacks.

Additional articles about events, people, sports, technology, and more may be found in the Advantages and Disadvantages section for students.

Nonetheless, the meaning of the word "audit" may be widened in other ways as well (from a business perspective). It's a catch-all word for a wide variety of endeavors whose primary purpose is to ascertain whether or not certain goals have been met. Tasks might be anything from the everyday (like IT support and business process improvement) to the unusual (like risk management and compliance audits). It is also important for a business that has been audited to understand the benefits and drawbacks of auditing. In this post, we'll take a closer look at the pros and cons of this approach.

A handful of Auditing's many benefits include the following:

1. The importance of auditing lies in the fact that it guarantees that public interest is protected by means of established rules and processes. To double-check that they're following industry standards and providing maximum benefit to the business, managers might use audits to verify the quality of their operations. In addition, audits might reveal whether there have been any shifts in management or other problems with the business's procedures.

2. Improvements in company performance may often be traced back to auditing, which is a method of testing the system and discovering gaps that should be filled. Changes in the system and potential for enhancement may be better implemented with the

aid of auditing. Through auditing, we can identify whether or not any one procedure is failing to meet standards or is being ignored by the team.

3.   Adds trust since an outsider verifies that there have been no undisclosed losses or difficulties with the company's finances throughout the auditing process. Incorporating external auditors, annual financial reports, and internal audit procedures are all useful tools for achieving this goal. Building trust in your company is crucial in today's market. The confidence gained by an audit helps you to conduct your company without worrying that your fraudulent activities may be uncovered.

4.   Stop corruption before it starts by conducting regular audits. The purpose of a financial audit is to evaluate the soundness of a business's finances. Companies, contractors, organizations, and institutions that receive government financing are not immune to embezzlement and other forms of fraud. Individuals, too, are subject to audits, and it is common practice to ask them to do so once a year. Auditors should be able to identify dishonesty in a wide variety of operational areas, including financial reporting, human resources, logistics, procurement, risk assessment, sales data, and more.

5.   Helpful for Setting Financial Goals - The auditing process includes audit planning and budgeting. As such, it is crucial in revealing previously unknown dangers or possibilities within the proposed actions. As an instance, if auditors intend to conduct an internal audit once every three years during the course of the complete cycle, they will have adequate time to apply fixes before any severe issues develop.

Problems with Auditing:

1.   Auditing can be expensive because of all the measures that may need to be put into place to guarantee compliance hiring an external auditing company is one example; subcontracting some tasks and closely monitoring their progress is another. The price of conducting regular audits may eventually make such inspections impractical.

2.   Auditors need specialized training - Auditing, in and of itself, may be a challenging procedure that calls for a great deal of expertise. In addition, auditing is a time-consuming and expensive process, especially for big corporations. Given their access to unencrypted customer information, accounting companies often demand exorbitant rates. Staff members may

utilize this information to perpetrate fraud or theft on the job, which is a major issue.

3. Infeasible to verify each and every trade - One major drawback of auditing is that it's hard to verify every single transaction that takes place inside a business. This is a difficulty for auditors in corporate environments, which need ongoing monitoring.

4. No good for startups since conducting an audit takes a lot of time and money. Most small firms lack either the personnel or resources to do audits in-house. These organizations would be better served by focusing their resources on eliminating the need for audits by enhancing the quality of their internal procedures and decision-making.

5. Bribery and other incentives that might greatly increase the value of audits are a constant temptation for auditors. Threats to the auditor may have the same effect on the outcome of the audit.

MODULE - 2
AUDIT PROCEDURES

Audit Procedures: Vouching – Definition – Features

Vouching is the process of verifying the correctness of numerical entries by examining the supporting documents. Vouching is the process through which an auditor verifies the accuracy of the accounting entries using supporting paperwork. The authenticity of a voucher is the litmus test of every audit. It verifies that the entry in the books of accounts is accurate. It's the process of looking at paper trails to make sure the numbers in the books add up and are legit.

Vouching, as defined by Dicksee, "consists of comparing entries in the books of accounts with documented evidence In support thereof."

If you believe Joseph Lancaster "The common misconception is that vouching entails nothing more than comparing the book entries to the supporting vouchers or documents. However, this is completely incorrect, since vouching entails an inspection of the ledger entries sufficient to convince the auditor that the entry has been correctly entered on the books of accounts and is backed by the supporting documentation."

This definition of vouching as an examination of the veracity of entries in the foundational books of accounts is obvious from the above. In a nutshell, vouching is an audit of the supporting documents for any accounting entry or transaction. Vouching does more than just make that the books are balanced and the transactions are recorded accurately. The auditor needs to know that everything is in order and that the books of account accurately reflect the financial situation.

Voucher
Examining Vouchers

A voucher is any piece of paper that may be used to verify the accuracy of the information recorded in a ledger. A voucher is any piece of evidence that may be used to verify the numbers recorded in the books of accounts.

Promotional coupons might look like these:

Examples of vouchers include bills, receipts, invoices, goods received notes, salary and wage sheets, goods inward and outward registers, stores records, cheque book counterfoils, pay-in slip book counterfoils, bank statements, bank pass books, delivery challans, agreements, material requisition slips, copies of purchase orders, minute books, memorandum and articles of association, partnership deeds, trust deeds, prospectuses, and so on.

The importance of vouching lies in the fact that it: • ensures the authenticity of transactions; • enables knowledge of transactions; • aids in understanding the significance of transactions; • helps with the equitable distribution of capital, revenue, and expenses; • identifies fraudulent or erroneous transactions; • makes decisions about the legitimacy of transactions; • complies with legal requirements; • guarantees accurate accounting and full disclosure.

The auditor has to keep these factors in mind as they vouch.

Vouching of cashbook
- The voucher's date.
- The title of the group
- A rubber stamp for ticking off audits
- Approval from the approved individual
- [When the total exceeds Rs.5000/-, a revenue stamp of Re.1 must be affixed.]
- The Deal is Related to Business
- Money and Profits
- Numerical and verbal representations of financial amounts
- No member of the client's staff may be asked for help while verifying payments. 9. Account manager.
- Invoices are not being accepted despite having receipts; 12) Vouchers are not present.
- Documents of Vital Importance
- Cash transaction affidavits
- Completion of all required paperwork
- Payee's signature
- Types of Payments
- A notation in the audit log
- Alteration
- Control number for vouchers
  The Reasons for Vending a Guarantee

The primary goals of vouching are as follows:
1. Keeping accurate financial records by recording all relevant business activities.

2.   To verify that all transaction entries are backed up by sufficient documentation.

3.   To ensure that no fictitious entries are made in the accounting records.

4.   Make sure that the books of account accurately reflect all company dealings.

5.   Ensure that a trustworthy third party authenticates all financial transactions.

Procedures for Conducting Audits

One definition of auditing techniques is the set of methods and tools that auditor employs in order to locate and analyze the evidences that have been tracked down via auditing processes.

The two words have different meanings; a process is a way of handling something, while a technique is a way of doing something. As a result, although it is possible to define a comprehensive list of methods (even with the inclusion of a new or better method or technique), it is more challenging to write a comprehensive list of procedures since they are tied to the goals to which they relate. While techniques tend to be more or less fixed and constrained, processes may take numerous forms, with the most appropriate one being chosen based on objective factors associated with the tasks at hand. Based on the same reasoning, we may differentiate between auditing processes and auditing methods in the ways that follow:

- Since there are many different kinds of audits, it would be impossible to compile a comprehensive list of audit processes, but it would be possible to describe a comprehensive list of audit methods.

- The processes (of audit) employed in various engagements emerge from the intelligent application of the available tools, and are hence referred to as "auditing procedures" (of audit).

- The focus of an audit procedure is on the more broad assertions that can be made about an account, such as its existence or occurrence, rights and obligations, completeness, valuation or allocation, presentation and disclosure, and so on, while the focus of an audit technique is on the examination of the evidences that have been traced as such by the audit procedure.

Fundamental Auditing Methods: It might be challenging to compile a complete checklist of auditing activities. The scope and nature of audits continue to be determined on the basis of judgment, tempered by experience. It is possible, however, to highlight the following as the most important auditing practices:

1. Inventory, purchasing, payroll, sales invoice preparation, stock valuation, depreciation accounting and analysis, invoice routing, etc. internal accounting controls are reviewed, tested, and evaluated.

2. Second, verifying the accuracy of the balances of debtors and creditors, and confirming the accuracy of the inventory at the lower of cost or market price in line with generally accepted accounting standards that have been consistently implemented.

3. A copy of the final inventory listing can be obtained and tested for clerical accuracy, as can the earnings records of employees, which can be compared to the original copies of appointment-cum-increment letters to ensure accuracy. The same is true for the appropriation of profit and the board's resolutions.

4. Invoices for sales may be compared to the total amount customers owe in order to perform a number of necessary 4 reconciliation, comparison, and confirmation operations. An example of this would be balancing the cost account records with the financial books. The bank's reconciliation statement serves as a reliable verification tool. By comparing the minutes of the board of directors for signs of pledges or assignments, we can check that the inventory in question belongs to the customer and that any lien on the inventory is declared appropriately.

5. Keeping an eye out for and asking questions regarding stale, slow-moving, outdated, or untouchable stock.

6. Keeping track of all inventory tags before and after a physical count.

7. Before attesting that the assets and liabilities that appear in the balance sheet exhibit a 'true and fair view' of the state of affairs of the business, the auditor's primary duty is to verify as to the evidences relating to the ownership of assets and existence of assets and liabilities, as part of auditing practices and procedures.

It will take the auditor a long time to do a thorough review of all of the company's transactions if they are substantial. When conducting an audit of a company's books, it is fairly uncommon practice for the auditor to just verify a sample of entries from each class, with the assumption that the others are also accurate if the sample checks out. It's called "test checking" for short. If a sufficient internal check system already exists, the auditor might skip the thorough checking phase. In the future, he may start using Test checking. It's a method of selecting samples from a larger whole that the auditor uses to speed things up by skimming over less important details. If, during Test Checking, he verifies that the records he has examined are accurate, then he will not need to do any more detail checking.

Comparison of Statistical Sampling and Test-Checking

There are two options for making a check list selection:

i.   Subjective evaluation
ii.   Systematic sampling

Test checking is the process used to ensure the correctness of a judgment-based approach. The practice of using samples to draw conclusions is known as statistical sampling.

Important Safety Measures - The auditor must take the following measures when doing the test check:

1.   First, the entries chosen for the exam must be generic enough to apply to all financial dealings.
2.   Second, it must be completely at random whatever products are chosen.
3.   Third, it is not applicable for use while vouching the cash book.
4.   No one in the client's office should learn which entries were chosen for the test check.
5.   The time frame used to verify data should vary from book to book and year to year.
6.   Where the law mandates a comprehensive audit, he should not use test checking.
7.   Seven, it's important to double-check some January and December entries.
8.   The test should be constructed in such a way that a significant amount of the work completed by each worker is evaluated.
9.   Test checking should not be performed on control accounts or the impersonal ledger.
10.   The auditor should choose the test on his or her own, without consulting any of the client's employees.
11.   Eleven. Double examine your bank statement and any entries for cash withdrawals and deposits.

Ultimately, the auditor's discretion and preferences will determine the scope of the test checking, but it's important to keep in mind that doing unnecessary checks is a waste of time and money. It's important to keep an eye on the scope of the test checking and make sure it doesn't become too robotic and unrepresentative. If the representative things picked for checking aren't chosen with great intellect and creativity, test checking will be useless.

One of the main benefits of using Test Check is the massive reduction in workload it provides.

Two, you may cut down on resources like labor and money.

Test checking may be highly successful if done correctly, and the additional time made available can be put to good use focusing on areas of high value.

The Downsides of the Test-Check Procedure

During a test check, the auditor is constantly worried that he may miss something crucial or that a mistake would go unnoticed.

Second, if the client's employees know that the auditor will be doing test checks, they may stop taking precautions.

In the event that accounting problems are discovered, the auditor cannot hide behind the fact that he performed a test audit. To guarantee that the Profit and Loss Account and Balance Sheet provide a truthful and fair assessment of the financial health of the company and its operations, respectively, the auditor must pick the test items with great care.

SPEEDY INSPECTIONS

It is preferable to conduct audits in an unexpected manner to prevent them from becoming regular, mechanical, and predictable. To do a surprise check, an auditor unexpectedly visits a client's office or place of business. The unexpectedness occurs in both the short and long term. During these unexpected inspections, neither the customer nor their employees are aware of what would be examined.

Verifying cash, shares, investments, and books of primary entry with such checks is a wise move. It helps in determining whether the internal control system is functioning well, which in turn aids in the prevention and detection of accounting fraud and mistakes.

CARDS USED

Checkboxes are used to monitor the auditor's productivity.

Ticks should be used cautiously during auditing. One of the first things to do is choose a color for the tick that stands out and can't be mistaken for the client's employees or internal auditors'. Second, decide which ticks you'll be using. All of the ticks need to go in the appropriate places so that the documents don't become unreadable and the records don't seem sloppy.

It's important to keep the customers' workers in the dark about the employment of various ticks.

STRICT INSPECTION AND REPORTING

According to Taylor and Perry, "Auditing in Depth" is "an in-depth investigation of the system used inside a company, including the tracking of specific transactions from beginning to end, with inquiries made into the records generated and their authorization at each step along the way."

In-depth audits are not the same as double-checking everything. It's an end-to-end analysis of the specific deals you've chosen to look at. This means that it is utilized in conjunction with test verification. If the auditor has chosen to thoroughly examine just 25% of purchase transactions, for instance, that's exactly what needs to happen. An audit should include a review of all relevant purchase documentation, including the Purchase Requisition, Tenders, Purchase Orders, Purchase Bills, Goods Received Note, Inspection Note, Purchase Journal, Stock Register, Bin Card, and so on. Accordingly, the auditor has to double-check the whole buying process. This allows him to assess the effectiveness of the company's bookkeeping and internal controls.

Vouching of trading transactions
COSTS THAT ARE JUST A PAIN IN THE POCKET

1. Locate the individuals responsible for Petty Cash.
2. Be sure you're not going to go over your Petty Cash budget.
3. Remember the Imp rest System's restriction.
4. Verify that the disbursement of petty cash is subject to frequent audits by an accountable individual.
5. On a regular basis, review Petty Cash Reconciliation Statements based on vouchers.
6. Ensure the Cashbook entry for Petty Cash reflects the movement of funds from the Imp rest system.
7. Check the signed invoices, bills, and receipts that accompany the petty cash vouchers.
8. Follow the mail outgoing register entries and postage costs for a complete audit trail. Look back to prior time frames to find reasonable justifications for unexpected shifts.
9. Double-check the column totals, subtotals, and sums.
10. Nominal ledger head of account tracking based on petty cash book entries.
11. Conduct a random check of the petty cash on hand on a certain day.
12. Take a look at the Suspense Vouchers / IOUs and make sure they're canceled in a timely manner.
13. Check the Petty Cash balance unexpectedly and compare it to the Petty Cash Book.

TRAVELLING COMMISSION ADVERTISEMENT

Payment is expected for all incurred costs, except those that may be verified without further evidence. The auditor is responsible for determining whether or not the directors are entitled to reimbursement for business-related travel expenditures and, if so, whether or not the expenses were undertaken in good faith.

The following details should always be included on a voucher for travel costs:

i.   Identify the individual or organization entitled to the refund by giving their name and position. The itinerary's finer points, so to speak. (High) The price of your train or plane ticket.

ii.   Arrival and departure timings and station-specific boarding/lodging costs/allowance amounts.

iii.   Anything else that was paid for but not reimbursed, such as porterage, gratuity, transportation, etc.

If flying was involved in getting where you need to go, the voucher should have the reverse of the airline ticket attached to it for inspection. The reported amount of a train or car ticket fee should be double-checked with a third party. Checking the rates of stopping allowance and boarding and lodging charges is important. T.A. invoices often lack documentation for miscellaneous itemized deductions. As long as it seems fair, most people won't question your spending. Official approval is required for all trip vouchers. The Board must approve any out-of-the-ordinary or international travel expenditures before they are paid.

Directors are not allowed to charge travel fees for attending Board Meetings unless such expenses are explicitly provided for in the Articles or payment is authorized by a vote of shareholders.

Vouching v/s verification

Point of Difference	Vouching	Verification
1. Meaning	The act of examining the vouchers is known as vouching. A voucher is any documentary evidence in support of a transaction entered in the books of account.	Verification an be explained as establishing the truth or securing some kind of confirmation with respect to the assets and liabilities appearing in the Balance Sheet of a concern.
	Vouching involves estabilishing the arithmetical accuracy	Verification goes beyond vouching. It seeks to establish that assets as stated in the Balance Sheet of a
2. Nature & Purpose	and the authenticity of the transactions of a concern. Vouching proves that an asset ought to exist.	concern exist in fact and that the liabilities are properly disclosed. Verification proves that an asset does exist.
3. Time	It is done during the whole year.	It is done at the end of the year.
4. Utility	Certifies correctness of records.	Certifies correctness of assets and liabilities.
5. Personnel	It is done by the junior staff of the auditor under the supervisionof a senior person.	It is done by the auditor himself assisted by senior.

Verification and valuation of assets and liabilities – Meaning

Spicer and Pegler have described verification as "it entails an enquiry into the worth, ownership and title, existence and possession and the presence of any charge on the assets". Verification is a method by which an auditor convinces himself about the correctness of the assets and liabilities shown in the Balance Sheet by scrutiny of the documented evidence available. Verification involves confirming the veracity, or confirmation of the assets and liabilities showing in the Balance Sheet.

Thus, verification entails checking:-

1. The presence of the assets
2. Legal ownership and possession of the assets
3. Making sure there are no liens on the property, and
4. Correct valuation

Of course it is not possible for the auditor to verify each and every asset. It was held in Kingston Cotton Mills case that "it is not part of an auditor's duty to take stock. No one contend that it is. He must rely on other people for the details of stock in trade in hand".

However, as per the decision given in Mc Kesson and Robins case the auditor must physically inspect some of the assets. Now the auditor has to report whether the balance sheet shows true and fair view of the state of affairs of the company. Hence, he is required to verify all the assets and liabilities appearing in the balance sheet. In case of failure, the auditor can be held liable for damages.

According to the 'statement of auditing practices' issued by ICAI, "the auditor's object in regard to assets generally is to satisfy that:

5. They exist.
6. They belong to the client.
7. They are in the possession of the client or the persons authorized by him.
8. They are not subject to undisclosed encumbrances or lien.
9. They are stated in the balance sheet at proper amounts in accordance with sound accounting principles, and
10. They are recorded in the accounts.

Points to be considered:

While conducting verification following points should be considered by the auditor :-

i. Existence: The auditor should confirm that all the assets of the company are physically existing on the date of balance sheet.
ii. Possession: The auditor has to verify that the assets are in the possession of the company on the date of balance sheet.
iii. Ownership: The auditor should confirm that the asset is legally owned by the company.
iv. Charge or lien : The auditor needs to examine if the asset is subject to any charge or lien.

v.   Record: The auditor should certify that all the assets and liabilities are recorded in the books of account and there is no omission of asset or liability.

vi.   Audit report: Under CARO the auditor is to report if the manangement has done physical verification of fixed assets and stock and the difference, if any, between the physical inventory and the inventory as per the book.

vii.   Event after balance sheet date : The auditor should find out if any event after the date of balance sheet has altered any items of assets and liabilities.

Verification Scope

The following details are required for verification:-

i.   Existence of the assets as of the balance sheet date

ii.   It was established that the assets were purchased for commercial use solely.

iii.   Which means the assets were legally obtained.

iv.   The assets have been legally transferred to the organization and the organization is the rightful owner.

v.   That there was no cost associated with using the assets, and

vi.   That all assets were accurately appraised and listed on the balance sheet.

Four verification targets:

The assets and debts to check for are as follows:

1.   To demonstrate an accurate assessment of assets and liabilities.

2.   See whether the balance sheet accurately reflects the company's financial position by doing your own analysis.

3.   It is necessary to determine who owns something in order to transfer or sell it.

4.   To unearth any potential fraud or mistakes

5.   Inquire into the adequacy of the internal controls in place for the purchase, use, and sale of assets.

6.   In order to check the numbers, the books must be reconciled.

7.   Verify the accuracy of the asset records.

Here are five reasons why verification is important.

The following are some of the benefits of verification:-

1.   Accounts are less likely to be tampered with.

2.   As a result, it prevents resources from being wasted.

3.   Accurate asset records and valuations are maintained.

4.   It provides a genuine and impartial picture of the company's health.

Verification methods:

1.   The term "inspection" refers to a hands-on examination of a company's possessions, such as its cash in the cash box, its merchandise, its certificates of stock ownership, and so on.
2.   As a witness, an auditor may be present when other parties check assets.
3.   Obtaining third-party written confirmation of the existence of assets is referred to as "confirmation."

Verification and valuation of different assets and liabilities

The word "verification" refers to the validation of certain transactions and the physical inspection of particular types of assets. The two terms—verification and vouching—are often used interchangeably, but the level of scrutiny that goes into each is different. Verification involves inquiring into the worth, ownership, existence, and possession of assets and confirming that they are free of any mortgage or charge, while vouching serves to attest to the veracity of the transactions and their numerical correctness. However, verification through physical examination and confirmation proves whether a particular asset actually exists without having any charge on the date of the balance sheet, whereas the mere presence of any entry regarding the acquisition of asset purports to prove that the asset ought to exist.

The actions required to verify assets are as follows:
1.   Examination of the estimates of worth;
2.   Verification of Asset Ownership and Title Documents;
3.   Visual examination of the Real Property; and
4.   Evidence of the asset charge;
5.   Disclosing, categorizing, and presenting the assets in conformity with generally accepted accounting principles and applicable law.

There is a lot that can be checked, therefore it's only fitting that the auditor has a significant role in the verification process. An auditor should make every effort to determine whether or not an asset is recorded at its fair value in the Balance Sheet, whether or not the company has exclusive ownership of the asset, and whether or not there are any liens or other claims against the asset. If the auditor does not carry out his responsibilities, he will be held responsible. In the case of

London Oil Storage Co. Ltd. "It is the job of the auditor to verify the existence of the assets listed in the Balance sheet and he would be accountable for any loss caused by the client if he fails in his duty," Chief Justice Alverstone said in Vs. Sear Hasluck & Co. (1904).

Verification is crucial not just for legal reasons but also to prevent the over- or undervaluation of assets like stock-in-trade, which may significantly affect a company's bottom line. As such, the Balance Sheet may not always reveal the true financial health of a company.

However, the auditor is unable to personally check each and every asset due to time constraints or a lack of expertise with the assets in question. According to the case "Kingston Cotton Mills," an auditor's responsibility does not include doing inventory checks. Nobody disputes that it isn't. The specifics of his profession are something he has to learn from others.

Once again, when we peruse the Mc Kesson and Robins case decision from 1939, we see that the auditor has to do on-site verification of certain of the assets. Title papers, such as negotiable instruments, shares, debentures, securities, etc., should be reviewed extensively on the final day of the accounting period if at all feasible. It is incumbent upon him to assure himself that the deals, if any, between the date of the Balance Sheet and the date of the audit, are genuine and supported by appropriate documentation. Although the legislation does not specifically require the auditor to take stock-in-trade, he is nevertheless responsible for verifying it using the purchase book, stock records, gatekeeper's book, etc.

Asset value determination
What This Means

To do an asset valuation, one must use generally accepted accounting standards to get an estimate of the fair value of the assets shown on the Balance Sheet. Overstating or understating the value of assets in the Balance sheet distorts the genuine and fair image of the financial situation and provides the inaccurate position of profitability, making accurate asset valuation crucial.

Officials' major responsibility is to determine how much the company's assets are worth. The auditor is tasked with determining whether the determined value is accurate. He may depend on the technical certification given to him by the specialists in the area for this purpose.

When doing an asset valuation, it is not enough to just verify the value of the assets held by a company as of the Balance Sheet date;

rather, a more in-depth analysis of the assets' worth is required.(a valuation of several assets).

The auditor must also verify that asset valuations are made in accordance with generally accepted accounting standards. For the sake of simplicity, we will refer to such assets as beneath for the purpose of calculating their worth.

1.Investing in Long-Term Assets

2.The Assets That Can Be Quickly Converted Into Cash

3.Using Up Resources

4.Non-Physical Resources

5.Valueless Paper Assets.

1. **Fixed Assets:** The "going concern value," or cost minus depreciation, is the standard method for valuing fixed assets. By "cost," we mean the sum total of the asset's purchase price as well as any additional costs paid for its production, acquisition, and setup. The value of an asset decreases over time due to factors including use, wear and tear, obsolescence, and more, and this decline is accounted for by a provision called depreciation. Values of fixed assets may be skewed if the depreciation allowance is not reasonable. The definition of a fixed asset changes depending on the kind of company.

2. Stocks, bills receivable, various debtors, etc. are examples of current assets that may be turned into cash at the earliest opportunity. Consistent with the concept of conservatism, the value of a current asset is determined by the lower of its original value (cost price) and its market worth (realizable value). Since their ultimate purpose is to be turned into cold hard cash as soon as possible, every potential value we may realize is crucial. This strategy is used to bolster a company's financial standing by offsetting potential losses due to a decline in asset value. The conservative accounting convention upholds this notion, which states that one should not expect profits but rather make allowances for expected losses.

3. Assets that depreciate over time as a result of their usage are considered wasting assets. First, the assets' potential worth in terms of units of output, etc., must be established, and then, the value must be lowered proportionally in light of the assets' actual usage. For assets of this sort, the value may be steady if they are not used over a certain time period. Therefore, we should dispose of these assets based on how often we use them. This approach, however, isn't always feasible, thus the "cost less depreciation" idea may have to be used instead.

4. Goodwill, intellectual rights, know-how, and similar intangible assets are often appraised at cost. The fair market value is used to determine the worth of intangible assets if they are acquired in a transaction other than a monetary one. Even though they have no current worth, intangible assets like these are nonetheless counted as such until they are entirely written off by the auditor. Their worth is to be calculated as their original purchase price less any depreciation that has been taken into account as of the date of the balance sheet.

5. Some one-time costs (such as legal fees or a stock issue discount) that won't be recovered for many years are treated as "fictitious assets" on the balance sheet until they've been written off in full. Because of this, all of them are examples of fictitious assets. They should be valued at the difference between their historical cost and any impairments that have occurred as of the date of the Balance Sheet.

Methods of Valuation - General Considerations

The numerous asset valuation concepts are outlined here.

First, there's the "cost price" (or "going concern value") technique, which takes into account depreciation to arrive at an asset's "true" value. Typically, this technique is used to determine the worth of long-term investments.

The asset's market value, or the price at which the item is currently trading, is referred to as the market value in (2). Whenever this is less than the cost of the item, it is used to determine the value of the present assets. Products that spoil quickly are often valued at their current market price.

Unneeded business property may have resale value on the scrap market if the company no longer has any need for it. The scrap value of an asset is the price at which it may be sold for scrap purposes.

The value at which an asset may be renewed is known as its replacement value (point #4). This is the market price at the time the balance sheet was created, which would be used to buy the asset.

The expected selling price, or the asset's realizable value, is the fifth definition. Commission, trading fees, and similar costs are typical deductions.

The opinion of the auditor on asset valuation:

Auditors take a somewhat different stance on value than they do on other parts of an audit. The auditor, as has previously been said, is not expected to have technical understanding about the assessment of assets. As a result, he must have substantial faith in the assessment provided by the board of directors, executives, surveyors, etc. Does it, however, absolve him of responsibility if the directors, specialists, surveyors, etc., misjudge the value of any or all of the assets in question? In cases where the auditor is reliant on the work of others and if assets are assessed using projected depreciation, the answer is an emphatic no. He must ensure that the company's management is providing an accurate picture of its current status. The auditor's responsibility in this situation is to ensure that the asset values are calculated in accordance with generally accepted accounting standards. He needs to make sure the estimate is accurate. In any instance, the accurate valuation of assets should be determined after a careful examination of all relevant paperwork by the auditor. If he has the slightest doubt about the accuracy of an asset's value, he should look into it.

Validation is not the same as assessment.

1. The difference between verification and valuation is that valuation attests to the accuracy of the worth of assets and liabilities, whereas verification attests to the existence, ownership, and purchase of assets.

2. Both verification and valuation occur annually, although at different times of the year.

3. Staff: an auditor checks the numbers, but the business owner sets the value.

4. Documentary proof for verification includes title deeds and payment receipts, while valuation documentation includes a certificate from the property owner.

Asset verification - example:

Cash on hand and in the bank:

A person's liquid assets consist of all of the following:

Money Physically Obtainable:

1. Verifying cash on hand requires extra diligence. No one can say for sure that the cash that was produced for auditing was ever in the custodian's possession.

2. This is why it's important for auditors to double-check the cash at some point after the end of the year, without alerting the client or his team in advance.

3. When there is more than one cash balance figure, as is the case when there is a cashier, a petty cashier, a branch cashier, and imp rest balance with employees, it is best to check all of them at

once if at all possible, to avoid the possibility of a shortfall in one balance being made up by a transfer of amount from another.

4. The cashier should be present throughout the counting of cash, and he should be required to sign a statement that confirms the accuracy of the count and the amount of cash on hand. If he is not there while the cash is being verified, he may later dispute the amount of real cash on hand, putting the auditor in a difficult situation.

5. If the auditor is unable to verify the accuracy of the Balance Sheet on that date, he must coordinate with his client to ensure that any remaining funds are transferred into a bank account before the end of the fiscal year. In the event of a balance at the factory, depot, or branch where cash cannot be examined at the end of the year, the same procedure should be followed.

6. If this is not practicable, the auditor must at least confirm all cash transactions up to the date of the cash count. The logical conclusion to draw from performed quickly after counting the funds on hand. The auditor has to sign the cash book for the day the cash balance was checked to show that the check was made.

7. The whole amount of any checks or drafts that are part of the cash balance must be reported.

8. The auditor must compare the entries in the rough Cash Book, or in a separate book detailing the daily balance, with the entries in the Cash Book to establish that the latter are accurate.

9. A responsible official should initial any slips, chits, or IOUs pertaining to advances made to employees that the auditor discovers in the cash balance. These should then be debited to the appropriate accounts.

Money in Motion (Remittance in Transit)

1. This is the sum that has been wired from a branch, depot, agent, etc. to the main office but has not yet arrived in the form of cash or a check. to put it another way, etc.

2. Such remittance in transit should be verified from subsequent period cash book/pass book as to whether actually it is received or not.

3. Reconciliation of H.O./Branch Accounts should also be checked.

4. If amount is deposited into bank, pay-in-slip can also be verified.

5. See that entry for remittance in transit is passed by only one party and is reversed in the next year.

Petty Cash

1. Petty Cash in hand should be verified with Petty Cash Book
2. Also check up the balance of Petty Cash Account in General Ledger.
3. Vouch the transaction of last month property to ascertain that ficititious payments are not entered into
4. Some of the points given for verification of cash in hand will be applicable for Petty Cash also.

Bank Balance :

1. To verify cash at bank, the auditor should examine the bank pass book and compare it with the balance as shown by the bank column of the cash book.
2. Check bank reconciliation statement with bank statement / pass book of subsequent period.
3. The auditor should get a certificate regarding the balance at the bank directly from the bank.
4. Ensure that the balance as shown by the cash book is brought into the balance sheet as 'Cash and Bank' and not 'Balance as shown by the pass book'.
5. The auditor should also see that the 'cheque outstanding' and 'cheques not yet collected' are genuine and not made up in order to conceal the deficiency. If some of these cheques are more than six months old, he should make inquires, and have them reversed in the books of accounts.
6. Cash in Fixed deposits with the bank can be verified by examining the deposit receipt, or getting a certificate from the banker.
7. If there are more than one bank account such as 'Dividend Account'. "Interest Account' etc. all such accounts should be checked and the balances should be verified upon the same date. Information regarding their balance should also be obtained from the bank directly.
8. If the bank account shows an adverse balance and the client has deposited any security for the overdraft, the auditor should enquire from the bank the particulars of the security and the amount of the interest charged.

Bills Due and Receivable

1. Bills Receivable that have not yet matured but are in hand on the date of the Balance Sheet should be reviewed by the auditor.

2.   Bank certifications are required to verify the specifics of any bill collection.

3.   If there are a lot of bills in the auditor's possession, he should compile a list of them.

4.   Bills that have been discounted but have not yet matured need careful examination, and he should check with the bank before include them as a note in the Balance Sheet's disclosure of contingent liabilities.

5.   The auditor must pay close attention to the Bills to ensure that they have been correctly drafted, stamped, and lawfully approved.

6.   He needs to see whether any debts are past due. If this is the case, the auditor needs to know what steps were taken, when they were taken, etc. Whether there are any invoices that have a low likelihood of being collected, he should check to determine if a sufficient bad debt reserve has been established to cover the loss.

7.   Bills that have been dishonoured must not be recorded as Bills Receivable, thus it is his responsibility to check on this. The auditor must also verify whether or not all required noting procedures have been followed.

8.   Many of the invoices that were due on the Balance Sheet date may have matured or been honoured by the time the auditor has visited his client after the Balance Sheet date. Because of this, the auditor must verify such invoices against the Cash Book or Pass Book and then reconcile the difference.

9.   Bills Receivable should also reflect the amount of the original bill due on the Balance Sheet date if it was renewed after that date, with interest on renewed bills appropriately accounted for.

10. In the event that the invoices you endorsed are returned as unpaid, you will get payment from the original drawee and the original endorsee would be debited.

Subsequent Loan Advances

There are several kinds of loans, including:

(a) Mortgages and other real estate-backed loans.

(b) Products-Collateralized Loans

(c) Securities collateral loans.

(d) Loans backed by the value of an insurance policy, and

(e) Borrowing that is secured by the borrower's own assets.

And therefore, generally speaking, an auditor's responsibilities are as follows, in any given situation:

1. Confirm that the purpose clause of the Memorandum allows for the issuance of such loans.

2. Analyzing whether or not an accurate loan ledger has been kept up to date.

3. Verification of each loan's collateral holdings. Interest rates in the loan agreement should be thoroughly reviewed. When payments, fines, interest, etc. are due.

4. He has to find out whether any loans are very unlikely to be repaid, in which case he needs to set aside money to cover the loss.

5. Unless it's a bank or a finance firm, an auditor has to verify that the money being advanced will be used for business purposes. The auditor must report whether or not the parties to whom loans are issued are regular in payment of interest and principal and whether or not the conditions of the loan are prima facie adverse to the interest of the firm, as required by Section 227(4A) of the Companies Act, 1956.

(a) Loans backed by real estate and infrastructure

1. Auditors are tasked with checking mortgage deed copies to ensure they are fully performed and recorded in the client's favour.

2. The title documents submitted with the mortgage deed must be reviewed by the auditor.

3. The valuer's certificate must be reviewed by the auditor to determine the security's value and adequacy, if applicable.

4. The auditor is responsible for verifying the existence of adequate property insurance and the timely payment of all required premiums.

5. The auditor is responsible for checking the Borrower's claims to the property.

6. If there is a second mortgage, the auditor must attest that the original mortgagee has been informed. To proceed, he must get the first mortgagee's acknowledgment of title deeds.

(b) Secured goods loans are included under clause

1. The auditor has to verify the products' authenticity and determine whether or not they are consistent with the description given by the borrower. He has to check whether the loan is secured by a dock warrant, a godown keeper's receipt, a railway receipt, a truck receipt, or any other kind of receipt.

2.   He is responsible for making sure that the godown is rented at market value and that the things kept there are adequately insured.

3.   The auditor has to check the worth of the merchandise by comparing it to its current market price. To some extent, he may trust the inspector's assessments on quality and quantity.

4.   The auditor has to look at the client's inventory turnover rate if the items are perishable.

(c) Securities-backed loans

1.   He should request a statement detailing the stocks and shares that were pledged as security and verify that all of them are completely paid.

2.   A transfer document should be checked by him to ensure it has been properly signed and stamped.

3.   He has to make sure that their true market worth is revealed.

4.   He must guarantee that the margin on the loans extended is enough.

5.   He has to verify that the fee was recorded accurately.

(d) Lending backed by insurance policies

1.   The policy's auditor has to verify that at least two years have passed since it was issued.

2.   The most recent premium receipt should be reviewed by the auditor to ensure that all premiums have been paid in full and the insurance is active.

3.   The auditor has to make sure the insurance company was notified of the assignment.

4.   The auditor has to verify that the loan was disbursed using the surrender value of the policy as attested to by the insurance provider.

5.   The auditor is responsible for confirming that the policy premium, if any, paid by the lender to maintain the policy in effect has been correctly deducted from the borrower's Loan Account together with the normal interest.

(e) Borrower-Guaranteed Loans

The auditor is responsible for reviewing the borrower's paperwork, which includes the Promissory Note, Guarantor information, and Borrower's Salary Certificate, among other things.

Miscellaneous Debtors

Sundry Debtors is the total amount that may be charged back to clients as payment for products and services provided.

1. After obtaining the client's schedule or list of debtors, the following process should be done to verify the accuracy of the 'Book Debts' or 'Sundry Debtors.

2. Debtors' balances may be confirmed directly by mail examining books at year's end.

3. Debts that have been labeled as "bad" or "doubtful" must be checked for their current status.

(f) Presentation or conformity with legal requirements

1. The auditor is responsible for sending the confirmation letter to the customer and ensuring that the confirmation reply is sent directly to his office from the client. Under the watchful eye of the audit team, this should be sent out no later than 15–20 days after the end of the year. When the response is received, it should be compared to the amounts recorded in the Debtors Ledger, and any discrepancies should be resolved.

2. After the aforementioned action is taken, he should examine the debtor's individual accounts with great care. Test Checks might be used in situations when there is a huge volume of debtors.

3. The auditor's attention should be directed into the ledger entries for discounts, refunds, cash received, rebates permitted, returned products, etc.

   After confirming that all of the debtors' balances are accurate, the auditor must next check the debtors in order to identify any problematic or dubious debts so that a provision may be made for them. If bad and irrecoverable or dubious debts are not appropriately prepared for, the financial statements will not provide a "True and Fair" image. In light of the debtor's age, the degree of inspection applied to payments received, the management's view, and any other relevant information (such as the debtors' financial standing), adequate provision must be made. The auditor will be held negligently responsible for any errors he makes in determining whether or not the provision is reasonable.

4. He is responsible for ensuring that Schedule VI of the Companies Act, 1956 is followed once he has determined the status of bad or doubtful debts. Debtors should be categorized as follows for this purpose:

a) Still outstanding after more than six months; and
b) Debt category

5. In addition, additional factors must be determined for disclosure, such as debts that are good and completely secured, obligations due from officers, directors, managers of the firm, etc.

6. Customers who have paid for their purchases using the hire purchase system do not need to have those items marked as "stock out on hire purchase" if not all of the installments are yet due.

7. Also, a client cannot be listed as a debtor at year's end if the products were sold on a "return or approval" basis.

8. In addition, anytime there are credit balances on certain debtors account, the same are not to be subtracted from other borrowers debit balances and net balance is not to be presented in the assets side, but rather the former is to be listed as Sundry Creditors.

Trademarks and Patents:

1. The patenting authority checks the patent grant certificate to ensure the patent is held by the rightful owner.

2. If it was bought, the agreement relinquishing ownership to the customer should be reviewed.

3. If the client has many patents, you should request a schedule including all of the relevant information about them or check the client's patent registry.

4. It is incumbent upon you to check that your patent rights are active and enforceable and that you have paid your renewal costs on time and credited your Revenue Account accordingly. If the patent has not expired, check the most recent renewal receipt.

5. Make sure the client's name is the only one on the patent registration.

6. Make sure the patent's expense is amortized during its working life.

7. If the patent is purchased, the money spent on it and any other associated costs must be written off as an investment.

8. If the customer develops the invention via their own investigations and lab work, only those costs actually expended in developing the patent should be capitalized.

Copyrights

1. The auditor has to look at the copyright assignment contract and the royalty payments made to the writers etc.

2. He must ensure that all transfers are recorded accurately.

3.	Clients who possess a large number of copyrights should be asked to provide a schedule of copyrights, with the auditor requesting all relevant details to verify that these rights are properly reflected in the financial statements.

4.	It is important to keep in mind that copyrights are worthless in the long term while calculating their potential value. Therefore, the worth is based on a revaluation basis and the length of copyrights.

5.	If a copyright is not being used to sell books, it should be cancelled that year. This is something that the auditor has to double-check thoroughly.

Expertise:

1.	Know how is recorded in the books only if it has been paid for. If it is developed in house, it cannot be capitalised. The auditor should keep his in mind while verifying know-how.

2.	Know-how can be of two types :

3.	The auditor has to make sure that any costs directly related to the production process (a) are deducted in the same year they were paid.

4.	The auditor has to make sure that any costs associated with (b) design, plant, and construction plans are capitalized, and that depreciation is calculated using the capitalized amount.

5.	If a single amount is to be paid for both forms of expertise, it is important that the two be kept apart as much as possible.

6.	The Income-Tax Act allows for the deduction of the cost of Know-How, within certain parameters.

7.	The auditor has to remember this when determining the tax due for the year in question.

Financial Assets:

The term "investment" may refer to a variety of different certificates, such as stock certificates, bond certificates, loan certificates, debenture certificates, and so on. This process is established for the purpose of verifying such securities.

1.	Get a list of holdings at the start of the audit period. Gather information such as the kind of investment, its purchase date, book value, market value, interest rate, the date interest or dividends were paid, the date on which they were declared, and any applicable tax withholding information.

2.	All the preceding information should be updated to include any investments bought or sold throughout the year.

3. Check the totals on this schedule against those in the general ledger and the balance sheet.
4. Verify the declared values of investments at the Balance Sheet date, based on stock exchange quotes or another appropriate technique.
5. On the date of the Balance Sheet, it is important to conduct a physical inspection of the certificates or securities.
6. Accrued earnings might be revised by comparing actual cash inflows with outstanding obligations.
7. Verify the contingent obligation on the Balance Sheet for uncalled liability on partially paid shares retained as investment.
8. Make sure that if the Balance Sheet shows an investment's book value is lower than it really is, a sufficient reserve is set aside to cover the difference.
9. Ensure the disclosure requirements of section 212 of Schedule VI of the Companies Act, 1956 are met with respect to the investment in subsidiaries.
10. To invest in a partnership, it is necessary to verify the partnership deed and a copy of the partnership's financial statements. Profit and loss allocation during the partnership term should be revised accordingly.
11. A proper authorization is required to certify investments held in the names of parties other than the business.
12. Collect a certificate from the parties involved for any investments that have been deposited with others as security or are lying with banks or share brokers.
13. Shares for which an application fee has been paid but not yet issued must be shown as such in the Balance Sheet.

Leasehold Property:

Leases and other rights to use property are often provided for certain terms of years. All rights revert to the original lessor after the lease term ends. The actions necessary to confirm leasehold rights are outlined below.
1. Read the lease carefully to learn about the premium, the length of the lease, and any additional requirements (such as those pertaining to maintenance, insurance, etc.).
2. A lease for more than one year must be given by a document registered with the Registrar in order to be legally binding.
3. Determine whether or not the lease's preconditions, the violation of which might result in the lease's termination, have been met.

4.   Refer to the sublease agreement to determine whether the sublease is lawful under the leasing agreement.
5.   Make that the lease's premium and acquisition costs are being amortised (deducted) throughout the lease's duration using a reasonable method.
6.   Make sure that, if any payment is to be paid upon the lease's expiration under the dilapidation clause, it is being done regularly and in a timely manner.
7.   If a lessee of leased land intends to build a structure on the property, the lessee should evaluate the situation and choose the proper manner of reporting the cost of this endeavor in the Balance Sheet.

Goodwill

1.   Goodwill refers to the difference between what a corporation paid for an operating business and what those assets are really worth on paper. The auditor may confirm this with the vendor's agreement and look for a precise amount paid or the difference between the purchase price and the value of the physical assets.
2.   Goodwill is recorded in the Balance Sheet once the firm has revalued its assets and created a Goodwill Account. If this is the case, the auditor has to examine the valuation's supporting documentation until he or she is happy with the results. If he is unhappy, that knowledge should be shared with investors.
3.   He must ensure that the surplus is placed in a reserve account for future use, such as a Capital Reserve or Revaluation Reserve, and that no dividends are paid out of it.
4.   Furthermore, he must check Schedule VI's disclosure obligation and make sure the facts are reported for 5 years from the date of revaluation.
5.   Goodwill that has been previously written off might be reinstated in the books of account to rectify the credit/debit discrepancy in the Profit and Loss statement. If an auditor is considering approving a particular strategy for generating Goodwill, they should do their due diligence to ensure it is appropriate. The board resolution is another source he should use. In the event that he is dissatisfied, it is necessary to inform the stockholders.
6.   The auditor has to make sure that if Goodwill was acquired in any other way, the relevant facts are fully declared and are backed up by documented proof.

Hardware & Equipment

1. In accordance with Section 227(4A) of the Companies Act, 1956, today's businesses must keep a Fixed Asset Register detailing such things as the assets' original purchase price, where they are located, how much they have depreciated, whether or not they were capitalized, etc. It is the responsibility of the auditor to request this kind of register be kept by the client and check to make sure that all physical assets are included with accurate descriptions.

2. All fixed assets must be physically checked by management under the same section's provisions. To this end, it is important for the auditor to inquire as to whether or not any such physical verification was performed. If this is the case, he has to inquire about the relevant paperwork. In the event of a disagreement, clarification as to why it occurred is required.

3. Invoices and other documentation relating to the setup of any new purchases made throughout the year will be checked for accuracy.

4. The fixed asset register's total value should match the amount recorded in the general ledger.

5. If any piece of equipment is sold, trashed, or transferred, the auditor should double-check the appropriate entries in the Fixed Assets Register to ensure that the item has been deleted.

6. The auditor has to make sure that depreciation is being taken into account for all plant and equipment and that the same method of depreciation is being used year after year.

7. The auditor has to verify that all of the client's equipment is owned outright and not subject to any liens or other claims. He must ensure that the mortgage paperwork have been correctly signed and that the mortgage is noted in the Balance Sheet if plant and equipment is being mortgaged.

Fixtures and Furnishings

- First, the auditor must guarantee that a comprehensive inventory of the client's furniture and fixtures is kept.
- The auditor is responsible for ensuring that all costs related to the acquisition of furniture and fittings are capitalized alongside the acquisition price.
- Third, the auditor should inquire as to whether the furnishings and fittings have been insured.
- It is the responsibility of the auditor to ensure that proper allowance is made for the depreciation of furniture and fittings.

- Fifth, the auditor may depend on the management certificate if he doesn't have time to physically verify the furnishings on a test check basis.

- He must also ensure that any broken or unsuitable furniture is completely written down in the books.

Freehold Real Estate (Land and Structures)

1. First, the auditor must check the client's property title documents to ensure that the property is freehold.
2. Second, if the property was bought during the year, the auditor must carefully review all of the documentation between the buyer and the broker or attorney.
3. Third, if a structure has been built on the freehold land, the bill from the construction company or an architect's certification must be provided as proof.
4. A certificate from the mortgagee to that effect should be acquired for verification if the title deeds have been lodged with the mortgagee.
5. If the title deeds are being held by a third party (such as a bank or a law firm) for safekeeping, the auditor should request a certificate from the holder of the account confirming this fact.
6. In case of doubt, the auditor should contact the client's solicitor to verify the legal standing of the property's title.
7. The auditor must verify that the property transfer is in the client's name and that the transfer is legally registered.
8. The auditor must check that every property is adequately covered by insurance.
9. An independent land and building account should be kept, and the auditor should verify this. Since no depreciation is often granted on land.
10. If the value of land and buildings has increased due to a revaluation, the auditor must verify that this fact is appropriately declared in the Balance Sheet in accordance with generally accepted accounting standards and the requirements of the Companies Act of 1956.

Automobiles

1. In the case of automobiles, the mileage or use technique is preferred because 1) it is easier to predict how long a certain vehicle will last and 2) it more accurately reflects how far a given vehicle is likely to go.

It is possible to calculate a write-off based on a percentage of the asset's cost multiplied by the number of miles driven and a specific year. For illustration purposes, let's say a car with an original price tag of Rs. 80,000 has accumulated 1,60,000 miles after being driven for just 15,000 miles in a single year. The depreciation for this vehicle would be:

$$8000 \times \frac{15000}{160000} = Rs. \ 7,500$$

2. Second, if the customer has a large fleet of automobiles, it is recommended that they keep a vehicle registry. In the absence of a dedicated vehicle registry, the General Ledger's Motor Car account balance should reflect the unique VIN and purchase price of each car.

3. Third, the auditor needs to check the registration book to see if the description matches the information provided by the client. The auditor has to make sure that the person in whose favor registration is filed really holds the asset for the client and confirms that he does not have any liens or claims against it.

4. The client often buys automobiles for the use of workers, who contribute a certain amount each month from their paychecks. After final payment is made, the customer officially transfers ownership of the vehicle to the worker. The auditor has to look at the appropriate documentation to verify the amount of money recovered and the amount paid to transfer it.

5. Fifth, the auditor confirms that anytime the client possesses a car, he should provide depreciation on it, even if the vehicle is owned by the employer and handed to the employee at no cost and the cost of maintenance is paid for by the client.

When an employee sells an automobile for scrap, an auditor should verify that the difference between the car's book value and the scrap price is credited to the appropriate revenue account.

Tools, patterns, dies, and the like that are not securely fastened together are considered to be in the "loose" category.

An auditor's responsibilities in confirming and appraising such assets may be summed up as follows.

1. For one, there's no need to have separate accounts for each of these assets since their useful life spans are so short. Because theft of such inconsequential items is always a possibility, the

auditor here should check to determine whether adequate safeguards have been put in place.

2. An auditor should ask a responsible officer for a list of all tiny tools, dies, molds, rigs, etc., and then conduct a thorough inspection of each item on the list. He must also verify that the list has been authorized by the proper authority.

3. Third, the auditor must ensure that tiny tools are not valued higher than their cost in the case of a company that created such tools in-house.

4. Typically, assets of this sort seem to vanish or be used up quickly. This means that the standard technique of depreciation cannot be used for these items. Montgomery's proposal in this context may be expressed. The alternative to depreciating such equipment is typically acceptable, and that is to charge the expense of replacement to maintenance. The auditor has to check whether the aforesaid recommendation has been implemented.

5. The auditor has to verify that the Balance Sheet accurately reflects the existence of this kind of asset.

Assets Obtained Via Hire Purchase Agreement
Equipment rented for a particular period of time
The auditing process should go as follows:

a) Ensure a board resolution authorizing the hire-purchase of an asset exists in the official meeting minutes.

b) Take your time reading the hire purchase agreement and make sure you understand all of the terms and conditions.

c) Make sure that payments are made on time and that the costs are deducted from operating income.

d) Verify that the asset's depreciation is included in the cash purchase price.

e) Verify that a current responsibility for the amount owed to the hired vendor is recorded.

f) A check bill agreement or any supporting documentation for a new purchase.

Animatronics

1. Live Stock Register entries should be double-checked against the company's ledger and financial statement.

2. The monetary worth of non-useful or deceased animals should be erased from the books.

3. Check to see whether there have been periodic headcounts.

Stockpiles and Extras

1. Stores and spare parts are an asset since they are consumable by the company and not for resale. Stores include things like lubricants, dyes, petrol, etc., and spare components of machines are kept for regular maintenance.

2. It is essential that the asset be identified as such on the Balance Sheet.

3. Third, the auditor has to get a documented inventory of supplies and replacement components from a competent official. If at all feasible, he should count the inventory personally to ensure its presence.

4. Fourth, keep in mind that the money spent on materials goes to the Manufacturing Account, whereas the money spent on replacement components goes to the Machinery Account.

5. Fifth, the asset should be recorded in the Balance Sheet at its acquisition cost. Due to its lack of useful life, it does not need depreciation allowances.

6. The loss due to breakage or waste on account of wear and tear, however, should be properly written off.

7. Seventh, the asset's value should be reviewed once a year.

Potential Resources

The following are some potential instances of dependent assets:

a) The opportunity to apply for stock in another firm at favorable terms;

b) Reimbursement of octroi for items sent at a later date;

c) Discounted but potentially dishonored debts payable from a prior endorsement;

d) Capitalization of uncalled shares;

Copyright infringement litigation, etc.

Neither the Balance Sheet nor the Companies Act require disclosure of contingent assets at the bottom of the assets section.

Transfer of funds in transit

When a company has both a main office and a branch office, and the main office transfers funds to the branch office to cover operating costs, the issue of remittance-in-transit arises. A "Remittance in Transit" occurs when either the main office sends cash to the branch office at the end of the year, but the branch office does not receive it until after the end of the accounting period, or when the branch sends its collection from customers to the main office, but the main office does not receive it before the end of the accounting period.

The auditor shall request and reconcile the main office's and the branch's bank statements to verify this item. It's possible that any funds received by a branch or headquarters in the first week of the new fiscal year were still in route on the final day of the old one. To reflect this cash in the books, the following entry is made:

Funds on the way-

1. To either the Main Office or a Branch Account.
2. Check the Cash Book/Pass Book for the current period or a later one to see whether money that was in transit was indeed received.
3. Lastly, review the Home Office and Branch Accounts Reconciliation.
4. If the money was placed into an account, check the pay-in slip to make sure the deposit was made.
5. Make sure that the entry you made in item (a) the previous year is deleted the following year.

Other Expenditures

To the extent they are not written off, the following are considered Miscellaneous Expenses in accordance with Schedule VI of the Companies Act, 1956:

(a) Initial Costs.
(b) Underwriting or Subscription Commission or Brokerage Fee on Shares or Debentures.
Allowable Discount for Issuance of Stock or Debentures
(c) Capital invested as interest
(d) Investment in Research and Development and Other Expenditures
(a) Initial, Expenses

1. These are the costs associated with forming a corporation, such as legal fees for preparing a Memorandum of Association, Articles of Association, Stamp Fees, etc.
2. Any auditor looking for information on preliminary costs should go to the prospectus or statement in place of prospectus.
3. Third, verify all agreements with key players including promoters, suppliers, and underwriters.
4. Finally, verify that the Board of Directors has approved the requested expenditures. The practice of obtaining receipts for money transfers is strongly encouraged.
5. The total amount of money spent on preliminary costs must not be more than what is stated in the prospectus or declaration of

non-prospectus. The shareholders' meeting is the place for such an excess to be authorized.

6. Share Premium Account (Section 78) may be used to deduct any initial costs incurred.

7. Preliminary costs must be deducted in a fair time frame (usually 3 to 5 years).

8. To the extent that they are not already written off, preliminary costs should be shown as Miscellaneous Expenditure on the Asset side of the Balance Sheet.

9. In the Profit and Loss Statement, preliminary costs that were written off throughout the year should be included in a separate section.

(b) Brokerage fees or commissions on the issuance of stock or debentures (Sec. 76):

1. Articles of Incorporation should permit this kind of commission.

2. Second, the commission rate cannot be more than 5% of the share issue price or the rate set out in the Articles of Association.

3. Commission rates cannot be more than 2.5% of the debentures issuance price or the rate set out in the articles of association.

4. The statement in place of a prospectus or the prospectus itself must include the amount of commission to be paid.

5. The Registrar should be provided with a copy of the agreement.

6. However, the aforementioned 5% or 2.5% limit does not apply in the event of brokerage (i.e. the proportion of commission owed to brokers who trade in shares and procure shares, etc.).

7. Payment in full must be approved by the Board of Directors.

8. It is possible to deduct any fees associated with the issuance of shares or debentures from the Share Premium Account (Section 78).

9. A fair number of years should be allowed for the write-off of such commission or brokerage (usually 3 to 5 years).

10. To the extent that commission or brokerage fees are not fully deductible, they should be shown as Other Expenses, Net, on the Assets side of the Balance Sheet.

11. Commissions and brokerage losses incurred during the year should be included in the Profit & Loss Statement.

12. Shares and debentures may be issued at a discount under Section79(c).

Auditors need to make sure:

1. First, the Company Law Board must provide its approval, and second, an ordinary resolution at a general meeting.

2. Second, unless otherwise authorized by the Company Law Board, the discount rate must not exceed 10%.

3. No such stock may be issued during the first calendar year after the issuance of the certificate of starting. In addition, the Company law Board must approve the issuance of such shares within two months.

4. Details on the sale price should be included in the prospectus.

5. The Share Premium Account (Section 78) may be used to offset any discounts that were applied while issuing shares or debentures.

6. Sixth, a reasonable number of years should pass before such a discount is written off. (typically ranging from three to five years).

7. Any unamortized portion of such a discount should be reported as a component of Miscellaneous Expense in the Assets section of the Balance Sheet.

8. The Profit & Loss Account must also detail any write-offs of discounts received on the issuance of shares or debentures during the year.

9. To defray interest costs, capital must be used in clause (d) (Section 208)

Auditors need to make sure:

1. This kind of interest is permitted when the firm has begun construction that will not be finished for many years, such as the building of plant and equipment.

2. The Articles of Incorporation or a special resolution must permit such an interest. In addition, such interest cannot be paid without first receiving clearance from the Central Government.

3. The annual percentage rate of interest (APR) cannot be more than 4%. It must be paid within the fiscal half-year that follows the fiscal half-year in which construction was finished.

4. It is important to double-check your bank statement entries with the interest you were really paid.

5. Interest paid from capital in accordance with Section 208 is not considered a diminution of capital.

6. Interest on delayed revenues may either be included in the 'Miscellaneous Expenditure' category or charged against the 'Cost of Construction'.

7. If the interest is moved to "Miscellaneous Expenditure," it should be depreciated over a reasonable period of time (i.e. 3 to 5 years)

You should break out the annual write-off total in your Profit & Loss statement.

Investment in Research and Development and Other Expenditures

Auditors need to make sure:

1. A vote of approval from the Board of Directors.
2. You should always request a receipt from the person or business you pay 2.
3. Receipts expected to be received later all costs should be deducted as soon as practicable (usually 3 to 5 years)
4. The amount that was written off has to be recorded in a distinct line on the Profit and Loss Statement.
5. This is an example of additional costs.

Extremely high levels of initial investment in advertising a new product.

Expenditures for R&D and similar activities.

An auditor is not a valuer.

Asset valuation is the process of estimating an asset's current market worth as of the balance sheet date. An important aspect of an auditor's job is to confirm the accuracy of asset values like these. It is the owners' fundamental responsibility to ensure that the assets are valued accurately in accordance with generally accepted accounting standards, since such assets are theirs by right of ownership. The auditor must conclude that all assets have been recorded at their "full and fair value." Auditors are not required to do their own valuations. But he just needs to check whether the values assigned are accurate and reasonable. That means he'll need all the wits, brains, and diplomacy he can muster to verify the stated valuations of the assets. Professionals like surveyors and valuers are often entrusted with the task of determining an asset's worth. Because of this, he may place trust in the certification provided by those experts, but he must make this fact clear in his report. No specialized training in asset appraisal is required of auditors. However, he should always look into the worth of assets himself using the data the firm provides. Furthermore, he often must rely on the assessment provided by the company's management team, investors, and owners.

That's why we say, "An auditor is deeply involved with principles." Since it is the auditor's responsibility to determine the asset's worth, he is the only one responsible for ensuring that the value established is accurate, fair, and truthful. For the simple reason that a company's financial health cannot be accurately represented in its Balance Sheet if its assets are mispriced. Although an auditor is not a valuer, he might be held responsible for incorrect asset valuation if he fails to independently verify the value of such assets. Therefore, if he ever has reason to doubt the accuracy of the reported value of any asset, he should say so in his report and absolve himself of any blame. Not even telling the board or the owners of the problem released him from responsibility. Although the auditor is not responsible for verifying the accuracy of the Balance Sheet or Profit & Loss Statement, he must exercise caution when doing so since outside parties rely on these documents when making business decisions.

This means that the auditor has to do due diligence before agreeing to the asset appraisal. He will not be held responsible for carelessness if he carefully and thoughtfully determines the worth of the assets.

Due to the auditor's limitless liability for an endless amount of time to an undefined group of individuals, he must exercise extreme caution when approving asset valuations. So, he isn't a valuer, but he has a deep connection to values.

CONFIRMATION OF OBLIGATIONS

What is meant by "verify liabilities" is to investigate the type, size, and existence of obligations.

It entails making sure of the following:

1. All obligations have been fully disclosed in the Balance Sheet's Liabilities section.
2. That all debts are directly associated with running the company.
3. That they are legitimate and right
4. That the amounts displayed in the balance statement are accurate representations of those amounts.

An auditor has a significant responsibility in establishing the veracity of the company's reported obligations in the financial statement known as the Balance Sheet. The purpose of checking liabilities is to make sure that the books haven't been tampered with by inflating or deflating numbers or by creating fictitious obligations. Most often, this kind of manipulation is used to either inflate or deflate the earnings of the organization, making the company's situation look stronger than it really is, in order to establish a hidden reserve. The Profit and Loss Statement and the Balance Sheet are both false due to the manipulation, and the latter cannot be relied upon.

Provide an accurate and balanced picture of the company's situation. Therefore, the auditor has to take every precaution to guarantee that the company's records accurately reflect all obligations. In addition to confirming the liabilities listed on the Balance Sheet, the auditor should also request management's certification that all liabilities, regardless of type, have been recorded in the books of accounts and that any contingent liabilities have been disclosed in a footnote to the Balance Sheet or otherwise accounted for.

ILLUSTRATIONS

Although share capital is not a corporate obligation, it must be confirmed by the auditor before he can provide a report attesting to the financial statement's accuracy.

The auditor's responsibilities consist of the following:

1. If the business is in its first year

a)   He has to read the Articles of Incorporation and the Memorandum of Incorporation.

b)   To determine the number of shares, the different classes of shares, the money received thereon, and the amount due from the shareholders, he must review the Cash Book, Pass Book, and Director's Minute Book.

c)   If the suppliers have been given any shares, he should look into the agreement between the vendors and the corporation.

d)   If shares are issued at a premium, he must make arrangements for the premium to be deposited into a special account.

e)   Verification of both allocation and call funds is required.

f)   If any shares have been forfeited or reissued, he shall verify this.

It is his responsibility to make sure the Companies Act is followed closely.

It's not the first year of business:

a)   Barring any changes or additions by means of new issuance or otherwise, the share capital would remain unchanged from the preceding year. He must see to it that the appropriate legal requirements are met.

b)   In a similar vein, he should review the provisions of the Act as set forth in Sec. 100 in order to learn how to decrease the share capital.

c)   If bonus shares are issued, the auditor needs to make sure the right resolution was passed, the correct capitalization entries were made, and the appropriate permission was obtained from the relevant authorities.

d)   If rights shares are distributed, the auditor has to review the cash book and the bank statements. With specific regard to Sec. 81, he has to make sure the necessary resolutions are approved and approval is obtained from the relevant authorities.

Reserves may be either broad in scope or narrowly targeted, and surpluses might follow suit. Particular reserves include a "sinking fund," "capital redemption reserve," and a "reserve for contingencies."

Following are some of the responsibilities of the auditor when confirming reserves:

1.   First, he has to make sure the conditions of transfer of profit to reserve are met by reviewing the Profit and Loss Appropriation account and looking for transfers to reserves.

2.   Before he transfers the money, he has to make sure the board has approved the action.

3.   Thirdly, he has to make sure that any changes to the reserve funds (such as increases or decreases from the previous year's total) are reported as required by law.

4.   Comply with all applicable legal requirements for reserve use.

5.   Make that the reserves are reported legally in the financial statements.

Money borrowed

The auditor should think about the following while checking the legitimacy of loans:

To determine whether or whether the Company has the authority to take out a loan, the auditor must first review the Company's Memorandum and Articles of Incorporation.

The auditor has to look at the loan documentation, including the agreement and any related emails.

The auditor must attest that the cash received on account of loans matches the receipts issued for the loans and the entries made in the cash book.

If the loan was secured by a mortgage, the auditor has to review the certificate of registration provided by the Registrar of Companies.

When an interest payment has been made, the auditor should double-check the Cash Book entries and the counterfoils of the receipts provided to the vendors to ensure that everything is in order.

Six, he has to double-check the loan payback by comparing the cheque book, bank pass book, and cash book counterfoils.

In order to certify that no interest is owed and that any recoupments of loans have been properly recorded in the books of account, the auditor may also request a confirming letter from the person that provided the loan.

The auditor should review the overdraft agreement and any collateral provided by the bank.

Creditors in the Commercial Trade:
1. To begin, the auditor has to get a list of debtors and cross-reference it with the purchase ledger, which he will already have seen.
2. Second, he must list all purchases, not just those made at the end of the year, in the creditors' records.
3. Third, with the client's permission, the auditor might request a statement of account be given in the event of doubt over the legitimacy of any creditors.
4. Fourth, he must verify the authenticity of the different debtis issued for discount, products returned, etc.

The auditor should inquire as to the rationale for any unpaid debts.

Liabilities That May Occur in the Future, or Contingencies

Liabilities that may or may not be incurred in the future to be paid are called contingent liabilities. It is the responsibility of the auditor to ensure that all liabilities, both existing and anticipated, have been recorded in the books as of the Balance Sheet date and are reflected in the statement.

Bills receivable that have been discounted with a bank and used may result in a liability to the bank if the acceptor does not pay in full on the due date of the discounted bills receivable. This is why a note in the Balance Sheet's footnotes explicitly details any potential liabilities that may arise in the future.

The responsibility for the amount uncalled must be determined once the amount called on shares owned and paid has been confirmed from the cash book.

Third, if the client has guaranteed a loan or overdraft for a friend or business partner, the auditor has to determine the client's obligation under the guarantee. It is important to determine potential liabilities in the event of a default on such a loan.

Liability for lawsuits against the corporation that are not recognized as debts: it is a liability in a case where damages may need to be paid but are in dispute. If there is a potential loss, it must be calculated and a notation added to the bottom of the Balance Sheet.

Responsibility for arrears of Dividend on Cumulative preference Shares: The auditor should review the Articles of Association, which should put out guidelines in this regard, and adequate provision should be made for such a liability.

Responsibility of AuditorBefore signing off on the financial statements, the auditor has to double-check the numerous contingent liabilities listed above. Bills Receivable which have been discounted and which have not matured at the date of the Balance Sheet, arrears of fixed cumulative dividends, etc. are examples of obligations for which no provision has been made in the books, but just a notation has been made at the foot of the Balance Sheet. The auditor has to look at circumstances where provision needs to be made in the Balance Sheet due to liabilities (such a lawsuit or tax liability) and determine how much needs to be set aside. The auditor has to look at the Director's Minute Book, as well as any contact with outside counsel and any data collected from company insiders. If he is not convinced that enough provision has been made for all such obligations, he must say so in his report. Keep in mind that the liabilities section of your Balance Sheet must comply with the provisions of the Companies Act in regards to the contingent obligation.

Tax Deduction Provision

First, the tax provision is required in the event of a limited liability corporation. The true cost of this account cannot be determined until the assessment is complete. Therefore, it is important to provide a reasonable estimate of the cost of this responsibility. Therefore, it is incumbent upon the auditor to verify the computation used to arrive at the anticipated provision.

But when the review is complete, the auditor must ensure that the accounts are amended to reflect the excess or short provision.

If the responsibility is being challenged in court and an appeal has not yet been filed, then the liability is said to be contingent. There must be accurate reporting of this information in the Balance sheet.

The contributions of workers:

Employees who handle money or inventory in a business or factory often have to put up some kind of financial security in case of theft or misappropriation. On lieu of cash, workers may be asked to endorse stocks held by a trustee in favor of the company. To keep in mind in this regard:

1. First, you should open a separate bank account to hold the cash or assets that serve as this kind of security.

2.   It has to be itemized on the liabilities side of the Balance Sheet.

3.   A verified schedule provided by the customer should be used to double-check the amount of deposits.

Bad and Doubtful Debts Reserve

The following is how you should check everything:

1.   First, the auditor has to verify the amount set aside for bad and doubtful debts by obtaining a certificate from a competent official of the firm.

2.   The likely number of bad and questionable debts may be determined by comparing the schedule of debtors with the balance of ledger accounts.

3.   A further check must be made to ensure that the reserve is sufficient. He has to look into the specifics of a firm and the regulations that must be followed there.

Payment Obligations

In order to ensure the accuracy of the Bills Payable, the auditor should:

1.   To begin, make sure that the Bills Payable Book matches the Bills Payable Account.

2.   Secondly, you must review the Cash Book to ensure that all paid Bills Payable have been recorded and that all returned Bills Payable have been inspected.

3.   The Bills Payable book and the Cash Book of the future years should be reviewed by the auditor to confirm the Bills Payable that have not yet matured as of the year's end. The auditor may request confirmation from the drawers if there is any uncertainty about the bill.

4.   The auditor should check the Balance Sheet to determine whether there is a charge that has been incurred on the company's assets as a result of paying the bill, and he should also verify that this charge has been properly recorded.

Proposed Dividend Payment of per Share

1.   A proposed dividend must be in accordance with the Companies Act and judicial judgments, particularly with regard to depreciation provisions, capital profit distributions, reserve transfers, and other similar things, before an auditor would sign off on it.

2.   The Profit and Loss Appropriation account entry and the board decision should both be verified by the auditor.

3.   Third, the auditor must confirm that the necessary provisions for gross dividend have been made in accordance with the Companies Act of 1956.

4.   The auditor should compare the names on the dividend list to the shareholders' list to make sure everything is in order.

Unpaid Expenses

Any remaining costs should have been accounted for in the current year's financial statements, and the auditor should receive proof of this from a responsible official. Cash Book entries may be used as proof of the amounts paid into different accounts. Verify that as of the date of the Balance Sheet, all unpaid costs have been reflected in the total. The following are important considerations.

1.   First, he has to make sure that everything has been recorded in the accounts, including rent, rates, interest, earnings, salary, audit fee, legal fees, etc.

2.   Second, he has to make sure that any entries made in the books based on invoices are not relevant to the year that is now being audited.

3.   Third, he has to compare this year's paid and unpaid costs with last year's to confirm that the two years are relatively similar.

4.   Finally, all past-due wages and salaries must be paid.

An Overdraft at the Bank

Overdrafts at financial institutions will be validated in the same manner as loans and advances. The difference is the bank loan or other kind of financial aid. The Bank Pass book should be reviewed by the auditor, and a summary of mortgaged assets should be requested. Remember that the Balance Sheet must accurately reflect the mortgaged assets.

Debentures

1.   The auditor must first review the firm's Articles of Association and Memorandum of Association to determine whether or not the company has the authority to issue debentures.

2.   Second, he must check the Registrar's registration certificate whether the debenture is a mortgage debenture.

3.   Third, he should make that all of the Trust Deed's requirements for issuing debentures have been met.

4.   Any money deposited into this account must be verified by the auditor against the cash book.

5.   The auditor is responsible for ensuring that interest on debentures is paid or given in a timely manner and in accordance with established policies and procedures.

6.   Debentures redemptions that occur throughout the year must be recorded in the Board of Directors' Minutes. Checkbook backs are like counterfoils. Various bank records include passbooks, cashbooks, reissued debenture certificates, and so on.

7.   Seven, he should make sure that the Balance Sheet accurately reflects the fact that the debentures were issued as collateral security.

Forgotten Dividend Payment

The auditor should use this approach to confirm any dividends that have gone unclaimed.

1.   First, make sure the dividend account has been correctly reconciled. Make sure a separate account is formed every year to receive dividend payments to ensure that dividends from different years are kept separate. Make that there are no lingering items in this Bank Accounts reconciliation, such as accounts debited by the bank but not accounted for in the books, etc., that might lead to an incorrect Unclaimed Dividend being recorded.

2.   Make that the proper entries have been made if a dividend is announced on shares and calls are behind.

3.   Make sure a comprehensive list of investors who haven't yet claimed their payout is compiled. This is important for two reasons: first, to demonstrate the correctness of the Member's Register, and second, to demonstrate that no errors were made in reconciling the Bank Account.

4.   The auditor should check that the number of shares listed as owned by each shareholder in the Share Register matches the number of shares that remain unclaimed in the Member's Register. Any dividend paid to a shareholder who has already transferred his shares, but who has not yet cashed in his dividend warrant, will likewise be shown here.

5.   Ensure that the money in the Unclaimed Dividend Account is delivered to the Central Government with information of shareholders who have not claimed the dividend if the statutory time limit of 3 years has passed.

Repeatedly missed calls

The auditor has to make sure the following about Calls Past Due:

1. Determine whether claims for payment are being made because of capital issued this year or if they are an ongoing consequence of capital issued in previous years.

2. Check the application money paid, shares issued, total shares money due, calls made, calls money payable, and calls paid to ensure the proper amount has been calculated for the call in arrears if it is related to capital issued throughout the year. To do this, he will need to do a thorough audit of the allocation of shares.

3. Check that shareholders have been contacted with reminders to pay any past-due calls from previous years. That notice will include a request for payment of the overdue principal plus interest if the Board has chosen to impose that penalty. See that such call moneys are paid with interest if any portion of the calls in arrears were received within the year on which interest was due.

4. In the event that a transfer application is received for shares for which there are outstanding call payments, you must ensure that no shares are transferred until all outstanding call payments have been paid in full.

5. If the Directors have declared a dividend, the dividend payable on those shares should be reduced proportionately, and if the Directors have decided to appropriate a dividend on those shares where calls are in arrears, the dividend should not be physically paid out, but rather appropriate accounting entries should be made crediting calls in arrears and debiting dividend payable.

6. Verify that the appropriate entries have been made in the books if the Board has enacted any Resolution forfeiting shares on which calls are in arrears, and that such shares have not been reissued continued to be recorded as a fully valuated component of capital, with arrears calls removed accordingly.

Fixed Deposits

1. An audit of a fixed deposit requires the auditor to bear in mind the following details:

2. Section 58A of the Companies Act of 1956 and the regulations of the Reserve Bank of India specify the procedures to be followed while accepting Fixed Deposits.

3. Director's fixed deposits of less than six months (but more than three months) shall not exceed 10% of paid up share capital and free reserves.

4. Third, the combined fixed deposits cannot exceed 25% of the company's paid-in capital and free reserves.
5. The maximum duration of a fixed deposit is 36 months.
6. No fixed deposit may earn more than fifteen percent per year in interest.
7. Below we set out the parameters within which brokerage fees might be paid.
(a) The maximum annual interest rate on deposits is 1% for the first year.
(b) between one and two years, up to 1.25 percent of deposit amount
(c) 2–3 years, up to 1.50% of deposit amount.
8. You should never let your cash on hand fall below 10% of your deposits due on March 31.
9. Customers who make deposits need to be given receipts.
10. Keep a record of your fixed deposits.
11. Please return fixed deposit returns to the Registrar by June 30. According to Section 45 MA of the Reserve Bank of India Act, 1934, the auditor must note the failure to send in the auditor's report.
12. Accrued interest that is not yet payable must be disclosed and recorded as a Current Liability.
13. Unsecured loans would include any fixed deposits received together with interest payable and accumulated.

Stock verification

Definition of Stock-In-Trade

(i) Accounting Standard 2 defines Stock as an Asset Held For:

(a) sale made in the regular course of business or

(b) throughout the manufacturing process before such sale or

(c) for use in manufacturing (i.e. consumable stores).

(ii) Checking Inventory

Stock verification entails a physical counting, measuring, and verifying to ascertain the amount of stock to be evaluated for stock value.

For the following reasons, verifying Stock-in-Trade is more complex than verifying any other asset:

(a) It's the company's most valuable asset right now, and it's always changing.

(b) A plethora of techniques for valuing tradable stock are available.

(c) Its valuation has a significant impact on annual revenue and profits.

(d) There is a higher possibility of deception or manipulation.

(iii) The reasons for checking inventory are these:
(a) Accurately calculating the year-end profit or loss.
(b) Providing accurate and complete information on the company's financial health.
(c) Preparing an accurate claim statement for merchandise lost in a disaster such a fire, flood, or earthquake.
(d) Establishing the worth of consigned goods.
(e) Stocks exchanged on a "Sale or Return" basis must have their worth determined.
(f) Identifying the legal owners of a company's shares.
(g) Verification that there are no fees associated with purchasing the shares.

The Auditor's Responsibilities Regarding Inventory Verification:

It is easy to see why verifying the closing stock is a crucial aspect of an auditor's job: the closing stock value is directly tied to the company's net income. The auditor is responsible for ensuring the following while checking inventory:

a) Figure out how inventories are taken and what factors are considered while setting prices.
b) Verify that the stock sheets have undergone a thorough internal review, i.e., that they have been verified as having accounted for pricing, extensions, and additions when calculating stock and are generally recognized as accurate by the managing director.
c) Double-check all sums and computations.
d) Compare the listed prices of a few key goods to the prices shown on real invoices.
e) Compare the amounts recorded on stock-sheets to the amounts recorded in stock books, if stock books are maintained.
f) Check to see that the stock was valued using the same methods as in prior years.
g) Make sure that old or unsalable inventory is priced fairly.
h) Evaluate the current and prior periods' gross profit as a proportion of revenue, and ivestigate any significant changes.
i) Items marked "Sold but not Delivered" must be left out of the tally.
j) Make sure you remember to include the items you purchased that weren't recorded in the invoice book.
k) Verify that the value of raw materials is taken at real cost and valued based on the cost of the items used and the salaries paid on them as of the Balance Sheet date.

The above may also have a percentage put on top in order to pay for the operating expenses of the factory, including those of the foreman, the utility company, the lighting company, the heating company, the depreciation company, and so on.

In the case of completed items, the works cost must be increased by a proportional amount to account for administrative expenses.

l)   Verify that products sold on approval are correctly accounted for at the end of the day.

m)   Make sure consigned items aren't included as inventory while acting as an agent.

n)   Carefully review the stock records, checking to see that they reflect just the client's items and not any assets bought.

o)   Verify that shares have been valued at either their cost or current market value.

p)   Obtain a certification from an appropriate official of the organization detailing the steps used when determining the value of shares of stock.

q)   A customer certification stating the following is required under clause:

r)   Inventory counts are counted by hand.

(i)   Everything in stock belongs to the corporation.

(ii) the technique for cutting off is carried out correctly. (A cutoff is an event that marks the transition between fiscal years.) the final inventory numbers on goods documents

When conducting inventory, it's important to have all relevant paperwork (received notes, items accepted notes, debit and credit notes, etc.).

(iii) The valuation method used this year is the same one used last year.

Case law-based requirements for the auditing firm's stock verification procedures

Kingston Cotton Mills Co., Ltd., Case I. (1896)

An inventory check is not considered part of an auditor's responsibility. The auditor is able to depend on other parties to provide information on the company's inventory. An auditor need not double as a detective, Justice Lopez said in the same ruling. The court ruled that if there are no red flags, the auditor may safely rely on the company's certification.

Second Case: Irish Woollen Company, Limited, v. Tyson and Others (1900)

It was decided that the auditor had no responsibility for inventory.

This is shown in Case 3 by Westminster Road Construction Co. (1932)

If the auditor has appropriate knowledge but fails to notice an overvaluation of work in progress, the auditor must provide compensation. If he does not consider all the facts, he will be negligent.

Fourth Case: McKesson and Robbins (1939)

It was decided that the auditor may use testing, observation, or a mix of the two to confirm inventory. The auditor was found at fault for signing off on a Balance Sheet that falsely claimed all available inventory was sold.

Place in India:

(a) If an audit is performed on a limited business, the auditor is obligated to state whether or not the final accounts match the books.

(b) The auditor must also make sure that the closing stock is included under the heading Current Asset as follows in Schedule VI of the Companies Act, 1956.

- Equipment and supplies
- Disorganized hardware
- Stock-in-trade
- Work-in-progress.

Management must do physical checks on completed items, storage, spare parts, and raw materials at regular intervals, per CARO.

Therefore, management has the main responsibility for checking, while the auditor should do test checks as per the Mckesson and Robbins case.

Check inventory counts to make sure they are accurate either by direct observation or by using a mix of the two.

Company sales and acquisitions shall be recorded in accordance with Section 209(1)(b) of the Companies Act, 1956.

If the auditor fails to mention that the company's books of account and annual stock-taking statement and statement of goods sold and acquired for the two years prior to the beginning of winding up are not in order under Section 541(2) of the Companies Act, 1956, he would be held accountable.

The auditor is required to do the following checks to ensure the accuracy of the inventory in accordance with the Statement on

Auditing Practices released by the Institute of Chartered Accountants of India (ICAI):

1. One, verify the physical inventory with a certificate from management. To ensure the management's certification of the stocktake's accuracy, an auditor must be certain that I the stocktake's processes were reasonable and (ii) the procedures were really followed.

2. The original stock sheets should be checked by the auditor. He should inspect a few random items and be present for at least part of the stock taking.

3. Third, whether there was an overabundance or a deficit discovered during physical verification, the auditor must confirm that the books were properly corrected.

4. The auditor is responsible for obtaining and reviewing confirmations from parties holding stocks that are not lying with the company (goods sent for processing, goods on consignment, etc.).

These precedents have so established the following principles:

a) Management has a responsibility to conduct a physical count of the shares to ensure that they belong to the shareholders. In most cases, an auditor lacks the personnel and technological expertise to conduct a thorough verification. Thus, the auditor has no responsibility for failing to conduct a physical inventory verification as of the Balance sheet date. The auditor is not responsible for inventory control.

Management's certification that the stock on hand as of the Balance Sheet date has been verified and valued is sufficient for an auditor to rely on, provided the auditor has conducted a thorough examination of all supporting documentation (as seen in the case of Mckesson and Robbins).

As a result of this debate, international accounting organizations have reached the consensus that it is not the auditor's responsibility to perform a physical stock-taking himself, but rather, he must ensure that verification of stock has taken place properly by either physically taking stock on the date of the Balance Sheet himself or by ensuring that his client performed the stock-taking in accordance with auditing standards.

Therefore, an auditor cannot avoid being accused of carelessness by only relying on the management certificate without also conducting tests and checks.

The Value of Inventory
What This Means
(i) A stock-in-trade valuation is the process of determining the fair market value of a company's shares at a certain point in time, usually at the end of the trading day.
(ii) The Role of the Auditor in Stock Valuation

1 The auditor must first make sure the valuation procedure hasn't changed.

2 If the stock valuation technique has changed from the previous year, the auditor must report that information and verify that the new approach is appropriate and generally accepted in the industry.

3 Third, the auditor must confirm that the stock was evaluated and documented using industry standard valuation methods. He has to make sure that the valuation is carried out in accordance with ICAI regulations.

4 The auditor should do a small number of valuation tests to ensure the stocks' computational correctness.

5 Fifth, the auditor has to make sure the stock hasn't been overvalued or undervalued, since this would skew the audit's genuine and fair assessment of the financials.

Schedule VI of the Companies Act, 1956 specifies that the values of stores and spare parts, loose tools, stock-in-trade, and work-in-progress must be stated separately, and the auditor must ensure that this is done.

A firm auditor's report under MAOCARO,1988 must include information on whether or not the company

a) He has examined the stocks and is certain that the valuation is fair and appropriate under generally accepted accounting rules.

b) Stocks are valued using the same methodology as the previous year. The auditor is obligated to disclose the impact of any change in the valuation basis.

c) Provision for loss was established based on physical inspection of damaged or unusable stocks, raw materials, or completed items, and

(d) A trading business has assessed the damage to its products and made a provision for the loss.

In order to comply with CARO, the auditor must confirm that the stock price was determined in a reasonable manner using generally accepted accounting principles. ICAI has established the rules that must be followed.

Auditing Practices Statement

Accounting Principles, Section b, Second Topical Group: Inventory Valuation

When doing a stock valuation, the auditor must see to it that the aforementioned conditions are met.

It is the responsibility of the auditor to ensure that the accounting policy for the value of inventory, including the methodology employed, is fully stated in the closing accounts.

Consignor's duty to inspect and appraise goods before accepting them

Buying and Selling on Consignment - What It Means

The principle (the consignor) sends products to the agent (the consignee) at another location so that the agent may sell the items on the principal's behalf in exchange for a fee.

Stock on consignment verification and appraisal:

(i) Unsold inventory must be physically counted and certified by management.

(ii) If there is unsold inventory, the auditor has to get a certificate from the consignee.

(iii) The amount that should be left with the consignee may be determined by looking at their account sale.

Items supplied on consignment are not considered to be for sale for the purposes of taxation or other legal requirements. Goods must be sold to a third party before revenue may be recorded.

(iii) In addition, the consignor must not charge the consignee any money for items that were delivered to the consignee.

(vi) Stock that hasn't sold should be valued at the lower of its cost or current market value, under clause. Both the sender and the receiver should include one-time costs into the total price. Loading, transportation, insurance, freight, octroi, unloading, etc. should all be included into the final inventory count and valuation. However, costs should not include selling and distribution fees.

Indicators of an auditor's competence

• Section 226 of the Companies Act, 1956 governs the requirements for becoming an auditor. Paragraph (1) of that section states, "A person will be qualified for appointment as an auditor of a company (public or private) only if he is a Chartered Accountant within the meaning of the Chartered Accountants Act, 1949."

If all the partners in the firm's India office are eligible for appointment as auditors, then the firm itself is qualified for appointment, and any partner in the office may perform auditing duties in the name of the firm.

• Cautions for auditors

Section 226 of the Companies Act of 1956 governs the procedure for disqualification of an auditor.

According to Section 226(3), the following individuals are ineligible to be appointed as corporate auditors:

A person who is indebted to the Company for more than Rs. 1000 OR A person who has given any guarantee or provided any security in connection with the Indebtedness of any third person to the Company for more than Rs. 1000.

a) After one year from the date of the implementation of the Companies (Amendment) Act, 2000, any person holding any security (a security would imply an instrument carrying voting rights) of such company.

b) According to Section 226(4), an individual is ineligible for appointment as auditor of a business if he is barred from serving in a similar capacity for any of the holding companies or subsidiaries of the company in question.

• Under Section 226(5), an auditor is considered to have resigned from his position if he is later found to be subject to any of the disqualifications listed in Sections 226(3) and 226(4).

i.   First auditors to be named

Section 224(5) outlines the essentials for selecting a company's first auditors.

ii.   Within one month after the date of registration/incorporation of the business, the board of directors may pass a resolution appointing the first auditors of the company.

The term of office for the auditors thus chosen shall be through the first Annual General Meeting.

iii.   Third, if the Board of Directors doesn't choose a first auditor within a month, the shareholders may do it themselves at a special meeting.

iv.   The company's shareholders have the right to replace the auditors chosen by the Board of Directors at any annual or special meeting.

v.   Fifth, just because an auditor's name is included in the Articles of Association does not mean he will automatically be designated as First Auditor.

Neither the company nor the First Auditor is needed to notify the Registrar of Companies of the First Auditor's acceptance or rejection of the appointment.

Appointment of the subsequent auditor:

i. The following are the most important considerations for selecting a company's subsequent auditor:

ii. The shareholders have the authority to nominate the auditor by a resolution at each Annual General Meeting, under Section 224(1).

iii. Any auditor nominated at the Annual General Meeting must be notified by the corporation within seven days.

iv. Third, the auditor has 30 days from the day he receives the company's notification of his appointment to respond to the Registrar of Companies in writing, using form no.23B, with his decision on whether or not to accept the position.

v. The term of office for the auditor thus chosen shall run from the close of one Annual General Meeting to the close of the next Annual General Meeting.

If an auditor accepts more than the allowed number of audit assignments from a firm at any one time, in accordance with section 224 of the Act, he will be guilty of professional misconduct.

i. First, during the first Annual General Meeting, shareholders have the right to vote to dismiss the auditor chosen by the board of directors. Without the consent of the Central Government, such Auditors may even be removed from office before the end of their term.

ii. In all other cases, the Central Government's prior consent is required before the company's General Meeting may dismiss the auditor.

iii. Third, an Auditor cannot be replaced when his tenure ends.

At the general meeting, a resolution requiring exceptional notice (of fourteen days) must be approved [Sec. 225(1)].

Company must provide retiring auditor with a copy of the notice of resolution upon receipt of such notification [Sec. 225(2)].

After being notified, a retiring auditor has the right to make a reasonable written representation to the business, which must be shared with the shareholders. Unless the notice is received too late, the corporation is obligated to provide such representation to the shareholders. It is also necessary to publish a notice of resolution that includes a statement of the fact of such a representation. An auditor may require a representation to be read aloud at a meeting if they did not obtain it in time to distribute it or if the firm was in default. [Sec. 225(3)].

Nonetheless, the business or any other interested party such as directors or shareholders may submit a petition to the Company Law.

It is the responsibility of the Corporate Oversight Board (CLB) to forbid the e) auditor from making such a statement if doing so will bring about harmful publicity or smear the auditor's reputation. Under such circumstances, the CLB may require that copies not be sent or read at the meeting [Sec. 225(3)]. If the federal government has nominated auditors, they, too, may be removed under these terms.

The corporation must notify the new auditor about the appointment of a new auditor within seven days of the appointment.4. Within one month after receiving such notification, the new auditor must notify the Registrar of his acceptance or rejection of the position, and he must also consult with the outgoing auditor.

MODULE - 3
INTERNAL CONTROL

Introduction

As with external controls, internal auditing is crucial. Internal control is the process of implementing and maintaining a system of internal checks and balances inside an organization to guarantee its effective and economical operation. You will get an understanding of the significance of internal controls and their goals at the end of this lesson. In addition, you will get a broad comprehension of auditing in the context of the digital realm as you are introduced to a number of different internal check systems.

Management would be ill-served without internal controls. It's a useful tool for management in carrying out its duties. This includes the system's own checks and balances as well as human-led measures like monitoring and auditing that have been put in place by the company. The management of modern businesses has challenges in obtaining reliable data because of the increasing complexity of their operations. Management can rest easy knowing the data it relies on is correct thanks to internal controls. Accounting data and other records are kept accurate and reliable via the use of internal controls, which are also used to pinpoint and strengthen the business's weak spots so that the company may better use its resources, protect its assets, and run smoothly.

Internal Control : Definition

Internal control is defined by the American Institute of Public Accountants as "the plan of organization and all the coordinated methods, and measures adopted within a business to safeguard its assets, check the accuracy and reliability of its accounting data, promote operational efficiency, and encourage adherence to prescribed managerial policies." The scope of internal control goes much beyond the duties of the finance and accounting teams.

"Internal control means not only internal check or internal audit but the whole system of control financial and otherwise, established by management to carry on the business of the company in an orderly manner, safeguard its assets, and secure as far as possible accuracy and reliability of its records," according to the Institute of Chartered Accountants in England and Wales.

By comparing the aforementioned definitions, it becomes clear that "internal control" encompasses a wide range of concepts. A system of checks and balances used inside a company to guarantee its economical and productive operation. Thus, internal control entails management's keeping a watchful eye and providing guidance over crucial areas like finances, purchases, and internal operations.

In order to run its operations smoothly and successfully, every company has to establish a reliable system of internal control. Accounting controls, budget controls, statistical analyses, and internal checks and audits are also included. It refers to the amount of safeguards put in place to ensure that a company's operations run smoothly. Any and all procedures that help an organization achieve the following goals are considered to be part of its internal control system.

IC's Reason for Existing

- To reduce or get rid of waste and inefficiency in corporate processes and protect company property.
- To improve productivity in business operations and safeguard the integrity of financial records.
- To evaluate the extent to which management's policies are being put into effect, and
- Assess the efficacy of all company operations and draw attention to any areas where improvement is needed.

Means of inside management

A system of internal controls is useful for keeping accurate financial records and maximizing the effectiveness of business processes. I want to have a serious conversation about them.

Money management with accurate books

This method guarantees accurate and trustworthy financial records in accordance with GAAP. The primary components of such controls are the organizational structure, as well as the processes and records, which deal with and are directly connected to the protection of assets and liabilities of financial records. Budgetary control, standard cost control, a self-balancing ledger, bank reconciliation, internal checks, and internal audits are all examples of financial controls used by accountants.

Transaction recording, asset protection, and management policy adherence are all areas that fall within the purview of accounting controls.

Power to administer

This regulation covers a large area. Accounting procedures also include controls. Organizational plans that include such controls tend to focus on maximizing productivity within existing systems. In a nutshell, they may be anything from a blueprint for running the company to detailed instructions for how tasks are to be completed, how information is stored, who has what kind of say, and how decisions are made. Time and motion studies, inspections for quality assurance, statistical analyses, performance evaluations, etc. are all examples of controls. A thorough examination of accounting controls is essential for an auditor because of the impact they have on the credibility of the financial statements. The accounting controls are his main area of focus.

The Role of the Auditor in Internal Controls

According to the Institute of Chartered Accountants of India's statement of auditing practices, "the duty of safeguarding the assets of a company is primarily that of management and the auditor is entitled to rely upon the safeguard and internal controls instituted by the management, although he will take into account the deficiencies, he may note therein while drafting his audit program." This statement explains the auditor's position with respect to internal control. This implies that an auditor's exclusive focus is on determining the efficacy of internal controls. If he discovers that the organization's internal checks and balances

system is insufficient, he should prepare to conduct a thorough investigation into those areas. Therefore, it is crucial that the auditor has a thorough understanding of the existing internal controls and how they are really used. His audit plan will benefit from this information. In addition, he may bring to management's attention any flaws in the internal control system.

Elements of a reliable internal control structure

A solid internal control system must include the following components:-
1. It is advised that a well-thought-out plan of organization be implemented, with effective delegation of functional duties. Without such an organizational framework, an internal control system will fail to meet its objectives.
2. The organization's assets, liabilities, income, and costs should be subject to stringent controls, thus it's important to establish a methodical system of authorization and record process. It has to

be crafted such that a) assets are safely stored and b) they are used appropriately, c) costs are spent for obtaining the necessary permissions, and d) revenues are accurately recorded.

3. In order for the different parts of the organization to carry out their responsibilities without hiccups, a system of sound practices and traditions should be established.

4. Since the organization's employees will be responsible for enforcing the internal control system, the company must hire a group of trustworthy individuals who have received enough training and are up to the task.

The system might be improved by instituting constant administrative oversight and frequent reviews.

1. Take Stock of Where You Are
What Is Internal Control?
Distinguish between financial and management accounting controls.
The following statements must be true or false:

a) An internal control system is not the same as an internal check.

b) Accounting control is beyond the scope of internal control.

c) All businesses must have an internal control system in place.

d) Time and motion studies and quality control are examples of internal controls.

e) A well-functioning internal control system facilitates the development of an audit that is both effective and efficient.

Internal Audit

An internal audit is a review of a company's internal processes performed by a dedicated team of auditors. The ability to regularly assess the accuracy of records is a crucial managerial tool.

To explain what is meant by "internal audit," "a service to management based on an impartial evaluation of ongoing activities inside an organization with the purpose of assessing their efficacy. It's a management control that determines how well other controls are working.

Defining Stettler's assertions as gospel, "Internal auditing is a method of providing management with an objective assessment of how well their business is doing.

Therefore, the overarching goal of internal auditing is to help management carry out their duties successfully.

provide impartial assessments, evaluations, suggestions, and remarks on the operations under scrutiny. In summary, an internal audit gives management confidence that checks and balances are functioning as intended.

For this reason, it is essential to conduct an internal audit of your company's accounting processes annually to verify that-

- Each and every financial deal has been accurately documented.
- The books are kept in a methodical manner and
- There will be no monetary or physical assets stolen from the company.

One of the responsibilities of an internal auditor in the present day is expanding. Verifying a small number of goods like stock, cash, and fixed assets, as well as performing the more standard job of validating the mathematical accuracy of the accounts using vouchers and documentation, is insufficient. Now, it is the internal auditor's job to document the process, evaluate the efficacy, and develop programs to enhance the accuracy with which controls are evaluated. His responsibilities include establishing defined goals for his own division, phasing those goals out over time, earning the trust of upper management, and providing tangible evidence of the value he adds via his work.

The internal audit is conducted in a manner similar to that of a third-party auditor. However, its exact shape varies from business to business, depending on factors like size and the nature of the operation. It is implemented in big organizations and executed by paid personnel trained in auditing procedures. Working for the company, it is his responsibility to eliminate any unnecessary expenditures. The internal auditor must adhere to the laws, regulations, standard auditing practices, and procedures set out for external auditors by the governing organizations of the auditing profession in the nation. While being professionally qualified to provide a thorough investigation of the business's operations, an internal auditor must also be familiar with the company's rules and programs. He will be in a better position to improve the efficiency of the internal audit system because to his professional experience and familiarity with the company.

Necessity

The primary goals of an internal audit are:

- Financial and statistical records submitted to management must be checked for accuracy and validity.
- To make sure that the company always uses proper accounting procedures.
- To aid in the speedy identification of mistakes and fraud.

All commercial dealings should have been conducted by duly authorized individuals with the right authorities.

It is the responsibility of the Internal Audit Department to conduct periodic reviews of the Internal Auditing System, provide recommendations for system improvements, and conduct ad hoc investigations as requested by the Management.

To ensure that the organization's obligations have arisen from lawful endeavors.

To that end, it's important to choose competent people for internal auditing roles, and it's also crucial to provide the internal auditor sufficient leeway to look at business dealings from more than just a purely financial perspective. The internal auditor's reports should go straight up to the executive team. He will have to work independently from the finance and administrative departments. We need to recognize him as an integral element of management and provide him autonomy in his role.

Differences between an internal audit and a statutory audit

An internal audit is a great aid to a statutory audit. When it comes to verifying the financial statements' veracity, internal and statutory auditors have a shared interest. The statutory auditor may focus on the big picture if internal controls are robust.

The role of the internal auditor is to inspect the workings of the company and to carry out assessment, compliance, and verification to guarantee that the company's policies, processes, regulations, and controls are being effectively implemented.

As a result of his assistance, the statutory auditor is able to more thoroughly examine the books of account. In most cases, the statutory auditor will accept the results of the internal auditor's thorough examination. Since the statutory auditor is legally obligated to report to many authorities, while the internal auditor reports exclusively to management, the scope of possible collaboration between the two is rather constrained. When performing his responsibilities, the statutory auditor must adhere to all applicable laws, regulations, and generally accepted auditing standards. The statutory auditor must do such test checks as are required to determine the efficacy of internal audit before accepting the results of such audits.

Both the internal auditor and the statutory auditor will verify and validate data via inspection of files and other means. Despite their shared characteristics, internal auditors and statutory auditors do not perform identical tasks and have different levels of authority or responsibility.

Differences between internal audit and statutory audit-

The following are the points of differences between internal auditand statutory audit:

Differences - Internal Audit & Statutory Audit

Internal Audit

Appointment – Internal Auditor is appointed by the Management.

Qualifications – Need not possess any specific expertise.

Status – Is an employee of the company.

Conduct of Audit – Is a kind of continuous audit.

Scope of Work – Determined by the management.

Statutory Audit

Appointment – Statutory Auditor is appointed by the Shareholders.

Qualifications – Must be qualified as per Sec 226 of the Companies Act 2013.

Status – Is an independent person.

Conduct of Audit – After preparation of final accounts.

Scope of Work – Determined by Law.

Fundamental principles of internal check

The term "internal check" refers to a mechanism that is used in business to ensure that the work of one employee is double-checked by other employees throughout the process of documenting the transaction itself.

According to Spicer and Pegler, an internal check system is "an organization of staff tasks wherein no one individual is authorized to carry out and record every component of a transaction" in order to limit the likelihood of fraud and increase the likelihood that no mistakes were made. As stated by De Paula, an internal check is "a constant internal audit carried out by the staff itself by means of which the work of each employee is independently examined by other member of the staff."

Therefore, in an internal check system, the staff's responsibilities are set up so that no single person is responsible for recording every detail of the transactions; rather, the entire workload is divided among the various members of the staff in such a way that the work of one person is automatically checked by other members of the staff.

Internal control relies on the following elements:

It is because checks are used in regular business.

Each member of staff is responsible for a certain aspect of the routine system, and the check is to be performed continually as part of the routine system.

Although each member of staff has their own responsibilities, their efforts complement those of the others.

It is becoming more and more common for auditors to acknowledge the need of an internal control system, especially for big businesses. When an efficient internal control system is in place, it lightens the load of the external auditor and allows them to focus on more high-level issues. To what degree an external auditor may rely on the system of internal check depends on the procedural tests he applies to determine the system's efficacy. However, if the auditor is found negligent, even though he examined the internal check in place in the organization before accepting it as acceptable, he will still be held responsible.

The Reasons behind an Internal Audit

Why To make it more difficult for dishonest employees to get by with their shenanigans and to cut down on the likelihood of fraud occurring in the workplace. In order to pull off any kind of fraud, at least two people must work together.

1. Quickly and simply identify fraudulent activity and remedy any resulting issues.
2. To put an ethical compulsion on the workforce.
3. Allocate tasks and responsibilities to each member of the team in a manner that makes it possible to hold each individual accountable for his or her actions.
4. Assigning tasks according to the concept of division of labour will help the whole team function more effectively.
5. To keep track of financial dealings in a way that can be trusted.

Importance of a well-designed internal auditing and monitoring system

- One employee may not be given exclusive authority over the documentation of the company's financial transactions.
- No one member of staff may have access to both the financial records and the physical assets.
- Assign specified tasks to each member of the crew.
- You should strongly urge all authorities and personnel responsible for cash, securities, or shares to take vacation time now to avoid the camouflaged fraud.
- It's important to give each employee a new challenge every once in a while.

- Mechanical devices should be used to try to stop the theft of money.
- A transaction must go via a certain chain of command and include many people.
- Books, vouchers, and other paperwork should be organized and made readily accessible for use as needed.
- All merchandise entering and leaving the store must be recorded accurately.
- The system might be improved by introducing a self-balancing ledger mechanism.
- No employee should be singled out or treated differently than others, and excessive dependence on any one employee should be avoided.
- The staff's responsibilities must be divided and assigned such that everyone's work is being checked on at all times.

Cash sales audit inside company

Given the higher potential for fraud in cash transactions, it is essential to have a reliable and effective internal control system. There are a few different channels that might effect cash sales: a) sales at the counter,

b) postal sales, or sales via the mail, and

c) sales through agents and representatives. This section elaborates on the internal check mechanism that must be used at all times.

A single salesperson should be assigned to one register and held accountable for all transactions that take place there.

The sales team must ensure that each representative has their own cash memo book. In order to easily distinguish between the many counters in an organization, the cash memo book must be printed in a variety of colors.

Each salesperson is responsible for keeping a sales tally. It's there where he should keep track of all the sales he makes. He must ensure that his cash sales summary matches the cash memos he has issued.

A carbon copy is required if cash is being sent through memorandum.

In no circumstances is the salesperson to be compensated in cash for the cash memos he issues.

A consumer must pay at the cash register in order to settle the salesman's cash note.

The following procedure should be followed in effecting sales:

1. The consumer must get three copies of the cash memo.
2. At the time of payment, the client must provide the cashier with all three cash memo copies.
3. Third, the teller must double check all of the information and be comfortable with the entire amount, both in terms of rates and quantities.
4. In the event that a cash payment is made, the cashier will mark any duplicate notes with a "cash paid" stamp.
5. Five, he'll keep one copy for himself and give the purchaser two.

In order to get their items, customers must produce the cash notes to the shipping department.

The products have been delivered, and the delivery staff will stamp the documents accordingly. One duplicate will be kept as proof of delivery, and the other will be given to the purchaser.

The salesman, the cashier, and the gatekeeper shall compile the summary and turn it in to the manager or officer in charge at the conclusion of each work day. If the totals add up, then the books may be considered accurate.

- Mail order and other postal sales
- The following are some examples of this:
- A separate register should be kept to track V.P.P. sales exclusively.
- If any items are returned, they must be noted in the register as well.
- You must record any cash payments received, together with any advances received for postal orders, in a ledger and deposit the entire money received in a bank account.
- Any products for which payment has not been received in full should be investigated further, and the V.P.P. record as a whole should be reviewed by a competent official.
- Mail orders should be properly filed, and the cash register should be reconciled with these orders.
- Commissioned sales agents and independent sales representatives

Large corporations often utilize agents and representatives to push sales and collect debts. The following is a suggested internal check mechanism to implement in this regard:

1. The representatives and agents must be given the authority to provide rough receipts to the consumers in exchange for the cash

they have collected from the customers. However, only the main office should provide the final receipt.

2. Customers should be instructed to contact corporate offices if they do not get the final receipt within an acceptable time frame.

3. Third, have your salespeople and agents wire the money they've earned back to headquarters as soon as possible.

4. Fourth, under no circumstances should sales representatives and agents be permitted to deduct their commission or other expenses from the money they bring in. Send in your final invoice to corporate for payment of any commission and other costs incurred.

5. The headquarters should automatically give the client frequent statements of accounts to keep them up-to-date.

It is recommended that the representatives and agents report to the main office on a regular basis with updates on their sales, cash collections, and names of any defaulters.

Those clients who have not paid their bills on time should be contacted by the main office with reminders.

They are not to have a base of operations, as stated in clause 8. On the contrary, they should be relocated periodically in order to maximize productivity and reduce the risk of fraud.

Procurement Validation Within Company Walls

i. Because of the increased potential for fraud in connection with the acquisition of products by a large company, it is necessary to develop a reliable and effective internal control system. The following is the standard method for making purchases and should be followed in this context.

ii. The purchasing department needs the amount and quality information from the department requesting the materials on the purchase requisition.

iii. Based on the request, the purchasing department will reach out to potential vendors to get price quotes.

iv. Once bids have been received, the order will be given to the supplier deemed to be the best in terms of quality, timeliness of delivery, competitive pricing, etc.

v. For their part, vendors are expected to start working on orders as soon as they are received. The goods are going to be accepted by the stores division.

vi. The stores department will provide a goods received note upon shipment confirmation, which will be checked against the order for accuracy. If everything goes as planned, the accounts department will get a copy of the supplier's invoice and delivery note, both of which will be signed off as proof that the products were received and put away.

vii. A senior official will approve payment of the invoice after double-checking the rates, quality, and other costs listed.

viii. Considering the above, the following purchase internal check mechanism is proposed:

ix. A distinct purchasing division is required.

x. Purchase orders will only be issued in response to requests from individual divisions.

xi. No verbal instructions will be accepted; all requests must be made in writing. Ideally, the order form would be a printed form with all the necessary information.

xii. The requests need to be submitted four times. The order, in one copy, must be submitted to the vendor. The second copy should be sent to the requesting department, the third copy should be forwarded to the accounts payable department, and the fourth copy should be kept by the purchasing department for record-keeping purposes.

xiii. Only the buy manager, or someone else authorized to do so, should sign any purchase orders.

xiv. The official seal must be included on all orders.

xv. The received products must be examined alongside the order document.

xvi. Compare the number, quality, and prices of the delivered items to the seller's delivery notes and supply invoices.

xvii. To confirm that the items have been received, the purchasing department should approve the supplier's invoice with a stamp.

xviii. A "Goods Received Note" must be made for each shipment after it has been inspected and evaluated. You should also provide the inspection report.

xix. The products cannot be put into stock without the approval of the procurement manager or an authorized official from the shops department.

xx. Once products have been received, a receipt should be generated and sent to the order dept. by the stores dept.

xxi. All shipments must be opened in the presence of an authorized employee.

xxii. Once the stores officer has confirmed that the products received are accurate, he or she should record them in the stock register.

Typically, the buying manager will affix a rubber stamp with the following certification on the supplier's invoice:

i. This is to certify that the items listed on Folio No. of Stock Register No. and Order No. on this date have been received and entered into stock.

ii. After the accounts department has reviewed the invoice, items received note, and purchase order, payment must be made.

iii. Invoices approved for payment should be rubber-stamped by the accounts payable team.

iv. The purchasing office must keep a separate register of purchases.

v. In order to prevent accounting shenanigans, a ledger clerk should have no access to the actual cash on hand or stock register.

vi. When making a purchase across different divisions of a firm or between other companies altogether, transfer notes are required.

vii. Employees are responsible for keeping track of their own money while making purchases for their own purposes.

viii. To keep track of items sent back to vendors, a dedicated "return outward book" must be kept.

ix. Claim payments will be credited to the customer's account. A duplicate of the credit note should be sent from the purchasing department to the accounting office.

x. Keeping a control account in the purchase ledger is a must. A monthly comparison of the ledger account with the supplier statements is recommended.

xi. Avoiding surplus and guaranteeing always-available essentials calls for a perpetual inventory management system.

xii. The Purchaser must review the Certificate of Receipt of Stock from the Authority to Whom Goods Are Delivered Before Authorizing Payment on Invoices for Goods Delivered Directly to Locations or Places of Work Not Under Their Control.

xiii. The purchasing office is responsible for placing orders based on indents, noting the order in the purchase day book, recording the goods received in the goods inward book, and forwarding the supplier's invoice, along with the inspection report and goods received notes, to the accounts payable office for payment.

xiv. By conducting an internal audit as described above, you may prevent accounting errors caused by the creation of fraudulent purchases, the duplication of invoices, and the theft of discounts and commissions from your suppliers.

Performing a Sales Audit within the Company

The sales and distribution model informs how the sales department is structured. The department's potential for sales suppression and account manipulation increases if it is not well organized. Property may also be stolen. As a result, it's important to have a solid internal check system, which may look like this:

1. Orders received from clients must be the basis for the fulfillment of sales.

2. Orders must be numbered and processed in order of receipt, and consumers must be notified that their orders have been received.

3. Thirdly, all orders received, those in progress, those that have been completed, and those that were denied must be recorded accurately.

4. After reviewing the order and the amount of supply of products, as well as the terms and conditions of sales acknowledged by the client, the sales must be authorized by responsible authorities.

5. Invoices must be made in quadruplicate and included with every sales order, as per Rule 5. The sales team should keep one copy, the client should get one, the accounting team should have one, and the shipping team should have the final copy.

6. Cash sales and credit sales should be handled by different divisions.

7. If you provide credit for purchases, keep track of your clients' good credit in a separate register. When the customer's request to purchase products on credit has been thoroughly reviewed, only then will the credit sale be approved.

8. The client must be provided with periodic statements detailing any outstanding balances and must confirm receipt of these statements.

9. Customers must be reminded on a regular basis that they have outstanding balances that need to be paid.

10. When all other means of collecting a debt from a consumer have been tried and failed, only then will the amount be written off as bad debt.

11. A debt may be written off at the discretion of the relevant authority.

12. The sales invoice clerk should have no access to either physical inventory or financial data.

13. The fact that the products were returned by the clients must be verified with the shipping and sales departments before the credit note can be created. Quadruple copies of all credit notes must be made. You should keep one copy for your records in accounting,

another for shipment, another for sales, and a final copy for the client.

14. If a transaction is canceled, the shipping department must be informed to halt the shipment of any products that have already been prepared for shipment.

15. Only the sales department is able to cancel the invoice (15). It is mandatory to print and number all sales invoices in sequential order.

16. A separate clerk is responsible for keeping the sales ledger.

17. Debtors should be issued statements on a regular basis.

18. Customers' ongoing balances should be confirmed on a regular basis in the event of credit sales. A higher-ranking employee than the ledger clerk must double-check the balance confirmation.

19. It is required that the control account and the sales ledger control account be reconciled on a regular basis.

20. A sales ledger control account must be kept in the general ledger.

21. Employees may only be given credit with management approval (paragraph 21).

22. Sales on consignment, hire buy, products on sales or return, etc., should all be handled by their own dedicated division.

23. There should be frequent checks of the stock held by the agents against the statements received from the agents.

24. No sales but unsold stock should be recorded for items sent on a sale or return basis but still unsold as of the balance sheet date.

25. Cash sales" suggests an internal method for verifying the accuracy of cash receipts. The sales department had an internal audit, which included the recommendations made for auditing cash sales.

Verification of Wage Payment Within the Organization

Wage and hour administration is crucial in any large firm, as is keeping track of all the many types of wage records, as well as figuring out how much to pay each employee and actually paying them. Therefore, it is important to devise a suitable system of internal check about salaries payment to reduce the likelihood of false identities, inaccurate salary records, and monetary theft. It is recommended that you use the following method of internal verification:

1. Workers should only be hired after receiving written approval from the Personnel Officer or the person with the power to make the appointment. It is recommended that the pay preparation

department get a copy of the appointment order with an endorsement.

2.   A separate team is responsible for keeping track of employees' attendance, managing their time off, paying their overtime, and handing them their paychecks. Each employee is accountable for accurately filling out their own salary sheet. It is also important for him to place his initials next to his finished work.

3.   The wage sheet must include sections for entering the employee's name, position, pay period, pay rate, and any other pertinent information about wage payment.

4.   The total salary drawn, deductions (with distinct columns showing the kind of deductions), net amount due, and employee signatures to acknowledge payment.

5.   Individual personnel files should be kept, including the hire date, pay grade, salary, etc. of each employee. Wage preparation must be endorsed with copies of all directives regarding salary raises, promotions, demotions, deductions for loans, medical insurance, ground rent, etc.

6.   Individual job cards must be kept in order to document each employee's efforts.

7.   Each employee must get a pay stub detailing both their gross and net salary.

8.   A separate register must be kept to track the names of employees who have been granted overtime. Without legal authorization, overtime labor cannot be assigned to any employee.

9.   Clocks that record time must be placed at the main factory entrance so that employees' entrance and exit may be tracked.

10.   A copy of each job's employee roster should be created and sent to the payroll department.

11.   Workers who are tardy to work must be recorded in a separate register and copied to the human resources department.

12.   A watch and ward system must be kept in order to record employees' arrival and departure times.

13.   Every employee's pay rate should be verified on a regular basis using a rate card.

14.   Payroll deductions and the resulting take-home pay must be carefully calculated, but that process must be double-checked by an outside party (see Rule 13).

15.   Only one person should input the names of employees, their pay rates, and the pay period onto the wage sheet. Someone else will figure out how much you owe in gross earnings. A third party is responsible for making the necessary deductions under the

different headings. A senior employee should calculate the net wages due and verify the wage sheet with reference to leave deductions, etc. Only the authorized signatory is permitted to sign the payroll sheet.

16. A job card must be issued to each employee in the event that they are to be paid on the basis of a piece pay system. The department foreman and the retail department receiving the manufactured items should both counter sign these cards.

17. Make three copies of the payroll sheet. Wage preparation must send one copy to the pay master for endorsement, send another copy to accounts, and save a third copy for their records.

Methods of in-house auditing and quality control

The auditor places a premium on the integrity of the internal control system and its implementation inside the business. To the extent that there is an efficient internal control system, the task of the external auditor is simplified. Because the internal check system handles the mundane and meticulous checking of transactions, he can focus on more important matters. If the internal control system is insufficient, the auditor should determine how much further, in-depth verification has to be done before he is satisfied with the veracity of the company's records. In order to rely on the internal check system, the auditor must first learn about the system currently in use inside the organization. This is done via a series of test checks. If the current system of internal checks is inadequate, he should conduct his own thorough audit of the books.

If he doesn't, he might be held responsible for any mistakes or scams that slip through the cracks. He should be careful to avoid slacking off while on the job. The audit plan he creates must take into account the system's vulnerabilities. To further improve the internal check mechanism, he should also recommend modifications to management. It is important to remember that although if a well-functioning internal check system inside an organization facilitates the auditor's job, it does not relieve him of any legal responsibility.

Difference between internal check and internal control

S.No	Basis	Internal Check	Internal Control
1.	Meaning	A system of allocation of responsibility, division of work, and methods of recording transactions, whereby the work of an employee is checked continuously by another.	It consists of all the methods and procedures adopted to assist in achieving the objective of efficient conduct of business. It includes internal check and internal audit.
2.	Scope	It operates in routine to double check every part of a transaction at the time of occurrence and recording of the same.	In internal control systems, work of one person is automatically checked by another.
3.	Objective	Its objective is to ensure that no one employee has exclusive control over any transaction or group of transactions and their recording in the books.	Its object is to ensure adherence to management policies, safeguarding of assets, prevention and detection of frauds and errors, accuracy and completeness of accounting records.
4.	Point of Time	Methods of recording transactions are devised where work of an employee is checked continuously by correlating it with the work of others.	In internal control system, checking is done simultaneously with the conduct of work. Every transaction is checked as soon as it is entered.
5.	Thrust of System	The thrust of internal check system is to prevent errors.	The thrust of internal control lies in fixing of responsibility and division of work to avoid duplication.
6.	Cost Involved	It is a part of internal control and a method of division of work, therefore does not add to the cost.	The system proves to be costly in case of small businesses because more number of employees are engaged.
7.	Report	The summary of day to day transactions work as report to the senior.	Internal control provide for built in MIS reports.

Audit of the Digital Setting (E.D.P. audit).

The primary purpose of an audit is to provide reasonable assurance that the financial statements fairly and accurately reflect the financial position of an organization as of a certain date and the results of its operations for the period ending on that date. Among the most crucial aspects of an audit designed for corporations of any size are:-

a) An analysis of the company's accounting and internal control procedures to see whether they meet its needs and ensure that all transactions are recorded accurately.

b) Conducting whatever checks and investigations are deemed necessary to ascertain if the systems are being operated properly.

An audit of financial records to confirm:-

The ownership, value, and existence of all assets shown on the balance sheet, as well as the accuracy of the recorded amounts owed on all accounts.

The profit or loss figure shown in the income statement is an accurate reflection of reality.

And to verify that the financial statements are accurate and in line with the supporting documents and legal standards.

The audit's overarching purpose and scope remain the same in an E.D.P. setting. However, the organization and methods used by the firm to accomplish effective internal control may need to be adjusted due to the introduction of computers into the process of processing and storing financial data. The auditor's study and assessment of the accounting system and associated internal controls, as well as the kind, timeliness, and scope of his other audit methods, may all be altered by the presence of electronic data processing.

The primary purpose of an EDP audit is to ascertain whether or not the audited computer system adequately protects assets, maintains data integrity, successfully achieves corporate objectives, and makes efficient use of resources. To guarantee success, a solid internal control structure is required. Despite the shift to an EDP setting, an audit's overarching goals and scope remain the same. However, the organization and method used by the firm to accomplish effective internal control may be impacted by the use of a computer, which alters the processing and storing of financial information.

While performing an audit of the digital books, the auditor should take the following additional measures.

1. A code list for the different accounts used in computerized accounting is required. The auditor has to get their hands on a list of these codes and double check their application.

2. In a manual accounting process, you can see every step of the way as it's being taken: preparing vouchers, passing entry, posting to the ledger, casting, balancing, grouping, preparing the trial balance, and finally, finalizing the accounts. When the books are kept digitally, however, it becomes impossible for the auditor to verify the accuracy of each and every step along the way. As a result, it is incumbent upon the auditor to verify the accurate and dependable operation of the computer system in question. To do this, he will need to pick out a subset of transactions to analyze and then compare the outcomes of the computer processing to the expected outcomes.

3. Floppy disks are used as a backup for data in the case of computerized accounting systems. It's been shown that these disks are influenced by

4. Conditions (such as heat, dust, etc.) The auditor must verify that the customer has taken reasonable measures to safeguard the disks in question.

5. He has to make sure the customer has taken reasonable precautions to prevent "Virus" from compromising the data on their machine.

6. He has to make sure that "Passwords" are being used to effectively regulate computer usage by different users.

7. He has to make sure the computers are serviced on a regular basis to keep them running well. As a result, there will be less potential for malfunction and data loss.

8. The correctness of input is crucial to the precision of computer output. He has to put in place a mechanism to regularly compare the results to the inputs.

9. Finally, he must make sure that only authorized personnel make modifications to the software and that these alterations are properly documented for future use.

INSIDE MANAGEMENT
Fundamental principles of internal check

Maintaining some degree of command over one's environment is a fundamental need for all humans, and this need has persisted through the centuries and in all sectors of human endeavor. In general, running a business is a difficult task, and it has become much more so as society and technology have progressed. Only recently has the idea of internal control been formally introduced into the field of business administration.

Control is a well-known tool in the commercial world for making the most of available assets and expanding upon available profit-making chances. Human employees and mechanical tools are essential to every organization, and both must be monitored for optimal performance.

They perform what they're supposed to do and there aren't any unnecessary losses or wastes that eat into the profits of the businesses.

Internal controls for a small firm run by a lone owner are different from those needed by a huge, complex corporation. If you're a little trader with a food store, you probably don't need more than a few of helpers. The assistants report to him, and he assigns them tasks. Always aware of his own financial standing, he is never caught unaware. He is aware of daily sales figures. He is familiar with the purchasing channels personally. He maintains a ledger of creditors and debtors. His helpers don't do much more than bring doors to clients and put everything in the right place.

As can be seen, the owner retains complete discretion and authority over all operational matters. As a company expands, however, its founder can no longer maintain tabs on every aspect of day-to-day business or monitor every employee's performance as they carry out their duties. As his company grows, he must hire additional workers and assign them specific responsibilities in order to keep things running smoothly. In addition to relying on these individuals to carry out the task and safeguard the materials, papers, and equipment entrusted to them, he must depend on them to do so in a remote capacity. Additionally, he must guarantee the upkeep of all machinery and structures. To achieve this goal, he must build an organizational structure that will allow him to get insight into the nature of the job at hand and the individuals accountable for it. Moreover, he must devise a system of delegating responsibilities and powers because, well, that's just the way it is. No one should bother him for guidance or a verdict since doing so would prevent him from giving his whole mental attention to issues that are more pressing.

Human nature is such that we tend to stray from the straight and narrow if we aren't kept in check. The work environment has to be monitored in a methodical way to make sure that the worker completes his tasks in the manner prescribed for the job and with due care for the tools and resources at his disposal.

Control system evaluation

The management's control system may be reviewed by studying, examining, and evaluating how well it is working. Finding out what management's controls and protocols are is the first step. The auditor may learn more about the nature, breadth, and effectiveness of the control system by reading business manuals, analyzing organizational charts and flow charts, and conducting appropriate interviews with officers and workers. It takes a lot of expertise and knowledge for an individual to get familiar with the ins and outs of how accounting data is gathered and processed, as well as the nature of the controls that ensure the data is accurate and safeguard the company's assets. Oftentimes, only a small fraction of this data is documented; for the auditor to get the information he needs, he must know whom to interview and how. In order to better retain the instructions and guidelines he reads in the handbook or learns via investigation, he should jot them down.

The auditor may use one of the following to learn about and understand the system being evaluated in order to conduct a thorough analysis of internal controls:

- The Narrative Record;
- A tally sheet;
- Questionnaire; and
- Diagram of Process

(1) All aspects of the system as discovered by the auditor during operation are described in detail in the narrative record. Such a system is better suited to small businesses, which means that it requires testing and observation before it can be put into action. Here are some of the major drawbacks of narrative records:

- Intuiting the system's workings is a challenging task.
- To identify areas where the system is deficient
- Add in costs associated with things like staffing changes, etc.

(2) A check list consists of questions and/or statements. He marks the area next to the instruction with an initial after he's through with it. Most check list instructions may be answered with a simple Yes, No, or NA. This is another example of a control feature that must be shown on the job. Here are some sample checklist instructions:
Are bids requested before orders are placed?
Do the purchases follow a formal, written order?
Is there a common format for the purchase order?
Do purchase order forms have sequential numbers already?
Have people who have nothing to do with:
(1) Work custody;
(2) Stock being received;
(3) The third step is inventory auditing.

Option 4: Invest in Stock

The principal/manager/senior examines the whole checklist to confirm the presence of internal control and assess the efficacy of its execution.

1. The third definition describes the internal control questionnaire as a thorough set of questions pertaining to internal control. The presence, functioning, and effectiveness of internal control in an organization may be assessed using this most popular form.

2. The questionnaire technique is preferable because it reduces the likelihood of forgetting or overlooking crucial steps in the internal control review process. All of the questions for the internal control assessment may be answered at once or in chunks if the questionnaire is designed well enough. Interim reviews are simpler to do. An further benefit of the questionnaire format is that it makes reporting control flaws systematic. Reviewing and documenting the status of the internal control system once a year is standard procedure. Typically, questions in the survey are worded in such a way that a "yes" response indicates a strong viewpoint while a "no" response indicates a weak one. There's room for clarification or more descriptions of "No" responses. When a question is not directly related to the company's operations, "Not applicable" is selected as an answer.

3. The customer receives the questionnaire once a year and is asked to have their relevant executives and workers fill it out. If discrepancies or apparent incongruities are spotted when reviewing the responses, the auditor's team will follow up with the client's workers to get to the bottom of things. Afterward, the responsible auditor will compile a report detailing the problems and making suggestions for fixes.

4. A flowchart is a visual representation of the many components of an organization's internal control structure. The most efficient technique to document the auditor's examination of the system is through a flowchart. Minimizing the need for lengthy expository writing, it allows for thought or presentation that would be impossible in any other format. It provides a bird's-eye perspective of the system, allowing for easy identification of issues with the flow of transactions and integration, as well as suggestions on how to fix them.

An in-depth examination of the complete manufacturing, trade, and administrative procedure, as well as a focus on the nature of the business's operations and the many channels of products and materials and cash, both internal and external, are also essential for the auditor. This will provide him the proper context from which to analyze the internal controls.

Advantages

*   The Auditor is permitted to depend on the safeguards and Internal Controls introduced by the Management in order to perform his duties, but he will, of course, consider any

inadequacies he may discover therein when preparing his Programme.

- Reasonable certainty that the accounting system is competent and that all accounting information that should be documented has been recorded is a prerequisite for an audit to be considered successful.
- The auditing and assessing of the Internal Control System is an integral aspect of the Audit Programme.
- Before deciding on the scope, time, and type of additional audit processes, the auditor should first familiarize himself with the accounting system and relevant Internal Controls, and then analyze and assess the activities of these Internal Controls.

Purpose of Audit: To ascertain, via examination of Internal Controls, if

(a) Whether or not mistakes and frauds are likely to be uncovered during routine company activities. Whether or not the Management has implemented and is effectively using an appropriate Internal Control System;

(b) Whether or not an efficient Internal Auditing division is in place;

(c) If administrative controls affect his job (for instance, when there is lax oversight over)

(d) Recruitment and enrolment of employees (of interest to the Auditor is the possibility of using fictitious names on the payroll sheet);

(e) How well the controls protect the assets

(f) To what extent and how efficiently is Management engaged in carrying out its responsibility for accurate documentation of transactions?

Questions to ask include:

(g) how trustworthy the management reports and records are;

(h) how thorough an examination of the various accounting areas the auditor must conduct;

(i) which auditing methods and procedures are most applicable under the circumstances;

(j) where control is lacking or excessive; and

(k) whether any helpful recommendations for strengthening the control system can be made.

THE ROLE OF THE AUDITOR

A brief summary of the auditor's function with respect to internal control would be as follows:

Management has primary responsibility for the security of the Company's assets. The Auditor may depend on • protections and Internal Controls put in place by the Management.

The Auditor wants to make sure that all transactions are carried out with Management's approval, that all transactions are documented accurately, and that assets are kept securely. That's why it's crucial to include an audit of the Internal Control System in your audit Programme.

The Auditor must have confidence that the accounting system is sufficient. 1.d that the required financial data has been recorded in a complete, accurate, and timely manner. In most cases, internal controls help provide this confidence.

The Auditor has to familiarize themselves with the accounting system and the relevant Internal Controls as part of the Audit's planning and programming stages. If he plans to depend on certain Internal Controls, he should learn about and assess how they work before deciding on the scope, frequency, and timing of other audit processes. Once he has a firm grasp of the Internal Control System and how it functions in practice, he may begin to create his audit plan.

If the Auditor evaluates the client's Internal Control System, he may alert Management to any flaws and provide recommendations for strengthening the system. It is possible that he will determine the extent to which the vulnerabilities have been addressed over the course of his examination.

Audit Methodology: The Auditor's knowledge of the Internal Control System informs the methodological choices made during the audit. If he finds holes in Internal Control, he may run further checks or expand the scope of existing ones to ensure everything is in order.

The presence and functioning of an Internal Control System is crucially important in determining a strategy for selective checking (test checking or sample checking).

As required by CARO, an organization's statutory auditor must issue a report covering several topics related to internal control, including: (a) Whether or not the organization has an adequate internal control system for the acquisition of inventory and fixed assets and the sale of goods and services, taking into account the organization's size and the nature of its business.

(a) Is there an ongoing failure to address significant gaps in the organization's internal control framework?

1. The Auditor's ability to determine the kind, scope, and timeliness of the necessary substantive audit processes relies on a firm grasp of the I.C.S.

Although Management is ultimately responsible for Internal Control, the Auditor-

2. In order to (a) determine the type, timeliness, and extent of other audit processes, the auditor must first (b) independently develop a knowledge of the accounting system and associated Internal Controls.

3. Third, if the Auditor determines that he can depend on a subset of Internal Controls, he will likely conduct a more limited set of substantive procedures than would otherwise be necessary. There might be variations in both the character and the timing of these occurrences.

4. It's possible that the auditor will choose an auditing procedure/test that isn't normally necessary in cases when Internal Control is poor. When he is satisfied, he may undertake more tests or expand the scope of existing ones to include a greater number of transactions or other things than he would normally review.

5. It is of no consequence, and does not relieve the Statutory Auditors of their responsibilities, that the Internal Control was designed by a Chartered Accountant who had also written a book on Internal Control. In order to design an effective audit program, the auditor has to have a firm grasp of, and evaluation of, the Internal Controls on their own.

CONTROL SYSTEM EVALUATION

The inherent constraints of internal control.

A fair but not complete guarantee that the aforementioned goals are met is all that can be offered by internal control. This is because internal controls have a number of problems of their own, including:

 (a) The cost-effectiveness of a control is a factor taken into account by management;

 (b) the possibility of human mistake;

 (c) the reality that most controls are not tailored to atypical transactions.

 (d) The possibility of collusion between parties outside of the entity and employees of the entity to circumvent controls; (e) The possibility that a person responsible for exercising control could abuse that authority, such as a member of management overriding a control; (f) The possibility that procedures may become inadequate due to changes in conditions and compliance may deteriorate; (g) Manipulations by management with respect to transactions.

EXAMPLES OF INTERNATIONAL CONTROL SYSTEMS FOR PROCESSING SALES, PURCHASES, PAYROLL, ETC.

1. Profits and Creditors
2. When it comes to Sales & Debtors, the most important Internal Control procedures are -
3. Invoices, Delivery Challans, and other papers should all be given a unique serial number, and any cases of missing paperwork should be looked into immediately.
4. There will be a wall built between the shipping department, the sales department, and the accounting department. The carrier is required to verify the delivery challan before the shipment is made.
5. The Purchase Order and the Delivery Challan must match up before the shipment can be made, and once it has, the two must be submitted in order.
6. Promptly get the customer's confirmation of receipt of sent products.
    Sixth, consumers should get invoices for all shipments in a timely manner when they have been created.
7. Seven, invoice prices must be in accordance with the normal price list, and any discounts or other adjustments to the list price must be approved.
8. Credit Notes must be properly authorized and checked with all relevant invoices, and returned products must be properly recorded.
9. Part delivery must be properly documented.
10. Sales ledger entries must be reconciled on a regular basis with the Control Account.
11. Mail-in checks must be documented, and "A/c Payee only" stamps are required for bearer checks.
12. After making a deposit, the cashier must double check the Cash Book with the pay-in slip from the bank.
13. Sales ledgers, cash receipts, and receipt issuing must all be handled by different employees.
14. Receipts and payments must coincide with bills.
15. The roles of those responsible for recording transactions and those responsible for obtaining balances must be clearly defined and separated.
16. Periodically, unbiased parties must compare sales ledger balance listings to the corresponding Control Accounts.
17. The aging analysis must be done, and it must be verified, on day 17. Previous payments should be followed up on.

18. Statements must be provided on a consistent schedule, client balances must be reconciled on a regular basis, and things that need follow-up throughout the reconciliation process must be monitored.

19. Before accepting any orders, credit limitations will be verified.

Crucial Purchase & Creditors Internal Controls Include -

Every purchase order must be accompanied by a valid purchase request and signed off on by an appropriate authority.

Before making orders, it is best practice to solicit bids.

The ordering process requires pre-numbering and serializing purchase orders.

Staffing levels in the Items Receiving Department should be sufficient to allow for thorough inspection, documentation, and proper storage of all goods.

Each Goods Received Note must have a unique serial number and be pre-numbered. Differentiating the following responsibilities is essential:

(a) Making Purchase Receipts;

(b) Noting the receipt of inventory in the Stock Records;

(c) Safekeeping and the right to distribute stocks;

(d) Goods-received-note-invoice comparison

Prior to publishing, invoices must be validated for accuracy and compared to the rates shown on the corresponding Purchase Orders.

Liabilities for goods must be properly pursued if Goods Received Notes have not been matched with invoices.

Those that come in at the end of the year should be properly noted.

When an invoice is received, it should immediately be logged in a dedicated Invoice Register. The Supplier Statements must be reconciled on a regular basis.

The Balance Sheet Control Accounts must be reconciled on a periodic basis with the entries in the Purchase Ledger.

Difference between internal checks and internal audit

S.No.	Basis	Internal Check	Internal Audit
1.	Meaning	Internal check is an arrangement of work in such a way that another person automatically checks the work of one person.	Internal audit is an independent appraisal of the operations of the company.
2.	Objects	The object of internal check is to prevent the occurrence of errors and frauds.	The object of internal audit is to detect errors and frauds.
3.	Scope of work	Internal check is considered as a device for doing the work.	Internal audit is a device for checking the work.
4.	Discovery of errors and frauds	In internal check errors and frauds are discovered during the course of doing the work.	In internal audit errors and frauds are discovered after the completion of the work.
5.	Commencement of work	Internal check is in operation during the course of transactions.	Internal audit commences only when accounting process is completed.
6.	Performance of work	In internal check no new staff is appointed to perform the work.	In internal audit the work is performed by a separate group of persons specifically appointed for this purpose.

Special areas of audit: Tax audit and Management audit

Tax audit: Tax audits are conducted to ensure that taxpayers are complying with tax laws and regulations and to identify any discrepancies or errors in their financial records or tax filings. The process of a tax audit typically begins with the selection of a taxpayer for audit, which can be done at random or based on certain criteria, such as a high income or a history of noncompliance. During the audit, the auditor will review the taxpayer's financial records, such as bank statements, invoices, and receipts, to determine whether their reported income and expenses are accurate. The auditor will also verify that the taxpayer has reported all of their income and that they have claimed all of the deductions and credits that they are entitled to. The auditor may also ask the taxpayer to provide additional information or documentation to support their claims.

If the auditor finds any discrepancies or errors in the taxpayer's records or filings, they may assess additional taxes, penalties, or interest. If the taxpayer disagrees with the auditor's findings, they have the right to appeal the decision.

Management audit: Management audit is a process of evaluating an organization's management and operations. The purpose of a management audit is to identify areas where the organization can improve its performance and to make recommendations for improving the effectiveness and efficiency of the organization's operations.

Management audits typically focus on areas such as financial management, marketing, production and distribution, and human resources. The auditor will review the organization's financial records, such as balance sheets, income statements, and cash flow statements, to assess the organization's financial health. The auditor will also evaluate the organization's marketing strategies, production and distribution processes, and human resource management practices.

The auditor will then prepare a report that summarizes their findings and recommendations for improvement. The organization can use the report to identify areas for improvement, and to develop and implement strategies for improving its performance.

It's important to note that management audit is different from financial audit, where the focus is more on the accuracy and integrity of the financial statements, but both are important for the overall well-being of the organization.

Recent trends in auditing

One of the major trends in auditing is the increased use of technology, such as data analytics and artificial intelligence (AI), to improve the efficiency and effectiveness of the audit process. This can include using data analytics to identify potential areas of risk, automating parts of the testing process, and using machine learning algorithms to analyze large amounts of data. For example, data analytics can be used to identify unusual transactions or patterns that may indicate fraud or other financial misstatements. Automation can also be used to perform routine tasks, such as testing for compliance with accounting standards, more quickly and accurately.

Another trend is the shift towards risk-based auditing, where the auditor prioritizes areas of the organization that are most likely to have material misstatements. This approach helps auditors to focus their efforts on the areas of the organization that pose the greatest risk to the financial statements. This can include assessing the internal controls over financial reporting, and performing substantive testing in areas where there is a higher risk of material misstatements.

Integrated audits is another trend where the auditor combines the financial statement audit with an examination of the organization's internal controls over financial reporting. This approach helps to identify and address potential control deficiencies and fraud risk before they result in material misstatements in the financial statements.

Overall, the use of technology and a risk-based approach is helping auditors to be more efficient and effective in identifying and addressing potential financial misstatements.

Relevant Auditing and Assurance Standards (AASs)
Standards for Auditing and Quality Control
ICAI is responsible for issuing auditing and assurance standards in India. To create auditing standards, ICAI established the Auditing and Assurance Standard Board (AASB) in 1982. In light of this, the Council has delegated power to the AASB to produce Statements on Standard Auditing Practices and Auditing and assurance Standards.

The Institute of Chartered Accountants of India, established under Section 3 of the Chartered Accountants Act, 1949, is authorized to make recommendations regarding auditing standards to the Central Government, which, after consulting with and reviewing the findings of the National Financial Reporting Authority, may then issue regulations implementing those recommendations. This authority is authorized by Section 143(10) of the Companies Act, 2013.

STANDARDS FOR AUDIT REQUIREMENTS
Each auditor must follow the auditing standards in accordance with section 143(9) of the Companies Act, 2013.

To avoid professional misconduct charges under clause 9 of Part 1 of the Second Schedule to the Chartered Accountants Act, 1949, a member must highlight any material departures from generally accepted auditing standards in his report if he is unable to perform an audit in accordance with those standards.

Goals and Duties of the Auditing and Assurance Standards Board (AASB) Purpose and Duties of the Auditing and Assurance Standards Board (AASB) Goal 1: Determine where new or revised Standards on Quality Control, Engagement Standards, and Statements on Auditing are needed by analyzing current and developing auditing procedures throughout the globe.

Second, to work with the Institute's Council to create official documents like the Engagement Standards, Quality Control Standards, and Auditing Statement.

To analyze the continued applicability of the current Standards and Statements on Auditing in light of the new circumstances and to revise them as appropriate.

To create guidance notes on problems arising out of any Standard, auditing issues relevant to any particular sector, or on general concerns, which may be provided with the authority of the Institute's Council.

Assess the current Guidance Notes for applicability under the new conditions, and update them as needed.

When questions arise about the Standards, it is the responsibility of the Standards Committee to draft General Clarifications to address them. Whenever it sees fit, the Board may, on its own initiative, create and distribute Technical Guides, Practice Manuals, Studies, and other materials to the public for the benefit of the public and the profession of accounting.

Institute's Auditing and Assurance Standards Board (AASB) creates auditing standards. The Auditing and Assurance Standards Board determines the areas where auditing standards need to be created and the priority with respect to their selection, and then follows the following method to accomplish so.

Study groups/task force formed to consider particular project to aid AASB in the formulation of Auditing Standards. The primary draft of the Standards is prepared by a research group/task force made up of a representative sample of Institute members.

The Committee then prepares an exposure draft of the proposed Standards based on the research groups' work and distributes it to ICAI members for feedback. AASB will complete the document after considering the feedback and then present it to the Institute's Council.

Following its evaluation of the draft, the Council makes appropriate adjustments in collaboration with the AASB and then Standards/Statements are released under the Council's authority. The Board also considers Indian law, culture, and business practices when developing auditing standards, as well as ISAs published by the International Auditing Practices Committee (IAPC).

QUALITY CONTROL, AUDITING, AND ASSOCIATED SERVICES STANDARDS LIST

The Institute of Chartered Accountants of India (ICAI) has released 43 Engagement and Quality Control Standards (formerly referred to as Auditing and Assurance Standards) that address a wide range of issues pertaining to audits and other Every single Chartered Accountant in India must follow these rules. A Chartered Accountant is guilty of professional misconduct if he is determined to have violated any of these rules. Except for SA 600 and SA 299, where equivalent provisions do not exist in ISA, these standards are entirely consistent with the International Standards on Auditing (ISA) released by the IAASB of the IFAC. As a whole, the term "Engagement Standards" refers to the following set of regulations published by the Auditing and Assurance Standards Board (AASB) at the Council's behest: iii (a) Standards on Auditing (SAs) - used for analyzing past financial data.

Standards on Quality Control (SQCs)

1. SQC 1, –Quality Control for Firms that Perform Audit and Reviews of Historical Financial Information, and other Assurance and Related Services Engagementsǁ

New/Revised Standards (Auditing, Review and Others)

1. SA 200 (Revised) issued under the Clarity Project, –Overall Objectives of the Independent Auditor and the Conduct of an Audit in Accordance with Standards on Auditingǁ

2. SA 210 (Revised) under the Clarity Project, —Agreeing the Terms of Audit Engagementsǁ

3. SA 220 (Revised) issued under the Clarity Project , –Quality Control for an Audit of Financial Statementsǁ

4. SA 230 (Revised) under the Clarity Project, —Audit Documentationǁ

Similarities and Differences between SA 710 and AAS 25

- Standard Auditing Practice Statements SA 210 AAS 26 Terms of Audit Engagement SA 260 AAS 27 Communication of Audit Matters with Those Charged with Governance
- The Auditor's Report on Financial Statements in Accordance with SA 700 and AAS 28
- SA 505 AAS 30-External Verifications
- Engagements to Compile Financial Information (SRS 4410) under AAS 31
- Aerial Refueling System, Model 4400, AAS Here are the 32 contracts we've gotten to carry out the agreed-upon financial data procedures:
- To the tune of 2400 AAS SRE Audits of 33 Financial Statements Commissioned
- Additional Considerations for Identifying Items in an Audit SA 501 AAS 34
- A35 SAE 3400

• Quality Control for Organizations that Conduct Audits of Financial Statements and Other Assurance and Related Services Engagements SQC 1 AAS 36 Examination of Projected Financial Statements

CLARIFICATION OF AUDITING AND ASSURANCE REQUIREMENTS BY ICAI

AAS-1 The Auditing Process: The Basics

For audits covering fiscal years that begin on or after April 1, 1985, the AAS must be used.

The Institute's first auditing standard, this Auditing and Assurance Standard set the bar high. The purpose of this document is to define and briefly explain the fundamental principles that form the basis of the auditor's professional responsibilities and that must be met in every audit. All work performed by others must adhere to these guidelines, as well as documentation, planning, audit evidence, accounting system and internal control, audit conclusions, and reporting.

Statement on Auditing Standards No. 2: Financial Statements

As of April 1, 1985, the Standard is to be used in all audits covering fiscal years. The goals and parameters of a general-purpose audit are laid out in this standard independent verification of a company's financial statements. The following are central aspects of an audit that are addressed by the Standards:

One of the main reasons for conducting an audit is so that an opinion may be expressed, based on the idea of a truthful and fair perspective.

Financial Statements: Management's Role in Relation to the Auditor's

The audit's scope, including its deciding criteria, the quality and quantity of audit evidence, disclosure considerations, and any previously unknown major misstatements.

Documentation for AAS-3

Any audit covering a fiscal year that began on or after July 1, 1985, must be conducted in accordance with the AAS.

To ensure that the audit was conducted in compliance with the widely recognized auditing standards in India, it is a fundamental principle that the auditor record all pertinent details. What counts as a working paper, and why they're necessary, are both defined in the Standard. The following are also addressed by the Standard:

Structure and Content Considerations for Form and Content, Volume of Related Documents, Long-Term Audit File, and Ongoing Audit File

Who Owns the Drafts and Where They Are Kept

AAS-4 In an audit of financial statements, an auditor is obligated to keep an eye out for signs of fraud and error.

Since April 1, 2003, audits covering fiscal years starting on or after that date must comply with the AAS.

This AAS was written to set guidelines on how an auditor should think about the possibility of fraud or mistake while doing an audit of financial accounts. The following is an outline of the AAS's material:

• Traits shared by fraud and mistakes

• The accountability of persons in positions of authority

Indicators of likely misstatement Evaluation and resolution of misstatements Responsibilities of management Auditors

Implications for Audit Report; Effect on Documentation; Management's Representations; Difficulties in Communicating with Auditors; Inability of Auditor to Complete Engagement

Risk factors for misstatements due to fraud or mistake, instances of altered auditing processes, and signs of suspected fraud or error are all included in the AAS's supplementary materials.

Auditing Documentation for AAS-5

All audits covering accounting periods starting on or after January 1, 1989, must comply with this AAS.

This AAS is intended to create standards based on the premise that the auditor should collect sufficient relevant audit evidence via compliance and substantive processes to allow him to make reasonable inferences therefrom upon which to base his judgement on the financial facts. The AAS also breaks out the different kinds of statements, as well as the internal vs. external evidence that supports them, and the elements that contribute to adequate suitable audit evidence. The techniques of collecting evidence are also addressed in the Standard, including inspection, observation, inquiry and confirmation, calculation, and analytical review.

Assessments of Risk and Internal Control (AAS-6)

For any audit covering a fiscal year that begins on or after April 1, 2002, the AAS must be used.

This AAS is meant to provide standards for how auditors should learn about and assess audit risk, as well as how they should go about doing these tasks, elements, including unavoidable danger, controllable hazards, and detectable hazards. Additionally, the standard goes into great detail on topics like the definition and three components of audit risk, the definition and inherent limitations of accounting and internal control systems, the control environment, control risk and its assessment, tests of control, inherent risk assessment and its relationship to control risk assessment, detection risk assessment, audit risk in small businesses, and communication of weaknesses.

AAS-7 Utilizing the Report of an Internal Auditor

All audits covering accounting periods starting on or after April 1, 1989 must comply with the Standard.

The AAS specifies how an external auditor should evaluate an internal auditor's report before deciding whether or not to rely on it. The Standard covers themes including the role and responsibilities of internal auditors, how they relate to their external counterparts, what criteria should be used to assess their performance, how they should operate together, and how their work should be evaluated.

Accounting Standard No. 8: Audit Planning

All audits covering accounting periods beginning on or after April 1, 1989, must be conducted in accordance with the AAS.

The AAS's overarching goal is to set standards predicated on the idea that an auditor should organize his work so that he may efficiently and effectively do an audit based on his familiarity with the client's enterprise. The AAS discusses the benefits of audit planning, where to go for information about the client's company, when and how to consult with the client, what to look for in an overall plan, how to create an audit program, and much more.

Methodology AAS-9 Based on the Product of Experts

For audits covering fiscal years that begin on or after April 1, 1991, the AAS must be used. This AAS addresses the auditor's role in utilizing an expert's work as audit evidence and the steps that must be taken. This idea is explained by the AAS of a "expert," instances when such a requirement can exist, criteria for determining whether or not to employ an expert's work, methods for assessing an expert's expertise and impartiality, citations to an expert auditor's report, and so on.

Using Another Auditor's Work (AAS-10) (Revised)

All audits covering accounting periods starting on or after April1, 2002 must comply with the updated AAS.

For the purpose of reporting on the entity's financial statements, an independent auditor (principal auditor) may rely on the work of another auditor (other auditor) with respect to the financial statements of one or more components included in the financial statements of the entity. This AAS addresses the procedures to be applied in such a situation. The term "component" is defined in the AAS. Details on documentation, coordination between the primary and other auditor, reporting concerns for the principal auditor, and division of duty are also covered, as is the necessity to evaluate the professional competence of the other auditor before relying on their work.

Statements by Management (AAS-11)

All audits covering fiscal years beginning on or after April 1, 1995 must be conducted in accordance with the AAS.

The AAS was published to provide criteria for the admissibility of management representations in audits, the methods to be used in assessing and recording such representations, and the steps to be followed if management refuses to submit such representations. The Standard discusses a wide range of related topics, such as when an auditor should seek management representations, the weight to be given to management representations compared to other audit evidence, the necessity of documenting management representations, the different kinds of management representations, the essential components of management representation letters, and so on. In addition, the Standard provides a sample management representation letter covering several aspects of financial statements.

Responsibility of Joint Auditors, AAS-12

For audits covering fiscal years that begin on or after April 1, 1996, the AAS must be used.

More than one auditor is often appointed to carry out audits of major organizations. Joint auditors are two or more auditors who work together to examine an organization's books and provide a consolidated report on their findings. This AAS addresses the auditors' obligations as professionals when they accept joint auditing engagements. Joint and several liability of joint auditors, responsibility for obtaining and evaluating information and explanations from management, scrutiny of branch accounts and returns, need for review of work performed by one joint auditor by other joint auditor(s), and reporting responsibilities are all discussed in detail in this AAS.

As per AAS-13, Audit Significance

For audits covering fiscal years beginning on or after April 1, 1996, the AAS must be used.

A misrepresentation (i.e., omission or erroneous statement) of substantial information is one whose omission or error might have a significant impact on the economic choices that users would make in light of the financial information. Instead of being an essential quality that the data must possess, materiality serves as a threshold for when the data stops being useless. The idea of materiality and its connection to audit risk are codified in this AAS. Thus, the AAS addresses issues like determining what constitutes a material misstatement, how auditors should weigh the risk associated with a finding, how audit evidence should be evaluated, what factors go into the total number of errors that need to be fixed, and how the auditor should go about fixing them.

AAS-14 Methods of Analysis

For audits covering fiscal years that begin on or after April 1, 1997, the AAS must be used.

When we talk about "analytical methods," we're referring to the process of examining and explaining statistically significant ratios and patterns, as well as the subsequent evaluation of fluctuations and correlations that don't make sense in light of these data or numbers that don't match up with projections. This AAS is intended to provide guidelines for the use of analytical methods throughout the auditing process. Therefore, the AAS covers topics such as the nature and purpose of analytical procedures, the role of analytical procedures in audit planning, the role of analytical procedures as substantive procedures, the role of analytical procedures in the final review of the audit, the degree to which auditors rely on analytical procedures, the investigation of unusual items, etc.

Audit Sampling per AAS-15

All audits covering accounting periods beginning on or after April 1, 1998 must be conducted in accordance with the AAS.

The term "audit sampling" refers to the practice of performing audit procedures on a subset (rather than all) of an account balance or class of transactions in order to gather and evaluate audit evidence about certain characteristics of the items chosen to draw or aid in drawing conclusions about the population as a whole. The Auditing Accreditation Standards (AAS) are a set of guidelines for both statistical and non-statistical sampling methods that are used to provide standards for the design, selection, and assessment of audit samples. Design of sample, audit goals, population, stratification, sample size and risk, tolerated and anticipated error, sample selection, evaluation of sample data, analysis of mistakes in the sample, projection of errors, reassessment of sampling risk; these are all topics addressed by the AAS.

The Status of AAS-16

For audits covering fiscal years that begin on or after April 1, 1999, the AAS must be used.

The term "going concern" is used to describe one of the key presumptions used to compile the financial statements, which is well known to the members. This AAS is intended to provide standards on the auditor's obligations in the audit of financial statements with respect to the propriety of the going concern assumption as the foundation for the preparation of the financial statements. Financial, operational, and other indicators of the suitability or otherwise of the going concern assumption, audit evidence, and illustrative audit procedures are all topics covered by the AAS in this respect.

Reporting and analysis in the event that the going concern assumption is deemed suitable, the going concern question is not addressed, or the going concern assumption is deemed incorrect.

Auditing Quality Assurance

For audits covering fiscal years that begin on or after April 1, 1999, the AAS must be used.

The objective of this Standard is to provide minimum requirements for the quality control policies and processes of an audit company in relation to audit work in general, as well as the procedures pertaining to the work outsourced to assistants on a specific audit. The AAS covers topics related to the quality control of audit work, including the goals of the quality control policies to be adopted by the audit firm, the instructions to be given to the assistants to whom tasks have been delegated, the monitoring of the assistants' work, the evaluation of the assistants' performance, and the factors to be taken into account.

Standard for Attestation of Accounting Estimates (AAS-18)
All audits performed on or after April 1, 2000, must adhere to the AAS.

In the lack of a reliable technique of measuring, accountants often resort to making estimates of the amounts of various items. The purpose of this AAS is to provide requirements for the examination of accounting estimates. Therefore, the AAS covers topics like the following: the nature of accounting estimates; audit procedures; reviewing and testing the process used by management; evaluating data and considering assumptions; calculating and testing results; comparing estimates to actual results; using independent estimates; reviewing subsequent events; evaluating audit results.

What Happened After AAS-19

All audits performed on or after April 1, 2000, must adhere to the AAS.

Subsequent events are those that occurred after the date of the balance sheet but before the date of the auditor's report. The auditor's responsibilities in light of later occurrences are spelled forth in this AAS. Reading minutes, examining management processes, and questioning pertinent personnel are all examples of audit techniques provided administration and all interested parties, etc. The auditor's reporting duties in light of later developments are also outlined by the Standard.

AAS-20 Business Acumen

All audits performed on or after April 1, 2000, must adhere to the AAS.

This Standard defines what constitutes knowledge of the company, why it is relevant to the auditor, and the responsibilities of the audit team in gaining that information. It also sets norms for how the auditor acquires and applies business knowledge across the board. The AAS addresses such issues as how to learn about the client's company before and after taking the assignment, where to get this information, how to put it to use, what other facets of your work will be influenced, and so on.

AAS-21, "Relevance of Legal Requirements in Financial Statement Audits"
All audits initiated on or after July1, 2001, must adhere to this AAS.

This AAS establishes guidelines for the auditing profession with respect to the auditor's duty to take into account applicable laws and regulations. Therefore, the AAS covers topics like who is responsible for ensuring compliance with laws and regulations, how auditors should think about whether or not a company is in compliance, what to do when auditing reveals a lack of compliance, how to notify management, users of audited financial statements, and regulators, and when an engagement should be terminated. Some possible signs of noncompliance are included in the AAS's appendix.

AAS-22 Opening Balances in the First Transaction
All audits initiated on or after July1, 2001, must adhere to this AAS.

For the purposes of this definition, "initial engagements" refer to audits of financial statements that are either being performed for the first time or that follow an audit of the prior period by a different auditor. When we talk about "opening balances," we're referring to the money in our accounts at the start of the time frame in question. This AAS sets the criteria for an initial audit engagement's opening balance sheet audit. As a result, the Standard is concerned with audit procedures for acquiring sufficient appropriate evidence in about initial deposits and balances. The Standard also instructs auditors on whether a qualified view or disclaimer of opinion is appropriate.

Relational Entities in AAS-23

All audits covering accounting periods beginning on or after April 1, 2001 must comply with this AAS.

The Institute released AS 18 on Related Party Disclosures as an Accounting Standard. This AAS is intended to provide guidance to auditors on how to handle related parties and related party transactions (both of which are described in ASC 18). The areas of focus for the AAS include management representations, audit findings, and reporting, as well as the presence and disclosure of related parties, transactions with related parties, and the examination of unidentified related party transactions. An example management representation letter involving linked parties is shown in the AAS appendix.

Auditing Entities That Engage Service Organizations: AAS-24 Considerations

Audits covering fiscal years that began on or after April1, 2003 are subject to this AAS.

The auditor whose client is a service organization may find helpful guidelines in this AAS. The client auditor may use this AAS to learn more about the audit reports prepared by the service organization's auditors. The AAS begins with an explanation of the term "service organization," and then goes on to detail the auditor's responsibilities with respect to the client, including how to determine the significance of the service organization's activities in relation to the audit, how to obtain the necessary information from service organizations, and the auditor's procedures in the event that such information is insufficient.

Comparisons to the AAS-25

Audits covering fiscal years that began on or after April1, 2003 are subject to this AAS.

This Auditing and Assurance Standard (AAS) is intended to define the auditor's duties with respect to comparables. However, it does not address circumstances where

Along with the audited financial statements are summary financial statements or statistics. As a result, the AAS elucidates the notion of comparatives in financial statements, as well as matching statistics and comparative financial statements. It addresses issues like how to conduct an audit when a prior period's financial statements were not audited, how to conduct an audit when a comparative period's financial statements contained material misstatements, and how to conduct an audit when a prior period's audit report contained a modified opinion. The AAS also includes example auditor's reports under the situations outlined in the Standard, as well as a discussion on financial reporting frameworks for comparisons.

Clauses Governing the Scope and Scope Limitation of an Audit, AAS-26

The AAS supersedes the Institute's Guidance Note on Audit Engagement Letters, and is applicable to audits of accounting periods commencing on or after April 1, 2003.

This AAS sets out requirements for auditors to follow when accepting to engagement terms with clients and when responding to client requests to modify engagement conditions to one that gives a lesser degree of confidence. An audit engagement letter's main components, a sample audit engagement letter for an audit of components, and the criteria that should be considered while drafting an audit engagement letter for repeated audits are all covered in the AAS. The AAS also devotes considerable attention to the auditor's responsibilities after an engagement termination.

Disclosing Audit Findings to Governance Entities (AAS-27)

This AAS is valid for all audits pertaining to accounting periods starting on or after April 1, 2003.

The word —governance‖ as used in this AAS refers to the function of those tasked with the oversight, control and direction of an organization. —Those entrusted with governance‖ are generally responsible for ensuring that the organization fulfills its goals, financial reporting, and reporting to interested parties. The AAS defines guidelines for communications of audit issues resulting from the audit of financial statements between the auditor and those responsible with governance of a company. The AAS consequently gives advice to auditors as to methods to identify relevant individuals, what are the audit items of broad interest to be notified, modes of communication, elements impacting communication, secrecy needs, rules and regulations etc.

AAS-28 Financial Statement Audit Report

Beginning with audits covering accounting periods that began on or after April 1, 2003, this Auditing and Assurance Standard must be used.

This AAS is meant to provide guidelines on how an audit of financial accounts should be conducted and what an auditor should include in their final report. The majority of this AAS may be used to auditor's reports on non-financial statement financial information. The AAS goes into great detail about ideas like what constitutes an unqualified opinion, what a qualified opinion is, what an adverse opinion is, what a disclaimer opinion is, what matters affect the auditor's opinion, and what matters do not affect the auditor's opinion, as well as emphasis of matter paragraphs and illustrative audit reports for each scenario.

AAS-29 Auditing of Information Systems in a Computerized Setting

All audits covering accounting periods starting on or after April1, 2003 must comply with this Auditing and Assurance Standard (AAS).

When one or more computers, regardless of size or kind, owned by the entity or by a third party, process financial information, including quantitative data, relevant to the audit, we say that we are in a CIS environment. This Auditing and Assurance Standard (AAS) was written with the intention of standardizing auditing practices in a computerized information system (CIS) setting. The AAS specifies requirements for the auditor's knowledge and ability to perform an audit in a CIS environment, including: factors to consider during audit planning; CIS environment specifics; risk assessment; audit procedures to mitigate audit risk; and audit documentation.

Confirmations from Outside Sources, AAS-30

All audits covering accounting periods beginning on or after April 1, 2003 must comply with this Auditing and Assurance Standard.

An integral part of any audit is the confirmations obtained from outside sources, and this Assurance Standard deals with just that. The Standard elaborates on a number of key aspects having to do with third-party verification. Considerations include the inherent and control risks, assertions addressed by external confirmations, timing of external confirmations, the design of the external confirmation request, the nature of the information being confirmed, the form of confirmations (both positive and negative), the characteristics of respondents, the evaluation of the results of the confirmation process, management requests, and so on.

AAS-31 Contracts for the Assembly of Economic Data

For all audits covering accounting periods beginning on or after April 1, 2004, this Auditing and Assurance Standard must apply.

The main difference between an audit engagement and a compilation engagement is that in the former, the accountant relies on accounting skills rather than auditing experience to gather, categorize, and summarize financial data. Assumptions underpinning the information being compiled are not often tested, since the accountant's primary responsibility is to simplify the data for the client. Furthermore, the accountant is unable to provide any guarantee or comment on the financial facts due to the techniques he uses to complete a compilation assignment. The AAS goes into great detail on important topics like the goal of a compilation engagement, basic principles in a compilation engagement (such as ethical requirements and management's responsibility), the essential ingredients of the terms of a compilation engagement (such as planning, documentation, and procedure), and much more. The AAS also addresses the unique issues that arise when a client uses an established financial reporting framework, when a client does not use a financial reporting framework, when a client is not in accordance with the accounting standards, and when a client uses estimations. Compilation engagement reporting is another area where the AAS offers in-depth assistance. For the convenience of its members, the AAS now includes an example engagement letter for compilation engagements as well as sample compilation reports for a variety of scenarios.

Accounting and Auditing Standard 32: Performing Mutually Agreed-Upon Procedures with Financial Data

For all audits covering accounting periods beginning on or after April 1, 2004, this Auditing and Assurance Standard must apply.

It is common practice for an auditor to issue a report detailing the facts they uncovered during an engagement to perform agreed-upon procedures, with the report itself being based on the auditor's findings regarding the elements, accounts, and items of financial statements that were the focus of those procedures. The AAS's overarching goal is to create uniform criteria for the nature, scope, and structure of the report issued by an auditor in conjunction with an engagement to execute agreed-upon processes on financial information. However, the AAS may also be utilized as a guide to carry out agreed upon processes using data that is not monetary in nature. Thus, the AAS 32 offers members with comprehensive advice on the goals of an agreed upon processes engagement, the underlying concepts involved in such an engagement (including ethical considerations), and the key components of the conditions of the engagement. The AAS also addresses the paperwork, methods, and proof that go into such endeavors. The AAS further specifies requirements for the form and content of the auditor's report. An example engagement letter and sample report format from the auditor are also included in the AAS.

An Agreement to Perform an Audit of Financial Statements in Accordance with Statement No. AAS-33

Review engagements for accounting periods commencing on or after 1 April 2005 are subject to the AAS.

Review engagements differ from audits in that they rely more heavily on the auditor's analytical techniques and questions. Listed firms in India's stock exchanges only have to submit their quarterly unaudited financial reports to a restricted examination by chartered accountants. Comprehensive advice on the sorts of methods and queries to be used by auditors is provided by the AAS on Engagements to Review Financial Statements. The AAS sets standards and provides guidelines on the form and substance of the report that an auditor produces in conjunction with a review, as well as the auditor's professional obligations. Scope of the review engagement, degree of assurance, conditions of engagement, and preparation are only few of the topics addressed by the AAS. standards for documentation, review methodology, findings, and reporting as they pertain to reviews. You can see examples of how an engagement letter, review process, and review report for both a qualified and unqualified opinion should look in the AAS.

Additional Evidence Regarding Item-Specific Audits (AAS-34)

With audits covering fiscal years that begin on or after 1 April 2005, the AAS must be used.

To supplement the guidelines given in AAS-5, "Audit Evidence," this AAS establishes rules on the auditor's duties, audit methods, and particular financial statement numbers and other disclosures. The auditor may rely on this AAS to help gather evidence for an audit in the following areas:

A Participation in the Actual Counting of Stocks. Subpart B: Claims and Litigation Inquiry

Section C focuses on the estimation and disclosure of the worth of investments held for a long time. In Section D, you'll find details on each segments.

This AAS goes into great depth about each of these points. For each of these sections, it specifies what is expected in terms of definition, processes, management representations, and audit findings and reporting.

AAS-35 The Analysis of Future Financial Data

Projection and prediction reports produced on or after April 1, 2007 are subject to this AAS.

This set of auditing and assurance standards (AAS) is meant to provide norms and give direction on engagements to evaluate and report on future financial information, such as examination processes for best estimates and hypothetical assumptions. The auditor must collect enough relevant evidence to conclude whether or whether Management's best estimates and assumptions on which the forward-looking financial information is based are reasonable and unreasonable assumptions, that they have been produced and presented in accordance with relevant accounting rules, that all key assumptions have been stated in a clear and understandable manner, and that they are based on a consistent basis with previous financial statements.

Rights, duties and liabilities of auditor

An auditor has several rights, duties, and liabilities in the course of conducting an audit.

Rights of an auditor include:

- The right to access the company's books, records, and other documents necessary for the audit
- The right to receive information and explanations from the company's management and employees

- The right to be indemnified by the company for any loss or damage suffered as a result of the audit

Duties of an auditor include:
- Conducting the audit in accordance with professional standards and the applicable laws and regulations
- Maintaining confidentiality and professional secrecy
- Communicating any significant findings or issues that arise during the audit to the company's management and, if necessary, to relevant regulatory bodies

Liabilities of an auditor include:
- Liability to the company and its shareholders for any loss or damage caused by the auditor's negligence or misconduct
- Liability to third parties, such as creditors or investors, for any loss or damage caused by the auditor's wrongful conduct
- Criminal liability for any fraudulent or illegal activities that the auditor may have been involved in or aware of during the audit

It's important to note that the specific rights, duties, and liabilities of an auditor may vary depending on the jurisdiction and the specific laws and regulations that apply to the audit.

Audit committee

An audit committee is a key component of a company's governance structure. The primary role of an audit committee is to provide oversight of a company's financial reporting process and internal controls, as well as to ensure compliance with laws and regulations. The audit committee is typically composed of independent directors who are appointed by the board of directors.

The primary responsibilities of an audit committee include:

1. Selecting, retaining, and overseeing the work of the independent auditors. The audit committee is responsible for selecting the independent auditors who will perform the annual audit of the company's financial statements. The committee also reviews the work of the independent auditors and evaluates their performance.

2. Reviewing financial statements and other financial information. The audit committee is responsible for reviewing the company's financial statements, including the balance sheet, income statement, and cash flow statement. The committee also reviews

other financial information, such as management's discussion and analysis, to ensure that it is accurate and transparent.

3. Ensuring compliance with laws and regulations. The audit committee is responsible for ensuring that the company is in compliance with all relevant laws and regulations. This includes ensuring that the company's financial statements are prepared in accordance with Generally Accepted Accounting Principles (GAAP) and that the company has effective internal controls in place.

4. Overseeing the internal audit function. Many companies have an internal audit function that is responsible for monitoring the company's internal controls and identifying areas for improvement. The audit committee is responsible for overseeing the internal audit function and ensuring that it is properly staffed and equipped to carry out its responsibilities.

5. Communicating with shareholders. The audit committee is responsible for communicating with shareholders and other stakeholders about the company's financial performance and governance practices. This includes providing regular updates on the committee's activities and responding to any questions or concerns that shareholders may have.

In addition to these primary responsibilities, the audit committee may also be responsible for other tasks, such as assessing the company's risk management practices, reviewing the company's code of conduct and ethics, and evaluating the effectiveness of the company's internal controls.

The audit committee plays a crucial role in ensuring the integrity and transparency of a company's financial reporting. By providing oversight of the financial reporting process and internal controls, the committee helps to ensure that the company's financial statements are accurate and that the company is in compliance with all relevant laws and regulations. The committee also helps to protect the interests of shareholders by providing regular updates on the company's financial performance and governance practices.

However, the Audit Committee alone cannot guarantee the integrity of financial reporting and internal controls. It is essential that management also plays its role in ensuring the company is following all laws, regulations and guidelines. The management should have a culture of compliance, transparency, and integrity.

It is important to note that the composition of the audit committee is also critical to its effectiveness. The committee should be composed of independent directors who are free from any conflicts of interest. This is important because independent directors are more likely to provide objective oversight of the financial reporting process and internal controls. Additionally, the committee should have at least one member who has financial expertise, such as an accountant or financial analyst.

In conclusion, the Audit Committee plays a vital role in ensuring the integrity of financial reporting and internal controls. The committee's responsibilities include selecting, retaining, and overseeing the work of the independent auditors, reviewing financial statements and other financial information, and ensuring compliance with laws and regulations. Effective audit committees are composed of independent directors who are free from conflicts of interest and have financial expertise. It is important for the committee to communicate regularly with shareholders and other stakeholders and to have a culture of compliance, transparency and integrity throughout the organization.

Auditor's report

An auditor's report is a written document that contains the results of an independent examination of an organization's financial statements. It is issued by an external auditor, who is an independent professional responsible for assessing the accuracy and completeness of an organization's financial records.

The auditor's report typically includes an introduction, a description of the organization and its financial statements, a discussion of the auditor's responsibilities, a section on the auditor's findings, and a conclusion.

In the introduction, the auditor provides an overview of the organization and its financial statements, as well as the purpose and scope of the audit.

The description of the organization and its financial statements includes information on the organization's operations, its structure, and the financial statements being examined.

The discussion of the auditor's responsibilities explains the auditor's role in the audit process and the standards that the auditor is required to follow.

The section on the auditor's findings is the most important part of the report, as it contains the results of the auditor's examination of the financial statements. The auditor will identify any significant deficiencies or material weaknesses in the financial statements and make recommendations for improvement.

In conclusion, the auditor will give an opinion on the fairness of the financial statements, and if the financial statements are free from material misstatement.

It's important to note that a 2000-word auditor's report is quite extensive and it would be best to consult with a professional auditor for a more detailed examination of the financial statements.

Auditor's report – Contents and Types

An auditor's report is a document prepared by an independent auditor or auditing firm that presents the results of an audit of a company's financial statements. The report includes a description of the scope of the audit, an opinion on the fairness and accuracy of the financial statements, and any recommendations or observations made during the audit.

There are several types of auditor's reports, including:

1. Unqualified Opinion: This is the most common type of report and indicates that the financial statements are presented fairly and in accordance with Generally Accepted Accounting Principles (GAAP).

2. Qualified Opinion: This type of report includes an unqualified opinion, but also includes a qualification or reservation about a specific aspect of the financial statements.

3. Adverse Opinion: This type of report indicates that the financial statements do not present a fair and accurate picture of the company's financial condition and do not comply with GAAP.

4. Disclaimer of Opinion: This type of report indicates that the auditor was unable to obtain sufficient evidence to form an opinion on the financial statements.

5. Emphasis of Matter: This type of report is added to an unqualified or qualified opinion and highlights a matter that is important to the users of the financial statements but does not affect the auditor's opinion.

6. Other Matter Paragraph: This type of report is added to an unqualified or qualified opinion and discusses any other important information that the auditor believes should be brought to the attention of users of the financial statements.

Auditor's Certificate

Independent Auditor's Report

To the Members of **«Name of Company»**

Report on the Audit of the Standalone Financial Statements

<u>Opinion</u>

We have audited the financial statements of «Name» ("the Company"), which comprise the balance sheet as at 31st March «Year Closing», and the statement of Profit and Loss and statement of cash flows for the year then ended, and notes to the financial statements, including a summary of significant accounting policies and other explanatory information.

In our opinion and to the best of our information and according to the explanations given to us, the aforesaid financial statements give the information required by the Act in the manner so required and give a true and fair view in conformity with the accounting principles generally accepted in India, of the state of affairs of the Company as at 31st March,
«Year Closing», its profit/loss and its cash flows for the year ended on that date.

Or

<u>Qualified Opinion</u>

We have audited the standalone financial statements of «Name» ("the Company"), which comprise the balance sheet as at 31st March « Year Closing », and the statement of Profit and Loss, and the statement of cash flows for the year then ended, and notes to the financial statements, including a summary of significant accounting policies and other explanatory information.
In our opinion and to the best of our information and according to the explanations given to us, except for the effects of the matter described in the Basis for Qualified Opinion section ofour report, the aforesaid financial statements give a true and fair view in conformity with the accounting principles generally accepted in India, of the state of affairs of the Company as 31st March « Year Closing » and profit/loss, and its cash flows for the year ended on that date.

Or

<u>Adverse Opinion</u>

We have audited the accompanying financial statements of «Name» ("the Company"), which comprise the balance sheet as at 31st March « Year Closing», and the statement of Profit and Loss, and the statement of cash flows for the year then ended, and notes to the financial statements, including a summary of significant accounting policies and other explanatory information.

In our opinion and to the best of our information and according to the explanations given to us, because of the significance of the matter discussed in the Basis for Adverse Opinion section of our report, the accompanying financial statements do not give a true and fair view in conformity with the accounting principles generally accepted in India as at 31st March « Year Closing », of its profit/loss and the cash flows for the year then ended.

Or

<u>Disclaimer of Opinion</u>

We were engaged to audit the accompanying financial statements of__________Company Limited (hereinafter referred to as the "Holding Company") and its subsidiaries (the Holding

Company and its subsidiaries together referred to as "the Group), which comprise the consolidated balance sheet as at 31st March « Year Closing », the consolidated statement of Profit and Loss, and consolidated statement of cash flows for the year then ended, and notes to the consolidated financial statements, including a summary of significant accountingpolicies (hereinafter referred to as the "Consolidated Financial Statements").

We do not express an opinion on the accompanying consolidated financial statements of the Group. Because of the significance of the matter described in the Basis for Disclaimer of Opinion section of our report, we have not been able to obtain sufficient appropriate audit evidence to provide a basis for an audit opinion on these consolidated financial statements.

<u>Basis for Opinion</u>

We conducted our audit in accordance with the Standards on Auditing (SAs) specified under section 143(10) of the Companies Act, 2013. Our responsibilities under those Standards are further described in the Auditor's Responsibilities for the Audit of the Financial Statements section of our report. We are independent of the Company in accordance with the Code of Ethics issued by the Institute of Chartered Accountants of India together with the ethical requirements that are relevant to our audit of the financial statements under the provisions of the Companies Act, 2013 and the Rules thereunder, and we have fulfilled our other ethical responsibilities in accordance with these requirements and the Code of Ethics. We believe that the audit evidence we have obtained is sufficient and appropriate to provide a basis for our opinion.

Or

<u>Basis for Qualified Opinion</u>

The Company's inventories are carried in the Balance Sheet at Rs. XXX. Management has not stated the inventories at the lower of cost and net realizable value but has stated them solely at cost, which constitutes a departure from the Accounting Standards prescribedunder section 133 of the Companies Act, 2013. The Company's records indicate that, had management stated the inventories at the lower of cost and net realizable value, an amount of Rs. xxx would have been required to write the inventories down to their net realizable value. Accordingly, cost of sales would have been increased by Rs. xxx, and income tax, netincome and shareholders' funds would have been reduced by Rs. xxx, Rs. xxx and Rs. xxx, respectively.

We conducted our audit in accordance with Standards on Auditing (SAs) specified under section 143(10) of the Companies Act, 2013. Our responsibilities under those Standards are further described in the Auditor's Responsibilities for the Audit of the Financial Statements section of our report. We are independent of the Company in accordance with the Code of Ethics issued by the Institute of Chartered Accountants of India together with the ethical requirements that are relevant to our audit of the financial statements under the provisions of the Companies Act, 2013 and we have fulfilled our other ethical responsibilities in accordance with these requirements and the ICAI's Code of Ethics. We believe that the auditevidence we have obtained is sufficient and appropriate to provide a basis for our qualified opinion.

Or

<u>Basis for Adverse Opinion</u>

As explained in Note X, the Group has not consolidated subsidiary XYZ Company that the Group acquired during 20XX because it has not yet been able to determine the fair values of certain of the subsidiary's material assets and liabilities at the acquisition date. This investment is therefore accounted for on a cost basis. Under the accounting principles generally accepted in India, the Group should have consolidated this subsidiary and accounted for the acquisition based on provisional amounts. Had XYZ Company been consolidated, many elements in the accompanying consolidated financial statements would have been materially affected. The effects on the consolidated financial statements of the failure to consolidate have not been determined.

We conducted our audit in accordance with Standards on Auditing (SAs) specified under section 143(10) of the Companies Act, 2013. Our responsibilities under those Standards are further described in the Auditor's Responsibilities for the Audit of the Consolidated Financial Statements section of our report. We are independent of the Group, its associates and jointly controlled entities, in accordance with the Code of Ethics and provisions of the Companies Act, 2013 that are relevant to our audit of the consolidated financial statements in India under the Companies Act, 2013, and we have fulfilled our other ethical responsibilities in accordance with the Code of Ethics and the requirements under the Companies act, 2013. We believe that the audit evidence we have obtained is sufficient and appropriate to provide a basis for our adverse opinion.

Or

Basis for Disclaimer of Opinion

The Group's investment in its joint venture XYZ Company is carried at Rs. xxx on the Group's consolidated balance sheet, which represents over 90% of the Group's net assets as at March 31, 20XX. We were not allowed access to the management and the auditors of XYZ Company, including XYZ Company's auditors' audit documentation. As a result, we were unable to determine whether any adjustments were necessary in respect of the Group's proportional share of XYZ Company's assets that it controls jointly, its proportional share of XYZ Company's liabilities for which it is jointly responsible, its proportional share of XYZ's income and expenses for the year, and the consolidated cash flow statement.

Information other than the financial statements and auditors' report thereon

The Company's board of directors is responsible for the preparation of the other information. The other information comprises the information included in the Board's Report including Annexures to Board's Report but does not include the financial statements and our auditor's report thereon.

Our opinion on the financial statements does not cover the other information and we do not express any form of assurance conclusion thereon.

In connection with our audit of the financial statements, our responsibility is to read the other information and, in doing so, consider whether the other information is materially inconsistent with the financial statements or our knowledge obtained during the course of our audit or otherwise appears to be materially misstated.

If, based on the work we have performed, we conclude that there is a material misstatement of this other information, we are required to report that fact. We have nothing to report in this regard.

Emphasis of Matter

We draw attention to Note X of the financial statements, which describes the effects of a ……………... in the Company's facilities. Our opinion is not modified in respect of this matter.

Key Audit Matters

Key audit matters are those matters that, in our professional judgment, were of most significance in our audit of the financial statements of the current period. These matters wereaddressed in the context of our audit of the financial statements as a whole, and in forming

our opinion thereon, and we do not provide a separate opinion on these matters.

(*applicable only in case of listed companies/companies in which disclaimer ofopinion is not made)

Or

Key Audit Matters

Key audit matters are those matters that, in our professional judgment, were of most significance in our audit of the financial statements of the current period. These matters were addressed in the context of our audit of the financial statements as a whole, and in forming our opinion thereon, and we do not provide a separate opinion on these matters. In addition to the matter described in *the Basis for Qualified Opinion* section we have determined the matters described below to be the key audit matters to be communicated in our report: **(*applicable only in case of listed companies)**

Or

Key Audit Matters

Except for the matter described in the *Basis for Adverse Opinion* section, we have determined that there are no other key audit matters to communicate in our report.

Responsibilities of Management and Those Charged with Governance for the Standalone Financial Statements

The Company's Board of Directors is responsible for the matters stated in section 134(5) of the Companies Act, 2013 ("the Act") with respect to the preparation of these financial statements that give a true and fair view of the financial position, financial performance and cash flows of the Company in accordance with the accounting principles generally accepted in India, including the accounting Standards specified under section 133 of the Act. This responsibility also includes maintenance of adequate accounting records in accordance with the provisions of the Act for safeguarding of the assets of the Company and for preventing and detecting frauds and other irregularities; selection and application of appropriate accounting policies; making judgments and estimates that are reasonable and prudent; and design, implementation and maintenance of adequate internal financial controls, that were operating effectively for ensuring the accuracy and completeness of the accounting records, relevant to the preparation and presentation of the financial statements that give a true and fair view and are free from material misstatement, whether due to fraud or error.

In preparing the financial statements, management is responsible for assessing the Company's ability to continue as a going concern, disclosing, as applicable, matters related to going concern and using the going concern basis of accounting unless management either intends to liquidate the Company or to cease operations, or has no realistic alternativebut to do so.

Those Board of Directors are also responsible for overseeing the Company's financial reporting process.

Auditor's Responsibilities for the Audit of the Financial Statements

Our objectives are to obtain reasonable assurance about whether the financial statementsas a whole are free from material misstatement, whether due to fraud or error, and to issue an auditor's report that includes our opinion. Reasonable assurance is a high level of assurance, but is not a guarantee that an audit conducted in accordance with SAs will always detect a material misstatement when it exists. Misstatements can arise from fraud or error and are considered material if, individually or in the aggregate, they could reasonably be expected to influence the economic decisions of users taken on the basis of these financial statements.

As part of an audit in accordance with SAs, we exercise professional judgment and maintain professional skepticism throughout the audit. We also:

• Identify and assess the risks of material misstatement of the financial statements, whether due to fraud or error, design and perform audit procedures responsive to those risks, and obtain audit evidence that is sufficient and appropriate to provide a basis for our opinion. Therisk of not detecting a material misstatement resulting from fraud is higher than for one resulting from error, as fraud may involve collusion, forgery, intentional omissions, misrepresentations, or the override of internal control.

• Obtain an understanding of internal control relevant to the audit in order to design audit procedures that are appropriate in the circumstances. Under section 143(3)(i) of the Companies Act, 2013, we are also responsible for expressing our opinion on whether the company has adequate internal financial controls system in place and the operating effectiveness of such controls.

• Evaluate the appropriateness of accounting policies used and the reasonableness of accounting estimates and related disclosures made by management.

• Conclude on the appropriateness of management's use of the going concern basis of accounting and, based on the audit evidence obtained, whether a material uncertainty exists related to events or conditions that may cast significant doubt on the Company's ability to continue as a going concern. If we conclude that a material uncertainty exists, we are required to draw attention in our auditor's report to the related disclosures in the financial statements or, if such disclosures are inadequate, to modify our opinion. Our conclusions arebased on the audit evidence obtained up to the date of our auditor's report. However, future events or conditions may cause the Company to cease to continue as a going concern.

• Evaluate the overall presentation, structure and content of the financial statements, including the disclosures, and whether the financial statements represent the underlying transactions and events in a manner that achieves fair presentation.

We communicate with those charged with governance regarding, among other matters, the planned scope and timing of the audit and significant audit findings, including any significant deficiencies in internal control that we identify during our audit.

We also provide those charged with governance with a statement that we have complied with relevant ethical requirements regarding independence, and to communicate with them all relationships and other matters that may reasonably be thought to bear on our independence, and where applicable, related safeguards.

From the matters communicated with those charged with governance, we determine those matters that were of most significance in the audit of the financial statements of the current period and are therefore the key audit matters. We describe these matters in our auditor's report unless law or regulation precludes public disclosure about the matter or when, in extremely rare circumstances, we determine that a matter should not be communicated in our report because the adverse consequences of doing so would reasonably be expected to outweigh the public interest benefits of such communication.

Or

Our responsibility is to conduct an audit of the Group's consolidated financial statements in accordance with Standards on Auditing and to issue an auditor's report. However, because of the matter described in *the Basis for Disclaimer of Opinion* section of our report, we were not able to obtain sufficient appropriate audit evidence to provide a basis for an audit opinionon these consolidated financial statements.

We are independent of the Group in accordance with the ethical requirements that are relevant to our audit of the financial statements and we have fulfilled our other ethical responsibilities in accordance with these requirements.

<u>Report on Other Legal and Regulatory Requirements</u>

1. As required by the Companies (Auditor's Report) Order, 2016 ("the Order"), issued by the Central Government of India in terms of sub-section (11) of section 143 of the Companies Act, 2013, we give in the 'Annexure A', a statement on the matters specified in paragraphs 3 and 4 of the Order, to the extent applicable.

2. As required by Section 143 (3) of the Act, we report that:

   a) We have sought and obtained all the information and explanations which to the best of our knowledge and belief were necessary for the purposes of our audit.
   b) In our opinion, proper books of account as required by law have been kept by the Company so far as it appears from our examination of those books.
   c) The Balance Sheet, the Statement of Profit and Loss and the Cash Flow Statement dealt with by this Report agree with the books of account.
   d) In our opinion, the aforesaid financial statements comply with the Accounting Standards specified under Section 133 of the Act, read with Rule 7 of the Companies (Accounts) Rules, 2014.

   e) On the basis of the written representations received from the directors as on 31st March, « Year Closing » taken on record by the Board of Directors, none of the directors is disqualified as on 31st March, « Year Closing» from being appointed as a director in terms of Section 164 (2) of the Act.
   f) With respect to the adequacy of the internal financial controls over financial reporting of the Company and the operating effectiveness of such controls, refer to our separate Report in 'Annexure B'.
   g) With respect to the other matters to be included in the Auditor's report in accordance with the requirements of Sec 197(16) of the Act as amended, we report that Section 197 is not applicable to a private company. Hence reportingas per Section 197(16) is not required. (applicable in case of Private Company)

Or

   With respect to the matter to be included in the Auditor's Report under section 197(16), In our opinion and according to the information and explanations given to us, the remuneration paid by the Company to its directors during the current year is in accordance with the provisions of section 197 of the Act. The remuneration paid to any director is not in excess of the limit laid down under section 197 of the Act. The Ministry of Corporate Affairs has not prescribed other details under section 197(16) which are required to be commented upon by us. (applicable in case of Public Company)

   h) With respect to the other matters to be included in the Auditor's Report in accordance with Rule 11 of the Companies (Audit and Auditors) Rules, 2014, in our opinion and to the best of our information and according to the explanations given to us:

The Company does not have any pending litigations which would impact its financial position.

The Company has disclosed pending litigations and the impact on its financial position - refer note________to the Standalone Financial Statements.

i. The Company did not have any long-term contracts including derivative contracts for which there were any material foreseeable losses.

Or

The Company has made provision, as required under the applicable law or accounting standards, for material foreseeable losses, if any, on long-term contracts including derivative contracts;

ii. There were no amounts which were required to be transferred to the Investor Education and Protection Fund by the Company.

Or

There has been no delay in transferring amounts, required to be transferred, to the Investor Education and Protection Fund by the Company.

Or

Following are the instances of delay in transferring amounts, required to be transferred, to the Investor Education and Protection Fund by the Company:

____

For «CA Firm»
Chartered Accountants
FRN: «Reg. No»

Sd/
-
«Sign»

Place: -«Auditors Place»
Date: «Date»
UDIN:

Membership No. «Membership No.»

Annexure 'A'

The Annexure referred to in paragraph 1 of Our Report on "Other Legal and Regulatory Requirements".

We report that:

i.

    a.   The company has maintained proper records showing full particulars, including quantitative details and situation of its fixed assets.

    b.   As explained to us, fixed assets have been physically verified by the management at reasonable intervals; no material discrepancies were noticedon such verification.

    c.   The title deeds of immovable properties are held in the name of the company.

ii.   As explained to us, inventories have been physically verified during the year by the management at reasonable intervals. No material discrepancy was noticed on physical verification of stocks by the management as compared to book records.

iii.   The company has granted loans to ....parties covered in the register maintained under section 189 of the Companies Act, 2013.

    a. The terms and conditions of the grant of such loans are not prejudicial to the company's interest;

    b. The schedule of repayment of principal and payment of interest has been stipulated and in such cases the borrowers have been regular in repayment of principal and interest.

or

The terms of arrangement do not stipulate any repayment schedule and the loans are repayable on demand with interest.

    c. There are no overdue amounts in respect of the loans granted to the parties listed in the register maintained under section 189 of the Act.

or

Since the term of arrangement do not stipulate any repayment schedule and the loans are repayable on demand, no question of overdue amounts will arise in respect of the loans granted to the parties listed in the register maintained under section 189 of the Act.

or

Amounts are overdue in respect of above loans. The total amount overdue for more than ninety days is..........and reasonable steps have been taken by the company for recovery of the principal and interest.

or

Amounts are overdue is respect of above loans. But there is no amounts overdue for more than ninety days. Reasonable steps have been taken by the company for recovery of the principal and interest.

OR

According to the information and explanations given to us and on the basis of our examination of the books of account, the Company has not granted any loans, secured or unsecured, to companies, firms, Limited Liability Partnerships or other parties listed in the register maintained under Section 189 of the Companies Act, 2013. Consequently, the provisions of clauses iii (a), (b) and (c)of the order are not applicable to the Company.

ii.   In respect of loans, investments, guarantees, and security, provisions of section 185 and 186 of the Companies Act, 2013 have been complied with.

Or

The company has complied with provisions of section 185 & 186 in respect of loans, investments, guarantees, and security except to the extent of:

S.No.	Non-compliance of Section 186				Remarks, if any
		Name of Company/ Party	Amount Involved	Balance as at Balance Sheet Date	
1.	Investment through more than two layers of investment companies				
2.	Loan given or guarantee given or security provided or acquisition of securitiesexceeding the limits without prior approval by means of a special resolution				
3.	Loan given at rate of interest lower than prescribed				
4.	Any other default				

iii.   The company has not accepted any deposits from the public covered under sections 73 to 76 of the Companies Act, 2013 except Rs.___________from__________. According to information and explanation provided to us, no order has been passed by Company Law Board or National Company Law Tribunal or Reserve Bank of India or any court or any other tribunal.

Or

The Company has not accepted any deposits from the public and hence the directives issued by the Reserve Bank of India and the provisions of Sections 73 to 76 or any other relevant provisions of the Act and the Companies (Acceptance of

Deposit) Rules, 2015 with regard to the deposits accepted from the public are not applicable.

ii. As per information & explanation given by the management, maintenance of cost records has not been specified by the Central Government under sub-section (1) of section 148 of the Companies Act, 2013.

iii.

    a. According to the records of the company, undisputed statutory dues including Provident Fund, Investor Education and Protection Fund, Employees' State Insurance, Income-tax, Sales-tax, Service Tax, Goods and Service tax, Custom Duty, Excise Duty, value added tax, cess and any other statutorydues to the extent applicable, have generally been regularly deposited withthe appropriate authorities. According to the information and explanations given to us there were no outstanding statutory dues as on 31st March
    « Year Closing »for a period of more than six months from the date they became payable, except:

Name of the Statue	Nature of the Dues	Amount (Rs. In lakhs)	Period for which the amount relates	Due Date	Date of Payment	Remarks, if any

    b. According to the information and explanations given to us, there is no amount payable in respect of income tax, service tax, sales tax, customs duty, excise duty, value added tax and cess whichever applicable, which have not been deposited on account of any disputes.

Or

According to the records of the Company, the dues outstanding of income-tax, sales-tax, service tax, goods and service tax, duty on custom, duty of excise, value added tax and cess on account of any dispute, are as follows:

Name of the Statue	Nature of the Dues	Amount (Rs. In lakhs)	Period for which the amount relates	Forum wheredispute is pending

iv. In our opinion and according to the information and explanations given by the management, we are of the opinion that, the Company has not defaulted in repayment of dues to a financial institution, bank, Government or debenture holder, as applicable to the company.

Based on our audit procedures and according to the information given by the management, the company has not raised any money by way of initial public offer or further public offer (including debt instruments) or taken any term loan during the year.

OR

Based on our audit procedures and according to the information given by the management, the company has not raised any money by way of initial public offer or further public offer (including debt instruments) or taken any term loan during the year.

ii. According to the information and explanations given to us, we report that no fraud by the company or any fraud on the Company by its officers or employees has been noticed or reported during the year.

iii. The company is a private limited company. Hence the provisions of clause (xi) of the order are not applicable to the company.
OR
According to the information and explanations given to us, we report that managerial remuneration has been paid in accordance with the requisite approvals mandated by the provisions of section 197 read with Schedule V to the Companies Act.

iv. The company is not a Nidhi Company. Therefore, clause (xii) of the order is not applicable to the company.
OR
The Nidhi Company has complied with the Net Owned Funds to Deposits in the ratio of 1: 20 to meet out the liability and the Nidhi Company is maintaining ten per cent unencumbered term deposits as specified in the Nidhi Rules, 2014 to meet out the liability.

v. According to the information and explanations given to us, all transactions with the related parties are in compliance with sections 177 and 188 of Companies Act, 2013 where applicable and the details have been disclosed in the Financial Statements etc. as required by the applicable accounting standards.

vi. The company has not made any preferential allotment or private placement of sharesor fully or partly convertible debentures during the year under review.
OR
The company has made preferential allotment or private placement of shares or fully or partly convertible debentures during the year under review and the requirement of section 42 of the Companies Act, 2013 have been complied with and the amount raised have been used for the purposes for which the funds were raised.

vii. Provisions of section 192 of Companies Act, 2013 have been complied with in case of non-cash transactions entered by the company with directors or persons connected with him

or

The company has not entered into non-cash transactions with directors or persons connected with him.

ii. The company is not required to be registered under section 45-IA of the Reserve Bank of India Act, 1934.

or

The company is required to be registered under section 45-IA of the Reserve Bank of India Act, 1934 and the registration has been obtained.

For «CA Firm»
Chartered Accountants
FRN: «Reg. No»

Sd/
-
«Sign»

Place:-«Auditors Place»
Date: «Date»
UDIN: **Membership No.** **«Membersh ip No.»**

Annexure 'B'

Report on Internal Financial Controls Over Financial
Reporting

<u>Report on the Internal Financial Controls under Clause (i) of Sub-section 3 of Section 143 of the Companies Act, 2013 ("the Act")</u>

We have audited the internal financial controls over financial reporting of «Name» ("the Company") as of March 31, « Year Closing » in conjunction with our audit of the financial statements of the Company for the year ended on that date.

<u>Management's Responsibility for Internal Financial Controls</u>

The Company's management is responsible for establishing and maintaining internal financial controls based on the internal control over financial reporting criteria established by the Company considering the essential components of internal control stated in the Guidance Note on Audit of Internal Financial Controls Over Financial Reporting issued by the Institute of Chartered Accountants of India. These responsibilities include the design, implementation and maintenance of adequate internal financial controls that were operating effectively for ensuring the orderly and efficient conduct of its business, including adherence to company's policies, the safeguarding of its assets, the prevention and detection of frauds and errors, the accuracy and completeness of the accounting records, and the timely preparation of reliable financial information, as required under the Companies Act, 2013.

Our responsibility is to express an opinion on the Company's internal financial controls over financial reporting based on our audit. We conducted our audit in accordance with the Guidance Note on Audit of Internal Financial Controls Over Financial Reporting (the "Guidance Note") and the Standards on Auditing, issued by ICAI and deemed to be prescribed under section 143(10) of the Companies Act, 2013, to the extent applicable to an audit of internal financial controls, both applicable to an audit of Internal Financial Controls and, both issued by the Institute of Chartered Accountants of India. Those Standards and the Guidance Note require that we comply with ethical requirements and plan and perform the audit to obtain reasonable assurance about whether adequate internal financial controls over financial reporting was established and maintained and if such controls operated effectively in all material respects.

Our audit involves performing procedures to obtain audit evidence about the adequacy of the internal financial controls system over financial reporting and their operating effectiveness. Our audit of internal financial controls over financial reporting included obtaining an understanding of internal financial controls over financial reporting, assessing the risk that a material weakness exists, and testing and evaluating the design and operating effectiveness of internal control based on the assessed risk. The procedures selected depend on the auditor's judgement, including the assessment of the risks of material misstatement of the financial statements, whether due to fraud or error.

We believe that the audit evidence we have obtained is sufficient and appropriate to providea basis for our audit opinion on the Company's internal financial controls system over financial reporting.

Meaning of Internal Financial Controls Over Financial Reporting

A company's internal financial control over financial reporting is a process designed to provide reasonable assurance regarding the reliability of financial reporting and the preparation of financial statements for external purposes in accordance with generally accepted accounting principles. A company's internal financial control over financial reporting includes those policies and procedures that

1. pertain to the maintenance of records that, in reasonable detail, accurately and fairly reflect the transactions and dispositions of the assets of the company;
2. provide reasonable assurance that transactions are recorded as necessary to permit preparation of financial statements in accordance with generally accepted accounting principles, and that receipts and expenditures of the company are being made only in accordance with authorizations of management and directors of the company; and
3. provide reasonable assurance regarding prevention or timely detection of unauthorized acquisition, use, or disposition of the company's assets that could have a material effect on the financial statements.

Inherent Limitations of Internal Financial Controls Over Financial Reporting

Because of the inherent limitations of internal financial controls over financial reporting, including the possibility of collusion or improper management override of controls, material misstatements due to error or fraud may occur and not be detected. Also, projections of any evaluation of the internal financial controls over financial reporting to future periods are subject to the risk that the internal financial control over financial reporting may become inadequate because of changes in conditions, or that the degree of compliance with the policies or procedures may deteriorate.

<u>Opinion</u>

In our opinion, the Company has, in all material respects, an adequate internal financial controls system over financial reporting and such internal financial controls over financial reporting were operating effectively as at March 31, « Year Closing », based on the internal control over financial reporting criteria established by the Company considering the essentialcomponents of internal control stated in the Guidance Note on Audit of Internal Financial Controls Over Financial Reporting issued by the Institute of Chartered Accountants of India.

For «CA Firm»
Chartered Accountants
FRN: «Reg. No»

Sd/-

Place: -«Auditors Place»   «Sign»
Date: «Date»   («Sign»)
UDIN: **Membership No.**   «Membership No.»

MODULE - 4
CONCEPTUAL FRAMEWORK OF CORPORATE GOVERNANCE

Introduction

The administration of a company is referred to as its "corporate governance." It is a method used for guiding and managing businesses. It involves making decisions for the company based on what those involved want. The board of directors and relevant committees really carry this out for the benefit of the company's stakeholders. To achieve success, it is necessary to strike a balance between personal and collective objectives, as well as between economic and social concerns.

Shareholders, the board of directors, and the management team all have a role in determining a corporation's performance and the direction it heads in, a process known as "corporate governance." No tension or unhealthy dynamics should exist between a company's owners and its management team. All proprietors need to make sure their employee is performing at or above par. You can't ignore these elements of good company governance.

The topic of corporate governance is concerned with the means through which investors ensure a reasonable rate of return on their capital. The relationship between shareholders and executives is delineated explicitly under corporate governance. It is up to the management to make the decision. The roles of owners and managers in today's organizations must be clearly defined and harmonized.

Strategy and decision-making are at the heart of corporate governance. The Board of Directors is given absolute power and duty as a result. With today's market-based economy, proper corporate governance is essential. Corporate governance is increasingly being pushed due to efficiency and globalization. Building value for a company's stakeholders is impossible without good corporate governance.

Strong and sustainable economic growth may be maintained with the help of good corporate governance practices. That way, both the interests of the majority and the interests of the minority shareholders are protected. In this way, the company guarantees that all shareholders may fully exercise their rights and that those rights are completely recognized.

The field of Corporate Governance is extensive. Institutional and social elements are both present.

The practice of good corporate governance fosters an atmosphere that is reliable, moral, and ethical.

THE MEANING OF THE TERM "CORPORATE GOVERNANCE"

For the purposes of this article, "corporate governance" will be defined as "the system through which firms are directed and managed" (Cadbury Committee, 1992). A more precise definition would be "the relationships among the management, Board of Directors, controlling shareholders, minority shareholders, and other stakeholders," as stated by the IFC. Corporate governance as described by the Cadbury Committee (UK), 1992

The method of guiding and controlling corporations is known as "corporate governance." All aspects of a company's operations are covered, and an effort is made to establish a balance of power between the company's shareholders, directors, workers, auditor, and management.

Second, "Corporate governance" refers to the structure in place to guide and regulate the operations of a company. The corporate governance structure lays out the rules and processes for making decisions about the organization, including the roles and duties of the board of directors, the management team, and the shareholders. This offers the framework for establishing organizational goals, as well as the mechanisms for achieving those goals and keeping tabs on progress.

Specifically, "Corporate Governance is the application of best Management practices, Compliance of law in true letter and spirit, and adherence to ethical standards for Effective Management and distribution of wealth and discharge of social Responsibility for sustainable development of all stakeholders," as defined by the Institute of Company Secretaries of India.

STATES ADHERE TO THE OECD PRINCIPLES OF CORPORATE GOVERNANCE

Incorporating a network of interactions among a company's leadership, board of directors, shareholders, and other interested parties, "corporate governance" describes the way in which businesses are run. Through corporate governance, the company's goals are established, and the processes for achieving them and keeping tabs on progress are mapped out.

Even while 'other stakeholders' are included in standard definitions of corporate governance, most discussions of corporate governance still center on the age-old conflict between disengaged owners (shareholders) and self-interested management. It has been claimed, rather ponderously, that there are two parts to good corporate governance:

Both the long-term connection, which incorporates issues like checks and balances, manager incentives, and open lines of communication with investors, and the transactional relationship, which focuses on issues like transparency and delegation of power, are important.

This suggests management and investors view one other with distrust and hostility. Much of the Cadbury Report's justification rested on this idea, and it's one of the reasons why the report gave such specific guidelines for how the board should act: consistency and openness towards shareholders are its watchwords.

Despite the critical nature of these characteristics, we prefer to adopt a more holistic perspective that contextualizes the Cadbury Code and subsequent codes (the Combined Code, Sarbanes-Oxley, King, etc.) and demonstrates how its recommendations emerge organically throughout the development of a company. One of the founders of this site, who also wrote an early book on corporate governance in 1992, defined corporate governance as consisting of five elements which the board must consider: long-term strategic goals; employees (past, present, and future); environment/community; customers/suppliers; compliance (legal/regulatory); and long-term financial viability.

PROS OF CORPORATE RULEMAKING

- Economic expansion and company prosperity are guaranteed by sound corporate governance.
- With investors' trust intact, a firm may more easily and successfully obtain money when it has solid corporate governance practices in place.
- One benefit is a decrease in initial investment price.
- The effect on the stock price is favorable.
- Owners and management are properly incentivized to advance the company's and shareholders' best interests thanks to this structure.
- To reduce waste, corruption, risk, and mismanagement, good corporate governance is essential.
- It's useful for creating and growing a brand.

- It guarantees that the organization is run in a way that benefits everyone involved.

COMPANY RULEMAKING IS ESSENTIAL

The following considerations emphasize the need of good corporate governance:

1. **Diversified Ownership:** These days, a company's shareholders may be found all over the globe, and the vast majority of them are disorganized and don't care much about the company's inner workings. Until a code of corporate governance is established, the concept of shareholders' democracy will remain restricted to the law and the Articles of Association.

2. **Modifying the Current Form of Ownership:** Institutional investors (both international and Indian) and mutual funds have become the main shareholders in the private sector's major corporations, marking a significant shift in the historical pattern of corporate ownership. These shareholders now pose the biggest threat to corporate management, requiring the latter to follow a code of corporate governance in order to improve their companies' public standing.

Public trust in corporate management is shaken by (iii) corporate fraud and (iv) corporate scandals. Everyone who owns corporate stock or is otherwise well-informed and socially sensitive is aware of the Harshad Mehta controversy, which is possibly the largest scandal in recent memory.

In order to restore faith in the business sector and so boost the economy, good corporate governance is a must.

GUIDE TO THE PRINCIPLES OF CORPORATE GOVERNANCE

The following are the cornerstones of good corporate governance:

1. **Transparency**

To be transparent is to have the attribute of being open and easy to comprehend. In the context of good corporate governance, it refers to the timely, complete, and correct dissemination of significant information to the company's stakeholders on the company's operating results and other pertinent data.

The public's trust in businesses may be built up via good corporate governance, which relies on open communication with shareholders. Companies should publish pertinent information regarding corporate issues in major publications on a regular basis (every quarter, six months, or a year, for example) in order to maintain public trust in the management of their business.

2.   Accountability

One's responsibility to account for the outcomes of actions committed on behalf of others is what we mean by "accountability." When discussing corporate governance, "accountability" refers to the expectation that the Chairman, the Board of Directors, and the CEO would utilize the business's resources (which they control) in a manner that benefits the firm and its stakeholders.

3.   Independence

A robust, non-partisan Board of Directors is essential for good corporate governance, since it will allow the company's senior management to make choices based on what's best for business rather than personal ideology. Good corporate governance is nothing but a pipe dream if the company's senior management isn't impartial.

COMPANY GOVERNANCE AS PER THE SEBI CODE

SEBI (Securities and Exchange Board of India) established a corporate governance committee, headed by Kumar Mangalam Birla, to advocate for responsible business practices. According to the recommendations of this committee, SEBI published corporate governance rules that must be included in the listing agreement between the business and the stock market.

Under the respective headings, below, you'll find an overview of SEBI's corporate governance guidelines:

(1)(a) The Board of Directors
The following are a few things to keep in mind in this regard:
i.   There should be a healthy balance of executive and non-executive directors on the company's board.
ii.   Whether the chairman is an executive or non-executive will affect the number of independent directors.

Independent directors shall make up at least one-third of the Board in the event of a non-executive chairman and at least half of the Board in the case of an executive chairman.

Without any other meaningful monetary link with the firm, "independent directors" are those who sit on the board of directors but are not paid as directors.
a) The Auditing Board

The following are a few things to keep in mind in this regard:

(1)   The business must establish a separate audit committee with the following members:

It must have a bare minimum of three members, all of whom must be non-executive directors; the majority of these directors must be completely unaffiliated with the company; and at least one must have experience in the field of finance and accounting.

The committee will be led by an independent director who will serve as chairman.

At the AGM, the Chairman will be available to address questions from shareholders.

(2)   The audit committee should have the authority to do things like I conduct investigations into anything that falls within its purview.

To (ii)inquire of any employee for information; (iii)seek the counsel of attorneys or other professionals; and secure the presence of outside experts if their presence is deemed required.

(3)   The audit committee is responsible for performing the following duties:

It is the responsibility of management to ensure that the financial statement is complete, accurate, and believable by monitoring the company's financial reporting process and the disclosure of relevant financial information.

Suggesting when an external auditor should be hired and fired.

Evaluation of the Internal Auditing Capabilities

- Communicating with external auditors on the purpose and parameters of the audit before it begins, and after it to address any issues that were uncovered.

- The company's financial and risk management policies will be evaluated

- Payment to Board Members, etc., Section c

- Within the Corporate Governance part of the Annual Report, the Board of Directors' compensation must be detailed as follows: I Salary, benefits, bonus, stock options, pension, etc. for each Director.

- Specifics on both the predetermined portions and the performance-based bonuses, as well as the metrics by which they will be evaluated.

Board Operating Procedure, Section d) Here are a few things to keep in mind:

There will be no more than four months between any two meetings of the Board of Directors in a given year.

For all the firms on which he serves as a director, he may not sit on more than ten committees or preside over more than five committees as chairman.

Management

Included in the annual report to shareholders should be a Management Discussion and Analysis Report, which delves into the following topics (within the constraints imposed by the company's competitive position).

i. Possibilities and dangers
ii. Success in other markets or with different types of products;
iii. Threats and worries
iv. Financial performance discussion in relation to operational performance
v. Changes that are noticeable in the realm of labor relations and human resources.

Shareholders

Here are a few things to consider:

When a new director is appointed or a current director is reappointed, the company is required to notify its shareholders of the following:

Briefly describe the director, including: 1. his background (summary); 2. the nature of his specialty; and 3. his accomplishments.

The number of firms where he serves as a director and/or on a board committee.

(ii) A Board Committee, led by a non-executive director, will be established to address investor and shareholder concerns including share transfers, failure to receive the Balance Sheet or dividends, and so on. The shareholders and investors grievance committee must be known as such.

Corporate Governance Report

The company's annual report will include a dedicated section for reporting on corporate governance practices.

Compliance

The company's auditors must provide a certificate attesting to the company's compliance with corporate governance requirements. The Directors' Report to shareholders and the stock market must include a copy of this certificate as an attachment.

The concepts, ethics, values, morals, rules, laws, and processes etc. that govern a company are the focus of corporate governance. A structure of duties and obligations for the management of the company's activities is set up by corporate governance.

Governing or managing the corporate bodies, i.e. ethics, values, principles, and morals, is what we mean when we talk about "corporate governance." Good corporate governance requires that the management fulfill their duties to the company's shareholders, creditors, workers, customers, the public sector, and the general public. With the aid of corporate governance, a structure may be set up in which a director is given extensive authority over the company's operations.

Because of economic liberalization and deregulation of industry and business, the notion of corporate governance evolved in India after the second half of 1996. The necessity for corporations to be more answerable to their stockholders and consumers grew with the era. The Cadbury Committee report on the monetary elements of corporate governance in the United Kingdom has sparked a discussion about Corporate Governance in India.

The need for corporate governance emerges when control of a company is divorced from its ownership. The success of a business depends on its attention to both financial and social factors. Equal treatment of producers, shareholders, consumers, etc. is essential. It has to do a good job of fulfilling its obligations to its workers, its customers, its communities, and, finally, to its governance.

In India, the "corporate governance notion" has been there since the Arthshastra era, when monarchs and their people governed businesses rather than chief executive officers. They have been replaced by corporations and shareholders, but the fundamentals of good governance remain the same.

The liberalization, globalization, and privatization of the Indian economy in the twentieth century contributed to its glitzy appearance. Capitalization, corporate culture, and business ethics were determined to be essential to the continued survival of corporations in the global market, and this occurred for the first time when the Indian economy came together with the global economy for product, money, and the labour market.

In order to ensure that the business's directors are not abusing their authority and are instead acting in the firm's best interests, the regulations governing the company must require that they do so.

In reality, "corporate governance" is merely the first step in expanding a company's operations and ensuring its success in the long run.

Historical Perspectives on Corporate Governance

Past, Present, and Future of Corporate Governance in India

As the business world evolves, good corporate governance has become a potent competitive and sustainability weapon. This is a crucial time for the firm, and everyone, from the CEO to the office cleaners, has to pull together to do what's best for the company in the long run.

Companies that want to grow, prosper, and compete in international markets by strengthening their strengths, overcoming their weaknesses, and running them effectively and transparently by adopting best practices in planning, management, innovative ideas, compliance with laws, and good relations among directors, shareholders, employees, and customers of companies need value-based corporate governance.

If Indian businesses want to succeed and develop holistically, they must commit to being dependable, creative, and timely service providers to their clients.

The term "Corporate Governance" refers to the system of rules and practices put in place by firms to ensure the well-being of its shareholders, workers, and customers in a global economy.

Good corporate governance is a standard for other countries, and Indian corporations that have implemented it will be recognized as leaders in their field. Ethics, values, and principles are ingrained and put into effect as part of a company's management practices thanks to corporate governance. Corporate governance plays a crucial role in fostering and sustaining a culture of honesty, openness, and responsibility inside a business.

A variety of structures meant to oversee corporations have been in place since recorded history began. In the Vedic era, kings had ministers and a set of laws, ethics, values, and principles to govern their state. In the modern era, these same elements can be found in corporate governance, which aids in the efficient management of corporations so that they can grow into global behemoths thanks to the effects of globalization.

Due in large part to their excellent corporate governance, several Indian companies including PepsiCo, Infuses, Tata, Wipro, TCS, and Reliance have established themselves as worldwide leaders.

These days, the law also plays a significant role in a thriving and expanding economy. Many laws and regulations, including the Securities and Exchange Board of India Act (SEBI), the Foreign Exchange Management Act (FEMA), the Cyber Laws, the Competition Laws, etc., have been passed and amended or repealed by the government and the courts so that they do not stand in the way of these corporations and the development of India. The courts have been quite helpful, especially in the quick resolution of business conflicts.

Companies have their own set of guiding ideas, beliefs, and philosophies that help them achieve their goals. Both large and small businesses publish annual reports in glossy periodicals that detail the company's successes and setbacks, as well as its financial standing and future plans. Some businesses have also shown an understanding of, and dedication to, environmental preservation, social responsibility, and the promotion of social advancement. One prominent firm that fits this description is Deepak Fertilizers and Petrochemicals Corporation Limited, which in 2005 was named the runner-up for business world magazine's CSR award.

In the current climate, stakeholders are accorded equal or more weight to shareholders, and they are given the opportunity to participate in the running of the firm by attending and voting at shareholder meetings and providing feedback on its operations.

From a prospective of the future, corporate governance plays an important part. All of the corporate entities have a very forward-thinking stance. They have a long-term strategy for the growth of their firm. They aren't afraid to try new things, and they embrace novel concepts; they also have an inspiring mission statement and lofty long-term ambitions.

Internationally recognised corporate governance norms are of utmost significance for Indian companies aiming to differentiate themselves in the global footprint, especially in light of the growing interdependence and free commerce among governments and individuals worldwide. Businesses should always strive to become better versions of themselves by providing higher-quality, more dependable integrated products and services. They need to be less covert in their dealings.

There has to be a commitment to corporate social upliftment, social responsibility, and environmental preservation as pillars of good corporate governance. It also entails doing something novel, productive, and beneficial for the benefit of all parties involved. Good corporate governance is essential in every jurisdiction, regardless of its financial, tax, banking, or legal system.

Consequently, good corporate governance is a means to a goal, and that objective should be business excellence.

CORPORATE GOVERNANCE: HISTORY AND KEY ISSUES

All of the major concerns in corporate governance are interconnected and must be addressed together for the sector to function effectively. Varying corporate organizations place different emphasis on the same set of corporate governance concerns.

Here is a rundown of the problems:

1. A company-wide emphasis on core values
2. Holistic perspective
3. Abiding by the rules
4. Openness, candor, and responsibility
5. Management of both corporate resources and personnel constitute,
6. Innovation
7. The need for changes in the judicial system
8. Globalization has aided Indian businesses in becoming industry leaders thanks to their focus on corporate responsibility and transparency.

What We Can Learn From Failed Corporations

One example of a company culture that is focused on ethics and values is Google. Corporations that want to survive the long haul must foster a strong company culture. Business governance best practices should include fostering a value-based corporate culture. It's an inviolable code of ethics and morals. One's "vision," one's "mission and purpose," one's "objective," one's "goal," and one's "target" are all examples of such guiding principles.

Second, a holistic perspective is a religious or spiritual outlook that is useful in managing a business or other organization. Adopting it isn't easy, but it's worth the trouble since it's the way to acquiring noble traits like tolerance and empathy.

Companies that care about their reputation, their employees' well-being, and their bottom line are the ones most likely to comply with the Securities and Exchange Board of India's (SEBI) Foreign Exchange Regulation Act, the Competition Act of 2002, the Cyber Laws, the Banking Laws, and other relevant regulations.

Accountability, transparency, and openness to the public are all crucial to effective leadership. Disclosed information should be complete and up-to-date, especially as it pertains to things like financial standing, performance, etc. Government trust in corporate entities depends on their openness, hence tax rates for corporations have dropped from 97% to 30% since the late 1970s. The market is very competitive, therefore companies need to be transparent or risk losing clients to their competitors.

Human Resource Management and Corporate Governance: The members of a company's personnel are like members of the extended family. Human resource management plays a crucial part in the success of any business because of the inextricable link between the two. Respect for one another and acknowledgement of each person's efforts are essential. The Human Resources team is responsible for ensuring that all employees and staff are given the greatest possible chances to demonstrate their value. As a result, Human Resource plays an important part in Corporate Governance.

In order to succeed, businesses need to be willing to take risks, and innovation—whether in the form of new goods or services—is a crucial part of this.

In today's period of rapid economic change brought on by globalization and liberalization, judicial reform has become an absolute requirement. Despite the beneficial function it has played for so many years, our legal system is undoubtedly becoming antiquated and outmoded. There are a number of competing interests at play, which contributes to the judicial system's slow pace. However, the judicial system need modifications to keep up with the times and the rising level of competition. To be successful, it must be able to settle conflicts quickly and cheaply.

In today's age of competition and owing to globalization, our various Indian Corporate bodies are becoming worldwide giants, and this is feasible only thanks to effective corporate governance.

Nine Takeaways from Bankrupt Businesses[6] The same way that there is a lesson to be learned from every narrative and every setback in business, there is also a lesson to be learned from every triumph. No of the cause of a company's loss, strong corporate governance requires that organizations take the necessary steps to recover and go forward.

Different corporate governance models have emerged in different parts of the globe on the basis of a wide range of theoretical and philosophical frameworks. More importantly, it seems that corporate leaders have strayed from the primary goal of increasing shareholders' wealth as economies have developed through time. These dynamics have prompted action on the part of capital owners who want to protect their holdings and generate adequate returns on their investments. There is a need for legislative protection for shareholders despite the fact that internal company control, external financial market forces, and the reactions of institutional investors have all been successful in protecting shareholder wealth.

A corporation is a separate legal entity with the ability to buy and sell property and engage into contracts for the production of products and services. In addition, the company may issue shares of stock to the public in order to obtain capital. In addition to receiving dividends from the company, shareholders would have some say in how it is managed via the people they elect to the board of directors. These executives are acting as representatives of the shareholders and are obligated to act in their favor. Common shareholders may benefit from a company's management team's efforts to increase shareholder value without sacrificing the interests of other stakeholders. For instance, if the company borrows some of the money it needs to finance its operations, the common shareholders will get a better return on their investment. This is because, in light of the tax incentives afforded to businesses, borrowing money is very cheap for the company. To put it another way, executive choices might end up shifting wealth from one set of shareholders to another. For instance, common shareholders may get larger gains from embarking on hazardous investment projects, whereas bondholders reap no advantages and incur greater risk. Wealth may also be squandered by corporate management. Many companies have gone bankrupt due to the conduct of its top executives, as can be seen from historical instances. However, managers of a corporation may benefit not only the owners of the capital, but also the workers, and ultimately society at large. If the well-being of one group were to rise without harming that of any other, it would be an example of Pareto optimality.

Internal Control Theory in Businesses

Maintaining a productive dynamic between the company and its many interested parties is key to good corporate governance. According to Roe, the American system of corporate governance developed as a consequence of the country's economic development and its democratic worldview. In fact, the government handed corporate managers too much authority by purposefully undermining commercial banks. Banks based in the United States were barred from holding any stake in a publicly traded company. The actions of major stockholders were further limited by U.S. law. This ensured that the distribution of stock ownership in American corporations was as even as possible. According to the Coase Theorem, this setup ensures that management will have to get the support of a large number of geographically dispersed shareholders in order to make decisions that are in everyone's best interests. Banks, as lenders to the company, are seen as having no business interest in the distribution of dividends to common shareholders, according to the political perspective on corporate governance. According to North, the current perspective on corporate governance displays both formal and informal contractual relationships amongst corporate stakeholders. Corporate structures may include compensation plans for investors and lenders, incentive programs for executives, and mechanisms for ensuring that workers' negotiating positions inside the company are fairly represented. The transaction costs associated with upholding and enforcing agreements inside this kind of artificially built system would be a burden. As a premise, the neoclassical approach holds that institutions are irrelevant. For instance, Modigliani and Mille postulate that a company's overall market value is unrelated to the ratio of debt to equity employed to finance its assets, provided that the market is aware of the firm's investment program. In instance, the firm's total cost of capital would not be impacted by its capital claims structure. The company's investment and finance choices would not be influenced by one another. By operating this way, the company's corporate governance structure would not aid in the production of shareholder value. Williamson (1988) challenges the neoclassical perspective by arguing that debt and equity are not just alternate finance vehicles but rather a different kind of governance. In addition, the nature of the assets themselves is the primary factor in determining whether debt or equity financing should be used for a certain project. Debt might be used to fund re-deployable assets, whereas equity should be used for non-re-deployable projects. In addition, the capital structure impacts how profits are shared among capital providers, as stated by Jensen and Meckling and Meyers. Enhancing shareholder wealth may not be consistent with maximizing the entire value of the business due to bondholders and shareholders sharing the risk of the company. The debt-equity ratio, as well as the firm's capital expenditures, may be significantly impacted by the incentive structure of the company's decision-makers. Managers have a long track record of either creating and adding value to their firms via shrewd investment and finance choices, or else transferring and redistributing corporate capital among stakeholders and eroding shareholder equity. In practice, the processes of investing, financing, and distributing a company's earnings are intertwined rather than separate.

The Real World of Corporate Governance

Owners of common stock are entitled to vote for candidates running for seats on the board of directors. The board of directors is in charge of overseeing the management team and making appointments as necessary. By decentralizing authority to shareholders, companies may give them more say in strategic decisions, employee evaluations, and the allocation of corporate earnings. In particular, this internal control mechanism is meant to reward strong business performance on behalf of both common investors and senior management. Ineffective managers may and should be fired by the board of directors. When shareholders are unhappy with the direction of a company, they might "walk away" by selling their shares at a loss. Alternately, big shareholders have pursued their goals of monitoring company management using either aggressive activities (known as "investor activism") or a pleasant strategy (known as "relationship investing"). As an added bonus, to the degree that U.S. company law allows it, rival managers would oust ineffective ones and acquire underachieving businesses. It is expected that the sum of the aforementioned measures would benefit the current owners. Following the business judgment rule, U.S. courts have stayed out of company matters. The foundation of business law in the United States is the idea that the board of directors reviews and approves the decisions made by company management. In particular, shareholders might anticipate rapid notification of business acts that materially affect their wealth. For this reason, American courts will often stay out of business conflicts unless they include fraud. Relationship investing is supposed to fill the void left by a board of directors without the ability or will to oversee management. One kind of hands-on company ownership is relationship investing. Large investors often take on a mentoring role with the company's leadership and exhibit affable, cooperative demeanor. Internal corporate control is an important part of building a successful company, and various investors prioritize different aspects of this process. Stakeholders' desire to hang on to a portion of businesses' profits is the driving force behind the corporate governance structure.

Competition

According to Oxford Dictionaries Online, "competition" is "the action or situation of seeking to earn or win something by conquering or establishing supremacy over others." In a competitive market, businesses compete for customers in order to increase sales or fulfill other goals. The ideal pricing for a product is the one where both the consumer and the seller come out on top. Businesses benefit from competition because it encourages efficiency and yields more goods and services at more reasonable rates for customers. This guarantees the most efficient use of all resources. Because people are able to afford more of higher-quality goods, the increase in consumer welfare is likewise substantial. Since it leads to economic expansion, fair competition is good for everyone: buyers, sellers, and the economy as a whole. In a free and open market, which is the goal of competition. It will lead to more economic freedom and lowered barriers to entry for new enterprises and rivals.

As a fluid idea, competition has no fixed meaning outside of the jargon of market and trade. Competition may be thought of as the antithesis of monopoly in this sense. Consumers aren't served by monopolies, which are bad for both free commerce and people's wallets, but competition has many positive effects. By a perpetual monopoly, all the other subjects of the State are taxed very absurdly in two different ways, first by the high price of goods, which, in the case of free trade, could be purchased at much cheaper rates, and secondly, by their total exclusion from a branch of business which it might be both convenient and profitable for many of them to carry on. This generosity was captured by Adam Smith in his famous book "Wealth of Nations."

Competition-Related Governance 1.10.5

Administration of Businesses In the context of law, the term "Corporate" is most often used to refer to a commercial entity. In a similar vein, "governance" refers to the use of power to steer or control a group. Thus, "Corporate Governance" refers to the framework through which the leadership of a company or other organization oversees and manages its operations for the benefit of its stakeholders. What we mean when we talk about "Corporate Governance" is the process by which a company decides how it will be led. It's a method of leading and managing a business. It's important to strike a balance between personal and collective objectives, as well as financial and non-financial ones. There are societal and institutional facets to it. Corporate Governance promotes an atmosphere that is reliable, moral, and ethical. For Margaret Blair, corporate governance is "the whole set of legal, cultural, and institutional arrangements that determine what publicly traded corporations can do, who controls them, how that control is exercised, and how the risks and returns from the activities they undertake are allocated," though other authors have offered competing definitions.

According to N.R. Narayana Murthy, Chairman of the SEBI Committee on Corporate Governance, Mumbai, February 8, 2003

Management's acknowledgement of shareholders' inalienable rights as the corporation's actual owners and of management's own position as trustee on shareholders' behalf is the essence of good corporate governance. Values, ethics, and the separation of personal and corporate money as they pertain to company management are at the heart of this concept.

It was the OECD that first coined the term "Corporate Governance" to describe the framework through which businesses are steered and managed. The Corporate Governance framework defines the roles of the Board, the Management, the Shareholders, and other Stakeholders, as well as the rules and processes for making decisions on the Corporation's affairs. In doing so, it establishes a framework for establishing and achieving Company goals, as well as for measuring and evaluating progress toward those goals.

The OECD also offers a broader definition as Corporate Governance refers to the Private and Public institutions, including laws, regulations and accepted business practices, which together govern the relationship in a market economy between Corporate managers and entrepreneurs (Corporate insiders) on one hand, and those who invest resources in corporations, on the other hand Good is a term used with great flexibility; Depending on the context, good governance has been said at various times to encompass: full respect of effective participation, human rights, the rule of law, multi- actor partnerships, and accountable processes, political pluralism, transparent and institutions, an efficient and effective public sector, legitimacy, access to knowledge, information and education, political empowerment of people, equity, sustainability, and attitudes and values that foster responsibility, solidarity and tolerance

Background on the Development of the Term "Good Governance"

- The term "good governance" first appeared in a World Bank report from 1989.
- Governance and Development, a paper released by the Bank in 1992, delved more into the idea and its potential applications.
- The Bank reframed "good governance" as a prerequisite for progress in 1997.

To foster and maintain human growth in its many dimensions requires good administration. The primary objective is to examine how the government helps its citizens (regardless of their background, religion, socioeconomic status, or political beliefs) make decisions that are in their best interests and give them the freedom to live a life that is free from harm while still being clean, decent, happy, and self-sufficient.

Something "Good" about Government

Good governance is the administration of public affairs and the distribution of public resources in order to address the collective needs of a population. As a result, ratings of nations have to include both the quality and quantity of public goods they provide. Human rights, democratization and democracy, openness, participation and decentralized power sharing, excellent public administration, accountability, rule of law, efficacy, equality, and strategic vision are all concepts that inform the policies that provide public goods.

Human Development Report authors stress the need of "good" governance as a democratic necessity for fighting corruption and giving citizens a voice in policymaking and holding their governments to account.

Essential Components of Effective Government

There are eight pillars of good administration. It's democratic in the sense of being open to input from all parties, consensus-driven, responsive, efficient, effective, fair, and inclusive. It ensures that the most vulnerable members of society have a voice in decision-making, that corruption is kept to a minimum, and that minority perspectives are considered. In addition, it adapts to the ever-changing demands of modern society.

Participation

When it comes to planning for the future, it's important that both men and women from civil society have a voice in the decision-making process. This facet of governance is critical for gaining buy-in and support for initiatives and improving the quality of their execution. A well-informed and well-organized participation is required. That's why it's crucial to have both free speech and assembly with a well-functioning civic society.

Adherence to the rule of law

An impartial legal system that is fair, predictable, and stable is essential to good governance. The rights of all people, and particularly those of those who are underrepresented in society, should be fully protected. An independent court and an unbiased, uncorrupt police force are essential for effective law enforcement.

Transparency

Decisions made and their enforcement are carried out in a way consistent with laws and regulations, making transparency in government a necessary requirement for effective governance. If you want people to trust you, you need to be open and give them all the information they need, and make sure it's presented in a way that's easy to grasp.

Responsiveness

Institutions must be able to meet the needs of all interested parties within a reasonable amount of time for there to be good governance. Mediation is required due to the number of parties involved, the diversity of perspectives represented, and the wide range of interests at play in modern society. An all-encompassing and long-term view of what is required and how to attain the objectives of sustainable development is essential for analyzing and acting in the best interest of the community.

Accessibility and fairness

Guaranteeing that all members of a society have access to resources that may contribute to their health and happiness is essential to the success of any society as a whole. The most marginalized members of society must be given the same chances as the rest of society if this is to succeed.

Proven efficiency and effectiveness

When it comes to meeting people's needs and making the most of available resources, good governance is all about the processes and institutions. The efficient use of resources and environmental preservation are both aspects of the efficiency idea.

Accountability

It's a must-have for effective leadership. Organizations in the public sector, the business sector, and civil society must all answer to the people and the institutions they serve. When making decisions or taking acts, any group or institution must answer to the people who may be impacted by those choices or actions. Only openness to the public and adherence to the law can ensure that those in power are held accountable.

Legal Order

A commitment to the rule of law includes upholding the principle of impartiality, rejecting corruption, and safeguarding the human rights of all people. These are the most important factors to consider as guidelines for excellent Governance in policymaking.

Importance of Responsible Leadership

The Constitution of India upholds a republican, democratic, and secular system of government, as well as the principles it enshrines. When referring to the political and administrative branches of government, "governance" denotes a political body responsible for their respective functions. The belief that man has the moral and intellectual capacity to rule himself justly and fairly is the bedrock of good government. Good governance refers to honest and competent government in a democratic system.

There are three aspects of good governance in particular that give it practical importance in the functioning of government.

The first is the extent to which the government has the authority and resources to make decisions and carry them out; the second is the nature of political will; and the third is the method by which a country's economic and social resources are managed for progress.

Furthermore, it shows how the general public feels about the government's different departments and how they're run. An example of "good" government would be one that works to eliminate poverty, hunger, terror, and violence while also fostering gender equality and protecting the environment for future generations. The United Nations defines good government as one that is open to citizen input and holds those in power to account. It comprises not just government agencies but also businesses and non-governmental groups.

To ensure human rights are protected, free from abuse and corruption, and with proper respect for the rule of law, it is essential that public institutions practice good governance in the way they handle and manage public affairs and resources.

This is a big deal because it holds the potential of securing all the rights that people have always fought for, including those to freedom of expression, peaceful assembly, and economic and political security. Installing administrative virtues and removing dysfunctional relationships is, thus, a key component of good governance.

The result is a government that is more efficient, trustworthy, and legitimate in its administrative structure, as well as more citizen- and community-oriented, compassionate, and open to sharing.

The Agency Theory and Business Management

In your own words, what does the term "agency" mean?

A person who acts as an agent does so on behalf of another. This means that workers act as representatives of their respective employers. However, agency is not limited to boss-employee dynamics. Contractors that work alone are also considered agents.

Representatives such as legal counsel, accountants, and public relations agencies act on behalf of their respective clients. Executive directors provide authority to the CEO to run the firm. An ordinary grocery shop acts as an agent for the corn chip producer. That's why it's important to remember that the agency connection encompasses not only the worker but a wide range of financial dealings. A principle is the person or organization that an agent serves.

One branch of economics known as "agency theory" analyzes the effects of financial incentives on agents. Agents may not share the principal's values and priorities, making it difficult to design effective incentives for them. Every year, millions of working hours are wasted as employees surf the Internet, send and read personal emails, and play online games instead of doing their jobs. Lawyers defending a company in court are paid by the hour, so they have an incentive to avoid settlements that would cut into their billings. (Such actions would be against the rules of professional conduct for lawyers.) It's very uncommon for auto repair firms to utilize second-hand or refurbished components yet charge for brand-new ones. All of these situations include an agent whose motivations are at odds with those of the principal.

The cost of incentives is central to agency theory. An agency connection is formed between you and the automobile rental company. The renter's actions are the problem, thus it's helpful to think of themselves as the agent even if the automobile rental business is technically an agency. Ideally, the agent would handle the business automobile as if it were her own. In contrast, the renter is aware that she isn't in her own vehicle and often drives more cautiously.

Exposition of Theories of Agency

Differentiating between the principals (the shareholders) and the agents (the executives recruited to run the firm or organization) gives birth to agency theories. According to agency theorists, the agent's interests often directly oppose those of the principals they serve (Johnson, Daily, & Ellstrand, 1996). Since they do not have a direct role in running the business, it is assumed that the principals incur a loss, or "agency loss," as a result of not being in charge. The agent receives a portion of the profit that would have been earned by the principal had he or she been responsible for running the business themselves. Therefore, agency theories recommend financial incentives to encourage executives to maximize owners' profits (Eisenhardt, 1989). To further safeguard the principals' interests, a board designed with agency theory in mind would likely use stringent control, supervision, and monitoring of the agent's work (Hillman & Dalziel, 2003). As such, the board is responsible to the shareholders and participates in the majority of the management decision making processes. Through the perspective of agency theories, a nonprofit board will demonstrate management by doing on behalf of the organization's stakeholders.

A two-tiered structure of control between managers and owners is assumed by agency theory in the context of corporate governance. According to agency theory, there will be tension and distrust between the two parties involved. Therefore, the corporation's fundamental structure is the interlocking contractual relationships among various stakeholders.

Features

In broad strokes, there are three factions inside the company with competing agendas. Leaders, shareholders, and debtors (such as banks). Since shareholders and bankers/managers tend to have different goals, tensions arise. Managers want for short-term gains that boost their own wealth, influence, and status, whereas shareholders favor long-term, stable expansion.

Function

With agency theory, we can pinpoint where different corporate interest groups are at odds with one another. Banks seek risk mitigation, whereas shareholders want profit maximization within certain limits. Risky as it may be for employees, managers take it on themselves to maximize earnings to advance their careers. Having these interdependent groups as the foundation of contemporary organizations isn't without its drawbacks, since it means that everyone is always vying for power over everyone else.

Costs

The idea of costs associated with maintaining the division of labor between loan holders, shareholders, and managers is a crucial discovery of agency theory. Managers have a leg up on the rest of the workforce because of their intimate familiarity with the company. This will help them seem good in the eyes of the public while hurting the bottom line of shareholders. Costs (such as lower earnings) are associated with limiting managers' authority, while pursuing profits via riskier projects might irritate financial institutions. The expense to an organization of keeping tabs on and restricting its management may be very high.

Significance

Firms, according to the agency theory of management, are not amorphous money-making machines but rather, units of conflict. This tension is not an exception, but rather an inherent part of how contemporary businesses operate.

Effects

If one accepts the premises of agency theory, then companies may be seen as collections of interconnected fiefdoms. Each fief has its own unique set of priorities and cultural norms, and these factors influence how each one sees the firm's mission. It is reasonable to presume that managers would act in a manner that maximizes their personal profit and reputation, even if it means shortchanging shareholders, when assessing how a firm operates. It's possible that management might be seen as a kind of institutionalized dishonesty due to the power differential that results from information asymmetry.

Agency Theory and Corporate Governance: What's It All About?

To better comprehend how agents and principals interact, agency theory is used. The agent's duty is to operate only in the principal's best interests while representing the principal in a commercial transaction. It's possible for principals and agents to have competing goals due to the fact that not all agents will always do what's best for the principle. As a consequence, there may be a number of issues inside businesses as a result of poor communication and conflict. When parties' goals aren't aligned, it may lead to friction and costly waste. The principal-agent dilemma results.

When a principal and an agent have competing goals, it's called the principal-agent issue. Businesses should work to reduce the likelihood of such events by implementing sound policies. Opportunities for moral hazard exist in these confrontations for people of good character. The agent's interests may not coincide with the principal's, but incentives may be used to change their conduct. The principal's interests may be restored via the use of corporate governance to alter the stipulations under which the agent acts. When a principal appoints an agent to act on the principle's behalf, the principal must do so despite knowing little to no details about the agent's track record in this area. Incentives for agents to cooperate with the principal's goals are essential. These incentives might be designed with agency theory in mind, taking into account the agent's underlying interests. Rules prohibiting moral hazard should be put into place, and incentives that encourage bad conduct should be eliminated. Better company policy may be crafted when the processes that cause issues are understood.

The Corporate Stewardship Theory

Introduction: Theory and Practice of Stewardship

Managers and executives, according to stewardship theorists, work for the same ends as the company's owners (Davis, Schoorman, & Donaldson, 1997). Therefore, agency theories imply the board shouldn't have too much sway. Executives' potential for excellent performance may be boosted if the board plays a facilitative role by giving them more authority (Hendry, 2002; Shen, 2003). Relationships including training, mentorship, and joint decision making are central to stewardship ideas, which advocate for them to be implemented between the board and top management (Shen, 2003; Sundaramurthy & Lewis, 2003).

Individual self-interest is the starting point for most theories of company governance. However, stewardship philosophy opposes selfishness. The foundation of agency theory is the analysis of how individuals and organizations manage the opportunity cost of separating ownership and control. Managers are thought to strive to better their own positions, while the board works to exert control over managers and, therefore, reduce the disparity.

Motivation

As per the tenets of the stewardship philosophy, managers should aim for more than just financial success. These include self-respect, helpfulness, reputation, accomplishment, contentment, and direction in life. Managers, according to the stewardship hypothesis, want to perform a good job, increase earnings, and provide satisfactory returns to shareholders. They do it not for the money, but out of a sense of obligation to the company.

Identification

The philosophies of agency and stewardship have divergent origins. When people exclusively think of themselves as autonomous entities, the agency issue arises. However, according to stewardship theory, managers do not see themselves mainly as separate persons.

Instead, they see themselves as integral to the company's success. According to stewardship theory, managers should integrate their own sense of identity and self-worth with the company's brand.

Policies

Certain policies are inherently associated with a stewardship style of corporate governance. Companies will lay out managers' responsibilities and requirements in great detail. These requirements will be very outcome focused and aimed at boosting the manager's confidence and self-esteem. The proponents of stewardship philosophy argue for autonomous managers. This implies that managers are intrinsically "company guys" who put the interests of the business ahead of their own. This independence will be put to work for the benefit of the company.

Consequences

The belief that the individualistic agency theory is overdrawn is central to the repercussions of stewardship theory. With everything else being equal, it is reasonable for board members to trust management. A board may rest easy knowing that a CEO who stays the course will not be motivated by the desire for personal wealth if he or she is not also the board's chairman. On the other hand, having the CEO double as the chairman is not a concern if there is no reason to believe he would abuse his position for personal gain. Stewardship theory, on the other hand, posits that, yes, managers do want to be lavishly rewarded for their work, but that no manager wants this to be at the price of the business.

CORPORATIVE GOVERNANCE FROM THE PERSPECTIVE OF SHAREHOLDERS AND STAKEHOLDERS

When asked to describe corporate governance, the Cadbury Committee in 1992 settled on the phrase "the system through which firms are directed and managed." The shareholder and stakeholder theories are among the most widely accepted frameworks for understanding effective corporate governance.

Concept of Stockholders

Foundered by Milton Friedman, the Shareholder Theory claims that a company's only duty is to maximize shareholder returns. The theory holds that because management was recruited by the shareholders in their capacity as agents, they owe the shareholders both legal and ethical duties of loyalty and care. Conformity to "the essential principles of the society, both those represented in law and those inherent in ethical custom" is the sole exception to the rule that says you should earn as much money as possible.

With the dawning realization that there are drawbacks to focusing only on shareholder interests, many businesses see the shareholder hypothesis as antiquated. Short-termism and increased risk-taking are only two of the many potential pitfalls. The failure of companies like Enron and Worldcom, whose management was under constant pressure to enhance returns to shareholders, might be considered as an application of shareholder theory.

Concept of Stakeholders

In contrast, the principle of stakeholder responsibility asserts that businesses have duties to more than simply their shareholders. To put it simply, a stakeholder is any individual or group that may have an impact on, or is impacted by, a company's decisions. Everyone from workers to clients to vendors to creditors to the neighborhood at large and even their rival businesses are all fair game.

Corporate social responsibility (CSR) is a concept that acknowledges the economic, legal, ethical, and charitable duties of firms in today's society; its initial proponent, Edward Freeman, acknowledged the stakeholder theory as a crucial part of CSR. Some of the top companies in the world today even state that CSR is at the core of their business strategy. While many businesses do have a "conscience," others use CSR as a PR tool to boost their image and reputation, but don't follow through with their good intentions.

Stakeholder theory has been in the news recently due to the controversy surrounding the tax practices of many large corporations in the United Kingdom, including Starbucks, Google, and Facebook. The corporations have taken legal steps to reduce their UK corporate tax obligations, but these maneuvers are commonly seen as immoral since they take advantage of loopholes in the British tax system. In response to public outcry over the company's tax practices, Starbucks has promised to pay an additional £10 million in taxes over the next two years.

The Implications of Stakeholders on Organizations

Shareholders, workers, consumers, the government, lenders, and others are examples of the many stakeholders. Every day, managers have a harder time making choices since they can't afford to ignore the interest of any one stakeholder in today's competitive climate. Managers would do well to consider all of the perspectives they'll need to account for in reaching a decision; even a seemingly little disagreement might have a catastrophic impact.

Ownership Interests of a Company's Shareholders

The ultimate goal of a company's shareholders is to increase their wealth via their investment in the company. Stockholders want to see the share price go up as much as possible, and if the company fails to meet their expectations, they have the option of selling their shares.

Workers and their own self-interest

Employees are the company's greatest resource and, in some cases, its competitive advantage. In addition to employer concerns, such as career advancement and compensation, employees have their own needs and desires. Managers lose both their jobs and the company's reputation if they put profit before employee satisfaction. British Airways' ongoing dispute with its cabin crew is a prime example of a conflict between management and workers. To maintain their competitive edge in the market, British Airways aims to save 62.5 million pounds annually through cost reductions (Holden, 2010). They've gone on strike for a total of 22 days this year, costing the company over 150 million pounds (Guardian, 2010). Freeman argued in a debate that the company should share its values with its workers (UVA Today, 2010). More than 150 million pounds were lost during strikes, and the company's market reputation and share price also took a hit due to the dispute, but British Airways' management is more concerned with increasing profit by cutting costs than they are about their relationship with employees.

The patron and his or her concerns

Companies only make goods, and often make decisions, based on what they think their customers want. Quality at an affordable price is of paramount importance to our customers. Customers nowadays are much savvier and critical than they used to be; a company can afford to lose billions of dollars but not its customers. In 2010, when confronted with a quality issue, Toyota recalled more than 9 million vehicles around the world, resulting in a loss of billions of dollars for the company (Conner, 2010). The company's stock price undoubtedly dropped after the allegations of using low-quality spare parts became public knowledge, button. February 5, 2010 when Akio Toyoda, president of Toyoda apologized and announced the recall of the Toyota cars, the companies share price ended 4.5% higher 74.71 on the New York Stock Exchange; Investors relieved that announcement as a concrete step to deal with the quality crisis (Reuters, 2010). (Reuters,

2010). This case also reveal that share price also get affected by customer satisfaction; as if customers are not satisfied, they can switch to some other product adversely affect sales and profit which ultimately affect the share price of the company

Creditors and their interest

The primary objective of lenders is to get back the amount with interest on time. Some scholars argue that lenders can secure themselves by contracts. But it doesn't mean that lenders are not at all interested in the market performance of the company. Lending institutes lend money to the firms by considering its market value and previous performance. That means they are not only interested in their returns on time but also in market value of the firm and long-term relationships.

Community and their interest

Business exist in a social environment, business and community have organic relationship. The stakeholder theory state that the main purpose of the businesses not only to maximize wealth but it should also do some social activities because business directly or indirectly affect the environment and society. Tata Group is committed to improve the quality of life of communities they serve (TATA, 2010)

Government and their interest

Governments principle purpose is to ensure that corporate operate according to the law imposed on it and do business by fair means. Government impose lawn the business in order to protect the rights of their citizens moreover they form apex bodies to keep eye on the businesses, as SEBI (Security and Exchange Board of India), its main purpose is to guard the interests of investors in securities and to standardize the security market (SEBI, 2010).

A corporation is created to address objectives which are much more than creating products and services, it has to serve the larger purpose of satisfying multilevel needs of the society. Healthy corporate governance practices are no longer the need of the law but have become essential for the very survival of the organizations, the current economic crisis has proven that beyond doubts.

The corporations have always faced the tug of war of protecting the interests of the shareholders (the legal owners) or the stakeholders which includes suppliers, creditors, government and communities.

This unit discusses certain current best practices as advocated by corporate governance groups and practiced by some Fortune public companies, with the understanding that best practices tend to evolve over time. We proceed on the assumption that a 'best practice' is one in which the benefits to the organization substantially exceed the cost of implementation. What is a best practice today may not be a best practice in the future.

CONCEPT OF CG

To put it simply, corporate governance is the framework of norms, procedures, and legislation that governs the management and operations of a corporation. A company's corporate governance is overseen by the board of directors, who are ultimately accountable for the business as a whole. In this sense, it describes the structure of authority inside a company. It is a method used for guiding and managing businesses. It involves making decisions for the company based on what those involved want. The board of directors and relevant committees really carry this out for the benefit of the company's stakeholders. To achieve success, it is necessary to strike a balance between personal and collective objectives, as well as between economic and social concerns.

THE CHARACTERISTICS OF CG

1. Shareholders, the board of directors, and the management team all play a role in corporate governance, which is the process by which these three groups influence the direction and success of a business. No tension or unhealthy dynamics should exist between a company's owners and its management team. The owners need to ensure that the worker's output is consistent with the expected output. You can't ignore these elements of good company governance.

2. The topic of corporate governance is concerned with the means through which investors ensure a reasonable rate of return on their capital. The relationship between shareholders and executives is delineated explicitly under corporate governance. It is up to the management to make the decision. The roles of owners and managers in today's organizations must be clearly defined and harmonized.

3. Strategy and decision-making are at the heart of corporate governance. The Board of Directors is given absolute power and duty as a result. Corporate governance is essential in today's market-based economy. Corporate governance is increasingly being pushed due to efficiency and globalization. Building value

for a company's stakeholders is impossible without good corporate governance.

4. Strong and sustainable economic growth may be maintained with the help of good corporate governance practices. That way, both the interests of the majority and the interests of the minority shareholders are protected. In this way, the company guarantees that all shareholders may fully exercise their rights and that those rights are completely recognized.

5. Institutional and social elements are both present. Good corporate governance fosters an atmosphere that is reliable, moral, and ethical.

Stakes in Having Corporate Governance Stakes in having corporate governance include:

i. Responsibility entails the need to explain one's actions when anything goes wrong at work, a concept known as "accountability." Good corporate governance is the foundation for responsibility.

ii. Assuming responsibility (a) guarantees that operational management (i.e. The Board of Directors is accountable to the Managers and Staff (BOD).

iii. Make sure the BOD is answerable to the shareholders if things go south.

iv. Fairness
The Shareholders' Rights are safeguarded by CG practices.

v. CG does not discriminate against any shareholder, including those who have a minority stake in the firm.

vi. Customer service that (c) Offers real solutions for those who have had their rights violated

vii. Transparency

(a) CG makes certain that all important facts, such as the company's financial status, performance, and ownership, are disclosed in a timely manner and are correct.

i. Independence
(a) CG sets up rules, regulations, and organizational frameworks to restrict or eliminate conflicts of interest.
As part of (b), CG selects "Independent Directors" and "Independent Advisers," whose only responsibility is to help the company make decisions without being swayed by any outside interests.

ii. Adhere to the regulations
(a) CG guarantees that everything is done according to the letter and spirit of the law.

According to SEBI, corporations need to implement sound corporate governance practices in order to maintain their listing. The significance of corporate governance

1. Brings out openness and honesty

Promoting honest and open monitoring of all of the company's activities is a key function of good corporate governance. It aids the firm in upholding its norms and policies. Directors may benefit from corporate governance's focus on their education and growth as decision-makers.

2. Get Your Hands On Some Foreign Funds

Foreign investment or "foreign capital" refers to financial resources obtained from sources outside of a country. Companies seeking funding from international capital markets must meet stringent requirements for productivity and openness. In order to achieve credibility and confidence from their customers on a worldwide scale, companies need to practice good corporate governance, which increases efficiency and transparency inside the firm.

3. The Safety of Investments

An further critical aspect of good corporate governance is safeguarding investor interests. Each and every investor hopes that their rights will be safeguarded by the company in which they have invested. Protecting shareholders' interests and boosting the effectiveness of business operations are both possible thanks to corporate governance.

4. Balanced Reporting and Holding Financial Parties Accountable

The term "financial reporting" refers to the process through which a business divulges its financial status to shareholders and the general public. Good corporate management ensures reliable financial statements. Workers and supervisors are held responsible for their actions in an effort to improve productivity as part of good corporate governance practices.

5. Shareholder Communication Is Strengthened

Voting rights in a company are referred to as "shareholder communication." It's a channel for investors to provide feedback with businesses. An effective corporate governance system is crucial for paving the way for open lines of communication between management and stockholders. There has been a shift in recent years toward valuing good company governance more highly. To better include shareholders in decision making, for instance, new measures were introduced to corporate governance in 2003.

6.   Builds a stronger brand and better reputation in the market

Good corporate governance practices may boost a company's popularity and standing in the market. Due to the fact that good corporate governance guarantees that rights are safeguarded, resources are used effectively, correct choices are made, etc.

7.   Improvements in the Worth of the Company

Investors' needs and confidence are met when there is more openness, responsibility from management, a solid reputation in the market, and a trustworthy track record. The result is a rise in the stock price.

THE REQUIREMENT FOR COMPANY LEADERSHIP

1.   Conspiracies Are Proliferating at an Alarming Rate

Stock exchanges, banks, financial institutions, businesses, and even government agencies are not immune to the misuse and theft of public funds. Companies should implement corporate governance measures to lessen the likelihood of financial mismanagement.

2.   Mergers and Acquisitions

The corporate sector is seeing a great number of mergers and acquisitions at the moment. Corporate governance is necessary to safeguard all stakeholders' interests in the event of a takeover or merger.

3.   Achieve SEBI Compliance

Compliance with SEBI's regulations regarding corporate governance is now mandatory for listed firms. It is in everyone's best advantage to comply with this SEBI mandate. Companies that violate SEBI regulations risk severe financial penalties.

4.   Urgent Call for Social Accountability

Nowadays, people place a premium on social responsibility. The BOD's responsibility includes safeguarding the interests of the company's many stakeholders, including its clients, workers, investors, vendors, communities, governments, and more. Corporate governance is essential for this to happen.

Effective Corporate Governance

The goal of corporate governance is to make your business more accountable and less vulnerable to catastrophic failures. The bankruptcy of energy company Enron and its insolvent workers and stockholders is a compelling case for the need of good Corporate Governance. Similarly to how an internal affairs division of a police force would root out and eliminate corruption, so too should well-executed Corporate Governance seek out and eradicate issues with severe ferocity. Below, we've included several arguments for why corporate governance is so crucial.

1.   Many changes have occurred in the ownership structure of businesses in the last few years. Most major corporations have a single shareholder that is a public financial entity like a bank or mutual fund. This means they are able to have significant influence on the firms' management. Management is coerced into implementing corporate governance. That is, they force upper-level leadership to improve practices like productivity, openness, and responsibility. They want management to create policies that benefit consumers, safeguard vulnerable populations, and preserve natural resources. Thus, corporate governance is the end outcome of the shift of ownership.

2.   These days, being socially responsible is seen as quite important. Directors have a responsibility to safeguard the interests of the company's many stakeholders, including its clients, workers, investors, vendors, and communities. Only by using corporate governance practices can companies achieve this.

3.   There has been an increase in the frequency with which scams, frauds, and other forms of corruption have been perpetrated in recent years. Every day, governments all across the globe, including India, waste and steal from the public coffers. Everything from the stock exchange to banks to corporations to government agencies is experiencing this. Many businesses have instituted corporate governance policies in response to the prevalence of such fraud and financial mismanagement.

4.   Shareholder Apathy: Most shareholders don't become involved in running their firms. They never miss the Annual General Meeting. India still lacks a postal voting system. Attendees at the meeting via proxies are not permitted to participate in the discussion. The strength of shareholder groups is low. Thus, directors abuse their authority for personal gain. Therefore, corporate governance is necessary to safeguard the interests of all parties involved in a business.

5.   Thanks to globalization, most major corporations now have international distribution networks. This means they need to court an international clientele and investment base. They must also comply with laws and customs of the host country. Corporate governance is essential for all of this. No company

can compete successfully in today's global economy without strong corporate governance in place.

6. There have been a lot of takeovers and mergers in the corporate sector recently. Takeovers and mergers need strict corporate governance to ensure everyone's best interests are protected.

7. The Securities and Exchange Board of India (SEBI) has mandated strict corporate governance standards for all listed firms. The goal is to safeguard the interests of the investors and other parties involved.

Goals of Effective Government

It is believed that the twin components of can best meet the purpose of corporate governance, namely, the general objective of wealth production and competitiveness for the benefit of all:

Improved company reporting, which for public and very large private companies will require the publication of financial statements and other information previously unavailable to the public. This "inclusive" approach to directors' duties requires directors to have regard for all the relationships on which the company depends and to the long, as well as the short-term implications of their actions, with the goal of achieving company success for the benefit of shareholders as a whole (eg. With employees, customers and suppliers as well as the wider community).

THE ELEMENTS THAT DETERMINE GOVERNANCE QUALITY

The commitment level of individual board members, the quality of corporate reporting, the amount of stakeholder engagement, and the integrity of the management all play a role in determining the governance quality.

i. Management integrity: A Board of Directors lacking in integrity may be inclined to abuse the confidence of shareholders and other stakeholders by making choices that favor insiders at the expense of other stakeholders.

ii. The efficacy of the Board is based on the combined abilities of its members in terms of knowledge and competence.

iii. Adequacy of the process: If the Board is not provided with appropriate and timely information for analyzing plans and the performance of the company, then the Board will be unable to properly monitor the executive management.

iv. The quality of a board is determined by the dedication of its individual members to the duties inherent to their position on the board.

v. Accuracy and disclosure in financial statements, as well as internal controls and auditor independence.

vi. Stakeholder engagement in management: Stakeholder involvement correlates with optimal resource use and the amount of new ideas provided to enhance the management structure and process.

vii. Transparency and timeliness in corporate communication with shareholders are two factors that contribute to the quality of corporate reporting. This aids investors in assessing management's stewardship abilities and making sound financial judgments. Corporate governance best practices will generally include the following: a definition of practices that defines good governance; a code of best practices covering the constitution of the Board and its various committees, defining their goals and responsibilities, exploring preferred internal systems, and disclosing requirements.

Excellent corporate leadership and management

All of us strive to be the best that we can be in our own fields of work. This is what will set us apart from the competition, and it's also the pinnacle of what we're capable of doing. In the business world, leaders must set an example. Good governance procedures serve as a model in this regard. "Corporate Governance" isn't simply a buzzword; it's a substantive idea with real worth. It's a crucial idea that may help any business improve and strive for greatness. When it comes to attaining Corporate Excellence, Corporate Governance is the most useful instrument available. To attain Corporate Excellence, businesses should pinpoint, evaluate, and formalize their core beliefs, core capabilities, and fundamental purposes. Today's technology was yesterday's magic, therefore for businesses to succeed, they need to think outside the box and behave responsibly. To succeed in any field, whether it is the economy, society, or production, good corporate governance is essential. Machines, computers, software, and the internet are not the exclusive proprietors of the future. All they are good for is as tools. The ideals of good governance are the single most important factor in harnessing them. The outcome is what matters, therefore we need to take responsibility for our acts and the outcomes they produce. The trust and respect of those with whom a business interacts is invaluable, and it is something that must be gained by deeds rather than demanded. Achieving greatness is dependent on, but not guaranteed by, good governance. In order to advance economically, good governance is essential. Benefit generation for shareholders (and other stakeholders) and social value are at the heart of Corporate Governance, along with transparency, accountability, investor protections, improved compliance with statutory laws and regulations. The only way to ensure a company's success is via good corporate governance. Every corporation now recognizes the need of maintaining a lean and healthy body in order to perform at its highest level in accordance with the tenets of good corporate governance. Any attempt by corporations to get around this fact and use quick fixes to succeed will backfire and undermine their good intentions. One's perspective will determine one's understanding of what constitutes business excellence or success. There are several ways to describe excellence. In the current economic model of the business, success is usually defined by a combination of factors, the most important of which are profit and the satisfaction of the firm's many stakeholders (including customers, workers, and shareholders). One can see that "Corporate Governance" concerns, as we understand them now, are given a lot of weight by focusing on things like revenue and profit growth, market share expansion, and market value increase (Stock Market Capitalization). Take a look at how stakeholders' needs are being prioritized in comparison to those of consumers, employees, and the company as a whole. It is believed that, in the long term, achieving corporate excellence is challenging without excellent governance, which is why the two ideas are so intrinsically linked.

We will have to regret in this time, not so much for the awful conduct of the wicked people, but for the dreadful silence of the decent ones," Martin Luther King Jr. said accurately. You can hear the message from a mile away. Companies with little resources must take the initiative to establish and adhere to a code of conduct if they are to succeed despite their limited resources. Keeping up with legislative changes and technology advances and comprehending their influence on his tasks and obligations will be difficult for professionals in the near future.

GUIDELINES FOR COMPANY MANAGEMENT

For a better understanding of corporate governance, it's important to know the four key principles:
1. Equality of treatment is what we mean when we talk about fairness, thus all shareholders should be treated the same regardless of how many shares they own. Moreover, workers, communities, and public authorities should all be treated properly.

2. In a nutshell, the Board of Directors has the power to make decisions and take action on behalf of the firm. And therefore it is incumbent upon them to take full accountability and use the power properly.

    The Board of Directors is in charge of the company's management, its affairs, the selection of the CEO, and the evaluation of the CEO's performance.

3. When a corporation is transparent, it is providing its shareholders and other stakeholders with clear information in a timely manner. The company's financial, social, and environmental standing should be accurately reflected in the information provided to investors, therefore it is imperative that any and all material items pertaining to the company's performance and activities be communicated promptly and accurately.

    Stakeholders' trust in a company's management and decision-making may be bolstered by open communication.

4. When we talk about a firm being accountable, we're talking about its duty and duty to explain its acts and behavior. The board should use sound risk management and internal control procedures, and provide shareholders with an objective and understandable appraisal of the company's performance and prospects.

    Stakeholders should be updated on a regular basis with a fair, balanced, and easily understood evaluation of the progress the firm is doing toward its business goals.

Corporate Governance Based on the 4 P's

1. Investors, shareholders, workers, members of the community, policymakers, and other stakeholders may all provide light on how a company's corporate governance structure serves its people.

2. The mission of the company should be clearly articulated and understood by all of its constituents. Good corporate governance is the result of a well-articulated goal and vision that are founded on the shared values of the organization.

3. Process encompasses the administration of processes, ensuring that processes are followed, and developing new ways to improve processes. Organizations with effective corporate governance have a system in place to guarantee that they never break the rules set out by the government or other relevant authorities.

4. Growth via efficiency may be achieved if performance is monitored, analyzed, and shared. enhancement and advocates for responsible business practices.

THE VALUE OF EFFECTIVE CORPORATE DIRECTION TO COMMERCE

1. Account for everyone involved
2. Brings about openness in all processes
3. Facilitates a positive public perception of the company
4. Establishes and promotes a culture of corporate social responsibility
5. Promotes moral behavior in the workplace

WITH ORGANIZATION

1. When workers are invested in their job, they perform better.
2. Various government agencies provide special privileges and exemptions.
3. In the eyes of the public, the company has risen in standing.
4. Customers are more likely to buy again.
5. Fraud and conflict are reduced.

AT MANY LEVELS AND TO MANY PARTICIPANTS

1. All major management decisions are better communicated to shareholders.
2. Employing practices at this organization are honest and open.
3. Products are of good quality and priced reasonably for the consumer market.
4. The profitability of an investment is optimized.
5. As a result of the organization's efforts to better the community and the environment, society as a whole benefits.

COMPANY MANAGEMENT THEORIES

In response to the fluctuating difficulties inherent in managing businesses, several theories of corporate governance have been developed. Corporate Governance refers to the framework established to ensure that major corporate decisions are carried out effectively. During the course of a company's operations, there are a number of theories that explain the interplay between the many parties involved in the enterprise.

1. Concept of Agency

The link between principals (such firm shareholders) and agents is outlined by agency theory (such as directors of company). In this model, business leaders are represented by "principals," who are responsible for hiring and supervising employees. Directors and managers, acting on behalf of shareholders, are tasked with operating a company's day-to-day operations. The shareholders depend on the agents to make sound judgments and take appropriate actions on their behalf. But it's not always required that an agent act in the principals' best interests. It's possible for the agent to give in to their own self-interest and opportunistic tendencies, causing them to fall short of the principal's standards. To put it simply, the central tenet of agency theory is the partitioning of property rights from managerial responsibilities. The notion advocates for holding individuals or groups responsible for the outcomes of their actions. Agents' priorities may be adjusted with the use of rewards and punishments.

2. A Conceptual Framework for Responsible Management

According to the steward hypothesis, a steward's job is to safeguard and increase the value of shareholders' investments via improved operational efficiency and productivity. Executives and managers in a corporation who act as stewards are there to safeguard shareholders' interests and generate profits for the business. When the organization achieves its goals, the stewards are happy and more likely to put in extra effort. For the sake of the company's shareholders, it advocates for workers and executives to have more leeway in their decision-making. The staff members are dedicated to their work and treat it as if it were their own.

3. Theory of Stakeholders

Management's responsibility to various interested parties was included into stakeholder theory. Managers have a wide variety of connections to manage, including those with customers, vendors, and other businesses. Managerial decision making is at the center of this theory, which holds that all stakeholders' interests are of equal weight and that no one group of interests should be prioritized above the others.

4. Towards a Theory of Resource Dependence

Directors' access to necessary resources is a central tenet of the Resource Dependency Theory. It explains how directors' connections to the outside world help a company acquire or maintain vital resources. Financial support is crucial to the success of any organization or business. The directors provide value to the company in the form of expertise, connections to important stakeholders (including suppliers, customers, government officials, and interest groups), and credibility. There are four broad types of directors: insiders, business professionals, support specialists, and important members of the community.

5. The Theory of Transaction Costs

According to transaction cost theory, businesses generate value by entering into a variety of agreements, either internally or with external parties. Each time you make a deal with a third party, you incur what is known as a transaction fee. When the market's transaction costs are too high, businesses sometimes choose to handle transactions internally.

6. Theories of Government

The method used by political theory is to cultivate voting support among shareholders as opposed to buying votes. It emphasizes how government favoritism determines the distribution of business power, earnings, and advantages.

Members of the Board of Directors of a corporation are typically chosen by the company's shareholders and are responsible for overseeing the management of the corporation. Business management is handled by professionals who are appointed by the board. Corporate governance models vary from country to country because of subtle but important regulatory variations.

Corporate Governance Structures

There are fundamental components of the corporate governance framework. These include the distribution of stock ownership, the major players in the business world, the make-up of the board of directors, communications and cooperation between these individuals, the legal and policy framework, the disclosure obligations of publicly traded companies, and the need for shareholder approval for major corporate decisions. As you may expect, these factors vary from one nation to the next. This diversity has resulted in many approaches to corporate governance. The following are descriptions of these versions of the models:

1. Corporate governance in the United States and other commonwealth nations, including the United Kingdom, Australia, Canada, India (to a significant degree), etc., is known

as the "Anglo-Saxon" or "outsider" model. The hallmarks of this model are:

i. A deep and liquid stock market: the great majority of publicly traded corporations in the United States and the United Kingdom are traded on stock exchanges. The capital market acts as a check and balance in these nations. The danger of a takeover causes a balancing of interests between shareholders and management.

ii. Company ownership tends to be highly fragmented, with the biggest voting bloc often comprising between 5 and 10 percent of shares in the United States and the United Kingdom, respectively. Due to widespread share ownership, shareholders have little influence on management. There are both private and institutional investors in the firm.

iii. Executive and non-executive directors are chosen by shareholders with voting rights proportional to their holdings, making up a unitary or single tier board of directors that prioritizes shareholder interests.

iv. Both inside and outside directors sit on the board of directors, with inside directors being either employees of the business (executive directors) or having close ties to the firm's promoters. Independent directors are not currently employed by or linked to the company's promoters.

The Anglo-Saxon system emphasizes a free market economy. A vast number of enterprises are publicly traded, and there is broad participation in the capital market. Companies are subject to the oversight of the stock market. And it's anticipated that shareholders who elect directors would be protected by the law and regulatory bodies. In terms of leadership, management, and advocacy, the board of directors is in charge. The day-to-day operations of a firm are overseen and directed by managers nominated by the board of directors. The influence of institutional investors (pension funds, mutual funds, insurance companies, etc.) on corporations is growing.

2. Corporate governance based on the "insider model" is common in countries like Germany, Japan, etc.

The German model is used in Germany, Switzerland, Australia, and the Netherlands. As a result, you may also hear this referred to as the "Continental Europe Model." Here are some of the hallmarks of the German model:

Because of limitations on company listings, debt is the primary source of financing in countries with a weak stock market.

i. In contrast to the free market, this system prioritizes banking institutions. A universal bank is a financial institution that offers both loans and equity.
Cross holdings and concentrated bank holdings are not publicly traded. Therefore, there is less of an established and liquid stock market. The stock market has little influence on corporations.

ii. Cross-shareholdings and concentrated ownership: big shareholders control the majority of German corporations. Franks and Mayer state that in more than half of the publicly traded corporations, a single person controls more than 50% of the voting stock. The common practice of cross holding results in pyramids of ownership. A small number of very powerful stockholders keep the company in their hands. Voting pacts, including capped voting systems and those with multiple votes, are also formed by block holders. The bank may even use its veto.

iii. A dual class share structure in which one class of shares has more voting rights than the other. This means that the concept of one share equals one vote cannot be used.

iv. Two Separate Boards: Every public limited company (AG) and private limited company (GmbH) with more than 500 workers has both an executive board (vorstand) and a supervisory board (Aufsichts crat). Executives with permanent positions are chosen by the board of directors. The executive board's decisions and actions are approved by the supervisory board, which is chosen by shareholders and workers. A place on the bank's board of directors is on offer to those who work there.

v. Employee Involvement In German corporations, workers elect between a third and half of the supervisory board's members. Other than the management team, the board of directors is made up of professional advisors, bank representatives, and representatives from companies with whom the company does business.

Thus, the main characteristics of the German model include concentrated ownership, cross shareholding, bank financing, a two-tiered board structure, a weak capital market, no legal protection for investors, and a lack of transparency.

The institutional incentives to make judgments in the near term are reduced under the German model, allowing for strategic planning over longer time periods. This approach prioritizes interactions between people. It's a way for workers to have a voice in the workplace. The needs of individual investors are ignored by this paradigm. Due to its lack of transparency, this paradigm is unfit for the international financial system.

3.   Modeled after Japan

Features that distinguish the Japanese approach to corporate governance include:

i.   Few Big Players (Keiretsu): The number of big players is rather low. Cross-shareholdings and business ties connect these corporations (like Mitsubishi and Mitsui). By virtue of their assets, most of these conglomerates are both horizontally and vertically diversified.

ii.   Consortium Financing: Banks and other financial institutions are the primary providers of capital for Japanese businesses. They're a source of financing for both debt and equity. There is one primary financial institution at their helm. Long-term relationships are formed between banks and their client firms, and the banks own a majority of the shares.

iii. Government-Industry Connections Many of these corporations hire former government officials, and they collaborate on government-backed boards. Appointing former government officials to boards of directors has become a common tactic for gaining special favors from authorities. These bureaucrats also ensure effective implementation of government policies. The government plays a dominant role of supervision and control over corporate activities.

iv.   Employee Participation Long serving and committed employees are offered membership on the board of directors. Senior managers and former employees account for 90 per cent of the company directors.

v.   Unitary Board Structure :Boards of major corporations represent the company as an integrated social unit. The entire board takes all major decisions of the company. In theory, the ultimate power to oversee the company's functioning lies with the board of directors. As a matter of custom, however, the board of directors typically cedes most of its power to the company president. The president and an operational committee made up of other high-ranking executives are responsible for vetting prospective board members and assessing the company's progress.

Thus, the main characteristics of the Japanese model are a high level of long-term company bank relationships, a high level of stock ownership by banks' cross holdings, a board of directors controlled by insiders, employee representation, retired government officers' board members, and emergency intervention by the main bank. This multifaceted model stands for a method of corporate governance that prioritizes trust and strong interpersonal connections.

Employees' long-term dedication to a firm is fostered through their involvement in corporate governance, as is the case in the Japanese Model. As opposed to the shareholder-centric Anglo-Saxon model, this one aims to keep everyone happy.

4. PRINCIPLES THAT ARE BASED ON THE FAMILY SYSTEM

Several developing and growing East Asian nations use a family-based style of business governance (India, Korea, Malaysia, Middle East, Brazil, Mexico, Chile, Turkey, Egypt, Kuwait, Saudi Arabia, UAE, etc). Some prominent features of this model include:

i.   Closely Held Companies: In most of the listed companies, the promoter's family is a dominant shareholder accounting for more than 50 per cent of the issued share capital. The founder, his relatives and associates dominate. The federal or state government is typically the largest stockholder in a public company. The company has been in the family for generations, and control has been passed down through the generations.

ii.   As a result of their ownership stakes and the web of interlocking directorships that binds them together, the family has absolute power over the company. Business families are held in high esteem, the regulatory framework is weak and outside shareholders have apathy. Banks and financial institutions provide considerable finance to family owned and managed companies. But they do not exercise much control. Their nominees on the board of directors of the borrowing company generally support the family control.

iii. Family Interest: The company is run primarily for the benefit of the family. Owners extract private gain by transfer of wealth through sale of assets at lower than market prices. Funds are sometimes diverted for family's interest. It's not uncommon for the interests of the controlling family and those of the minority shareholders to be at odds. Managers act primarily for the controlling family. Family based model fills the monitoring gap of market mechanism because the family exercises an effective control. It is driven by long term interest of creating wealth for the family. But the model expropriates the minority interest. Tensions within the controlling family may hamper the functioning and performance of companies. Corporate governance practices are not very sound and effective.

The family-based model of corporate governance is changing due to globalization and liberalization. Internationalisation of capital markets, global competition, increasing role of financial institutions, tightening of regulatory framework are the major forces due to which companies in developing countries are improving their corporate governance practices. For example, Indian companies which want to raise capital abroad and get listed on foreign stock exchanges are adopting international standards concerning accounting and public disclosure.

This safeguards against promoters using their influence on independent directors to further their own agendas. The current "government-approach-based regime," which is seen as restrictive and limits entrepreneurial growth, will be replaced by a more relaxed system that encourages self-regulation through increased levels of disclosure. India's business law environment would become more modern with the recognition of new forms of organization like the "one person-company" and "small company" concepts. Intercompany loans are governed by the Act as well. Independent directors must make up at least one-third of a company's board, as required by the Act.

a) To put it simply, corporate governance is the framework of norms, procedures, and legislation that governs the management and operations of a corporation. In this sense, it describes the structure of authority inside a company. It is a method used for guiding and managing businesses.

b) The scope of having corporate governance is: Accountability, Fairness, Transparency, Independence, Compliance with rules.

c) The goal of corporate governance is to make your business more accountable and less vulnerable to catastrophic failures. It is felt that objective of corporate governance, i.e. the overall objective of wealth generation and competitiveness for the benefit of all can best be achieved.

d) The commitment level of individual board members, the quality of corporate reporting, the amount of stakeholder engagement, and the integrity of the management all play a role in determining the governance quality.

e) There are 4 main principles of corporate governance which include: Fairness, Responsibility, Transparency, Accountability.

f) 4P's of Corporate governance are : People, Purpose, Process & Performance.

g) Good corporate governance provide many benefits to business, shareholders, invertors etc.

h) In response to the fluctuating difficulties inherent in managing businesses, several theories of corporate governance have been developed. Theories are: Agency Theory, Stewardship Theory, Stakeholders theory, Resource Dependency Theory, Transaction Cost Theory, Political Theory.

There are different corporate governance models: The Anglo-Saxon Model (The Outsider Model), The Insider Model, German Model, Japanese Model, The Family Based Model.

E-governance, expands to electronic governance, is the integration of Information and Communication Technology (ICT) in all the processes, with the aim of enhancing government ability to address the needs of the general public. The basic purpose of e- governance is to simplify processes for all, i.e. government, citizens, businesses, etc. at National, State and local levels.

In short, it is the use of electronic means, to promote good governance. It connotes the implementation of information technology in the government processes and functions so as to

cause simple, moral, accountable and transparent governance. It entails the access and delivery of government services, dissemination of information, communication in a quick and efficient manner.

IMPORTANCE OF E GOVERNANCE

1. Information delivery is greatly simplified for citizens and businesses.

2. It gives varied departments' information to the public and helps in decision making.

3. It ensures citizen participation at all levels of governance.

4. It leads to automated services so that all works of public welfare is available to all citizens.

5. It revolutionizes the functions of the government and ensures transparency.

6. Each department and its actions is closely monitored.

7. Public can get their work smartly done and save their time.

8. It provides better services to citizens and brings government close to public. Public can be in touch with the government agency.

9. It cuts middlemen and bribery if any from the picture.

ADVANTAGES OF E-GOVERNANCE

1. **Speed:** Technology makes communication swifter. Internet, smartphones have enables instant transmission of high volumes of data all over the world.

2. **Saving Costs:** A lot the Government expenditure goes towards the cost of buying stationery for official purposes. Letters and written records consume a lot of stationery. However, replacing them with smartphones and the internet can save crores of money in expenses every year.

3. **Transparency:** The use of e-governance helps make all functions of the business transparent. All Governmental information can be uploaded onto the internet. The citizens access specifically access whichever information they want, whenever they want it, at the click of a mouse, or the touch of a finger.

   However, for this to work the Government has to ensure that all data as to be made public and uploaded to the Government information forums on the internet.

4. **Accountability:** Transparency directly links to accountability. Once the functions of the government are available, we can hold them accountable for their actions.

   Through e-governance, the government plans to raise the coverage and quality of information and services provided to the general public, by the use of ICT in an easy, economical and effective manner. The process is extremely complicated which requires, the proper arrangement of hardware, software, networking and indeed re-engineering of all the processes to facilitate better delivery of services.

TYPES OF INTERACTIONS IN E-GOVERNANCE

1. **G2G (Government to Government):** When the exchange of information and services is within the periphery of the government, is termed as G2G interaction. This can be both horizontal, i.e., among various government entities and vertical, i.e ., between national, state and local government entities and within different levels of the entity.

2. **G2C (Government to Citizen):** The interaction amidst the government and general public is G2C interaction. Here an interface is set up between government and citizens, which enables citizens to get access to wide variety of public services. The citizens has the freedom to share their views and grievances on government policies anytime, anywhere.

3. **G2B (Government to Business):** In this case, the e-governance helps the business class to interact with the government seamlessly. It aims at eliminating red-tapism, saving time, cost and establish transparency in the business environment, while interacting with government.

4. **G2E (Government to Employees):** The government of any country is the biggest employer and so it also deals with employees on a regular basis, as other employers do. ICT helps in making the interaction between government and employees fast and efficient, along with raising their level of satisfaction by providing perquisites and add-on benefits.

Thus, E-governance can only be possible if the government is ready for it. It is not a one day task, and so the government has to make plans and implement them before switching to it. Some of the measures include Investment in telecommunication infrastructure, budget resources, ensure security, monitor assessment, internet connectivity speed, promote awareness among public regarding the importance, support from all government departments and so forth. It has a great role to play, that improves and supports all tasks performed by the government department and agencies, because it simplifies the task on the one hand and increases the quality of work on the other.

DISADVANTAGES OF E-GOVERNANCE

1. **Loss of Interpersonal Communication:** The main disadvantage of e-governance is the loss of interpersonal communication. Interpersonal communication is an aspect of communication that many people consider vital.

2. **High Setup Cost and Technical Difficulties:** Technology has its disadvantages as well. Specifically, the setup cost is very high and the machines have to be regularly maintained. Often, computers and internet can also break down and put a dent in governmental work and services.

3. **Illiteracy:** A large number of people in India are illiterate and do not know how to operate computers and smartphones. E-governance is very difficult for them to access and understand.

4. **Cybercrime/Leakage of Personal Information:** There is always the risk of private data of citizens stored in government serves being stolen. Cybercrime is a serious issue; a breach of data can make the public lose confidence in the Government's ability to govern the people.

5. **Speed:** Technology makes communication swifter. Moreover, internet, smartphones have enables instant transmission of high volumes of data all over the world.

6. **Saving Costs:** A lot the Government expenditure goes towards the cost of buying stationary specifically for official purposes. Letters and written records consume a lot of stationaries. However, replacing them with smartphones and internet can saves crores of money in expenses every year.

7. **Transparency:** In addition to saving cost, use of e-governance helps make all functions of the business transparent. All Governmental information will be uploaded onto the internet. The citizens access whichever information they want, whenever they want it, at the click of a mouse, or the touch of a finger. However, for this to work the Government has to ensure that all data as to be made public and uploaded to the Government information forums on the internet. Thus, it is not possible to withhold uploaded information.

8. **Accountability:** Transparency thus directly links to accountability. Once we have visibility over functions of the government are available, we can hold them accountable for their actions.

9. **Technical:** There are technical problems in implementing **e-governance transformation**. Information and Communication Technology infrastructure is the main challenge for Electronic governance transformation. Architecture should be in place to provide a uniform set of guiding principles models and standards. Governments must build an effective telecommunication infrastructure.

10. **Privacy:** Privacy and security of confidential reports is the main problem. There are concerns about hacking defence information and other data, tracking the website, mismanagement of private information are big challenges.

11. **Security:** Security of information and systems against disclosure or destruction of data is one of the main concerns. It includes the security of documents and network security. Maintenance and E-infrastructure should be protected in the form of firewalls and data accessibility should be limited. The security technology like encryption and digital signatures should be used to protect user IDs, credit card numbers, passwords, and other data.

12. **Lack of Training and Qualified Personnel:** Lack of digital skills is one of the main challenges in developing countries. Appointing and training the personnel to acquire appropriate

technical and functional skills is very much essential for governance to be successful.

13. **Digital Availability:** Accessing the internet might be a challenge. Since there is a lack of internet skills and internet availability, all citizens cannot access the internet. Lack of computer literacy is one of the main challenges.

Digital Transformation of **e-governance** has the potential to administrate systematically. It is an instrument to run a government for its citizens. The services can be provided to citizens on time and on demand. The criminal cases register1ed in police stations cannot be manipulated if the files are digital. **Digital transformation in the public sector** will be a boon to the country if it is successful.

GREEN GOVERNANCE
MEANING

Environmental problems caused by human behaviour have become increasingly serious in recent decades, thereby driving global green governance issue to become an important research agenda. The proper governance structure design and governance mechanism arrangement can effectively coordinate the relationship between human and nature. Open innovation activities can effectively deal with the externalities of resources and environment and then relatively balance the economic value and green value of organizations, which is an effective green governance mode, reflecting the characteristics of the main subject composition and mechanism operation of green governance.

Green governance is a systematic approach to help organisations work in environment friendly manner and to strive towards sustainable development. Environmental regulation is increasing rapidly around the world. Therefore, business and other organisations have to efficiently track and manage their green efforts. They want to improve the bottom line through more efficient use of energy and other natural resources.

Auditing and Corporate Governance

Green governance requires organisations to:

(i)   Clearly articulate a strategy with well defined goals concerning green economy.

(ii)   Understand the risks involved in meeting the goals and objectives.

(iii) Comply with both prescribed regulations and the internal policies.

(iv)   Solicit ideas from key stakeholders on what can be done to meet the defined objectives and goals.

(v)   Evaluate comprehensively the portfolio of possible initiatives.

(vi)   Focus on effective and efficient implementation of chosen initiatives.

SEVEN STEPS FOR TRANSITION

Rula Qalyoub has suggested seven practical steps for transition to green economy, these are:

Political Commitment: Political commitment to the green growth path presupposes that fiscal and monetary tools are used to steer economies away from business-as- usual. This would include investing in research and development (R&D), demonstration, deployment and the commercialisation of different renewable technologies in production and consumption activities. For example, in the wake of the 1990s financial crises both Finland and Korea made stategic moves to increase R &D funding for renewables while scaling back on other public expenditures coupled with phasing out fuel subsidies. Currently, Finland and Korea have the competitive advantage in innovative technologies in renewable energies. Korea's New Green Deal established 17 new growth ventures and supported funds to research potential alternative energies.

Legal and Regulatory Framework: If decisions and policies are not anchored in a binding and enforceable framework, they become merely olrnamental in nature. While we do not need to green all regulatory systems concurrently in order to respond to climate change challenges, legal standards must be assessed in a systematic approach. Legal reform require revisiting existing laws and tuning their jurisdictions through amendments and directives. In some areas, this may require energizing the legal stand by conducting gap analysis, which entails comparing current environmental laws and procedures with international best practices in order to assess the current incentive

system. The model of Kalundborg in Denmark demonstrates that wise planning can generate income and economic growth without adding environmental pressures. This distinctive example of using wastes from certain manufacturing operations as raw materials for industry was the result of coordinated efforts and a sustainability mindset in action.

Financial Instruments: Policy makers backed by a regulatory body have the power to initiate a paradigm shift using three simultaneous measures. Firstly, putting proper mechanisms in place to prevent natural resource use and abuse. This entails reevaluation of the two types of resource usage, one being resource-use intensity and the other the depletion of natural stock. Secondly, government bodies need to reevaluate subsidy provisions and redirect funds towards ventures that provide permanent solutions to energy security issues. Finally, to reduce the financial risks associated with provate green investment the government should boost their R & D support, providing stimulus packages aimed at increasing the efficiencies of existing systems and supporting the development and demonstration stages of the renewable energy agenda.

Technology Viability: Even with financial instruments in place, the choice of renewable technologies may prove to be a significant chalenge. There are three steps by which choices in technology can be tested, the first of which is to use public funds to support working groups to debate the type of renewable technology most suited to current geopolitical and climatic conditions. The criterion of technology debates must be in line with technology suitability in order to meet the designated goal and to avoid duplications of efforts. Secondly, government funding for frequent sensitivity analysis will enable a clear vision of all options regarding renewable technologies. Thirdly, governments should champion resource-gap assessments. Such dialogues promote stakeholders to participate in finding solutions by acknowledging resource gap difficulties. This gap analysis should be sponsored by different government bodies in coordination with practitioners, research groups and venture capitalists at the national and local levels.

Human Capital Formation: Investments into human capital is a crucial expenditure that should not be compromised and as part of public funding ought to enhance the know-what, know-how and the know-why. Education, vocational training and research are extremely vulnerable areas during economic downtuirns. During recessions, governmental bodies (at both local and national levels) exercise greater budgetary discretion and often downsize publicly funded activities such as education and training. Stripping educational budgets reduces the value of human capital that could otherwise help to stimulate the economy out of recession. It is during economic downturns that education and other human capital building vehicles need extra support to fund training and facilitate the formation of a cadre that fits the new green ideal. Lessons can be learned from Finland where during the economic crisis in the early 1990s, the government made a commitment to avoid cuts on essential services favoring R & D and educational institutions. Finland experienced a quick recovery from recession with a world-class educational system and highly skilled workforce.

Institutional setup: Institutional adjustments are required which will adopt and adapt ot innovative solutions, otherwise institutions will face "creative destruction" through inaction. The Village Council of Wild poldsried in Bavaria, Germany, passes a local green initiative in 1997 with modest goals to attract new industries and to bring in new revenue. The council equipped new installations with solar panels, built biogas digesters and installed seven windmills. Today the villages sell power back to the national grid generating 321 percent more energy than it requires. This far, returns on this investment have amounted to US$5.7 million for 2,600 villages (though the proportion of initial public investment is hard to tell).

Common language: Common language entails the standardizations of targets, benchmarks, indicators and measurement units and methods. Moreover, common language is about a unified code of practices, streamlined green accreditation of products and services, and consistent decision making processes on green issues across government. This is an important criterion as it eliminates the ambiguities and doubts associated with an emerging breed of buzz words which quickly become redundant and which government officials frequently need to relearn. Choice of target thresholds and indices may be important in order to establish a benchmark comparison but ought to be used with caution. By and large, instruments ought to be modified by region and reflect local environmental circumstances. This may require some trial and error but more importantly requires having the necessary human capital base to provide knowledge both of local conditions and on the availability and viability of tools.

LEGAL PROVISIONS RELATING TO GREEN GOVERNANCE IN INDIA

The Department of Commercial Affairs (MCA) provides the legal framework for companies to support sustainable development and, through the amendment of the Indian Companies Act of 1956 in 2013, has made arrangements for initiatives respectful of the environment. Now the law is known as the Indian Companies Act, 2013

Legal provisions related to green initiatives The Corporate Affairs department is important to all its stakeholders, including:

- More than a million companies are incorporated under the Companies Act of 1956 or 2013.

- 28,000 companies are covered by LLP (Limited Liability Partnership).
- CA (auditor)
- CS (company secretariat)

From 2008, MCA will become the electronic administrative portal of the Ministry of Enterprise.

A. Electronic submission Under Annual electronic filing, companies registered under the Companies Act of 1956 must file electronically the following documents to the ROC :

- P&L A/C FROM XXIII ACA Income Tax Return Report to be Filed by All Businesses
- Annually 20B Form to submit declaration form by capital companies
- Annually the declaration form 21A must be submitted by companies without share capital Certificate must be submitted [from companies selling Rs. Have deposited 10 lakh capital at Rs. 5 crore.

B. Registration of companies Companies can register via the MCA portal. It is also set up for, Registration of companies under Section 8 of Companies Act and foreign companies.

C. Digital signature ,certificate Services The Information Technology (IT) Act 2000 contains certain mandatory provisions for the application of digital signatures to documents submitted in electronic form to confirm the security and accuracy of the documents submitted electronically. This is a safe and accurate way to^submit a document electronically. Just as such Business LLP advice under the MCA21 Electronic Governance program submitted by the person authorized to sign the documents with digital signatures.

D. Corporate Sewa Kendra For any problem related to Companies can contact Corporate Sewa Kendras to consult business creations, electronic filing and public documents. A single DIN cell for questions about the DIN also arise.

E. Business data to be managed electronically Form Any publicly traded company or company with no less than 1000 shareholders, obligation Holders and other holders of securities manage their administration electronically (form.16)

F. Postal voting A company makes decisions by correspondence only for matters announced by central government. In a postal vote, voting takes place within 30 days after sending by post or electronically.

G.   Dividend payment Section 123 of the new law states that a cash dividend can be paid by: check or money order or. electronically to the shareholder who is authorized to pay the dividend.

H.   Transfer of decisions in circulation: Section 175 of the 2013 Law provides that "it is to be assumed that a decision by the Board of Directors has only been taken in a circular procedure if it is included in the project, through the accompanying documents, by manual delivery or by post or by post or electronically can contain email or fax."

I.   Electronic voting Every listed company or a company with no less than 1,000 shareholders offers him convenience Members must grant GM their voting rights electronically. A member is authorized grants each CEO the right to vote electronically and the company can confirm any decision (regular / special) regarding an electronic voting system.

J.   Meeting notification "A report of every rejection, messages and subsequent returns are made by or on behalf of Company as proof of delivery. The company is not responsible for defects in communication beyond their control. If the member does not provide an updated email, address, the company is not in default. Meeting announcement: A company can bet Summons via electronic mode. A message can be sent by e-mail text or attached to an email or as an electronic link or URL statement to access this notification when posted on the company website. Can be electronic mode any communication from a company through her secure computer program that is authorized to store the acceptance and document of such communication with the copyright holder communication to the last email address provided by the member. The meeting is convened through distribution report at least 7 days, this can be done electronically. General meeting; can be electronically stored in the prescribed manner for at least 21 days.

(A)   Document delivery: A document can be delivered on an electronic company.

(B)   Inspection and copies of documents in electronic form: The company examines documents in electronic form or provides copies of these documents

Indian law provisions on CSR are scattered across legislations in different areas and need to be collated under a single umbrella for corporates to be able to develop a systemic or institutional approach to CSR and their responsibilities to stakeholders. With some additional policy input and legislative changes, the existing corporate governance legal system can provide the enabling environment for improved Green Governance integration by corporates within their business. Within the field of board responsibilities towards stakeholders, the scattered provisions on board responsibility towards certain stakeholders, as well as the liability of directors for a company's non-compliance with environmental and labour laws make it clear that Indian law intended for the board to be responsible, at least to certain stakeholders. However, what is missing is legal or regulatory guidance regarding a comprehensive approach towards stakeholders, which includes philanthropic initiatives.

CLASS ACTION SUITS UNDER THE COMPANIES ACT 2013

In a class action suit, a large group of people, having same or similar injuries caused by the same person, collectively bring a claim to court, represented by one or more persons. This form of lawsuit is also called a Representative Action. One set of persons representing a larger group approach the court for redressal of their grievances.

The rationale behind such suits are – firstly to protect the interest of members of a class who are geographically dispersed and secondly to reduce the duplication of the litigation as it combines the various proceedings initiated in different parts/jurisdiction bearing same cause of action(s).

Further it also makes adjudication possible; otherwise as per the rule of necessary party all the members of a class are required to be made plaintiff, which otherwise would have made the adjudication impossible.

In January 2009, India witnessed one of its biggest corporate scandals – the 'Satyam scandal' also referred to as 'India's Enron'. Satyam Computers Services Limited (''SCSL'') was under the microscope for fraudulent activity and misrepresentation of its accounts to its board, stock exchanges, regulators, investors and all other stakeholders. Thereafter, shareholders of SCSL, approximately 300,000 were unsuccessful in claiming damages worth millions due to the absence of the provision for filing a class action suit under the Companies Act, 1956. American investors on the other hand were able to claim their part of damages in the US Courts through a class action suit against SCSL.

The concept of class action was first introduced in the US in the year 1938. 'Class Action', which is also known as 'Representative Action', is actually a form of lawsuit where a large group of people collectively brings a claim to the court through a representative. A class action suit is filed generally when a number of people have suffered the same or similar injuries. Often many of the individuals' injuries are relatively minor, such that they might not pursue legal redress on their own. Together, however, the value of the claims of the class add up, and claiming as a class helps consolidate the attorneys, evidence, witnesses, and most other aspects of the litigation.

CLASS ACTION SUITS UNDER VARIOUS LAWS 8.3.2a Class Action suits under Companies Act, 2013:

1. A suit can be filed or any other action may be taken by any person, group of persons or any association of persons affected by any misleading statement or the inclusion or omission of any matter in the prospectus under the following provisions of the Act. (Section 37)

Section 34 – Criminal Liability for misstatements in prospectus Section 35 – Civil Liability for misstatements in a prospectus Section 36 – Punishment for fraudulently inducing persons to invest money.

2. A class action suit can be filed by members or depositors of the company or any class of them if they are of the opinion that the affairs of the company are being conducted in a manner prejudicial to the interest of the company or members or depositors. (Section 245)

3. **Class Action suits under Code of Civil Procedure:**
   There are no limits on the subject matter except for actions that cannot be filed in the civil courts at all, such as mismanagement suits. All persons having same interest in the suit can make an application for the class action suit.

Class Action suits under Competition Act:

A class may dispute an agreement which causes an appreciable adverse effect on competition within India or abuse of dominant position by an enterprise. Any person, consumer or their association can bring the action. E.g. Price Fixing Class Action suits under Consumer Protection Act: The suit under this Act is restricted to disputes relating to goods and services sold/provided or delivered or agreed to be sold/provided or delivered. Consumers of the goods or services aggrieved can bring the action under this Act.

ADVANTAGES OF CLASS ACTION SUITS

1. **Clubbing of similar applications and bar on futile litigations:**
   When the facts are similar in suits filed in different dominions by the members of the same class, standing against the same or

similar defendants, it makes sense to combine them all and adjudicate it under one roof. Clubbing of similar claims/suits would also result in efficiency of judiciary, as the same would save precious time of judiciary from adjudicating the similar dispute numerous times. Hence Class Action Suits against similar defendants/respondents seeking similar relief may be consolidated into one. Further the legislature also intends to bar the future class action on same subject matter.

2. **Reduction of Cost:** The cost of bringing a claim to the settlement under the present mechanism at times is very expensive as well as time consuming particularly while filing of suits under Civil Procedure Code, 1908. Further the territorial jurisdiction of the civil court also leads to duplicity of litigation leading to multiplicity of cost for same cause of action. It therefore makes far greater sense for people to share the costs of litigation by teaming up with others in a similar position. If as a group, only one set of counsels are instructed and the factual cases of each member are identical the legal cost will be far less than that would have been if instituted individually.

3. Class action suits would allow individuals to hold some of the world's most powerful companies and organizations accountable for their actions. These lawsuits will cover a wide range of issues including the mismanagement of monies invested with a company, securities law related fraud, malfunctioning of accounts, restraining company to act ultra vires or in breach of the articles of association of the Company, etc.

4. Class action suits will provide a window to the small shareholders to redress their grievances irrespective of their jurisdictional limitation.

ELIGIBLE ENTITIES ACCORDING TO THE COMPANY'S ACT, 2013

A class action suit can be filed against following persons to claim damages or compensation or demand any other suitable action from or against:

➢ the company or its directors for any fraudulent, unlawful or wrongful act or omission.

➢ the auditor/audit firm for any improper or misleading statement made in audit report or for any fraudulent, unlawful or wrongful act or conduct.

> any expert or advisor or consultant or any other person for any incorrect or misleading statement made to the company or for any fraudulent, unlawful or wrongful act or conduct or any likely act or conduct on his part.

RELIEFS UNDER CLASS ACTION SUITS

Following orders can be sought from Tribunal by Members/Depositors:

(A)   To restrain the Company from:

> committing an act which is ultra vires to Memorandum of Association (MOA) or Articles of Association (AOA)

> committing breach of any provision of MOA or AOA

> acting on resolution which is void (due to suppression of facts/misstatements)

> doing an act which is contrary to the provisions of this Act or any other Act

> taking action contrary to any resolution passed by the members.

(B)   To claim damages or compensation or demand any other suitable action from or against:

> the company or its directors

> the auditor/audit firm for any improper or misleading statement made in audit report or for any fraudulent, unlawful or wrongful act or conduct

> any expert or advisor or consultant or any other person for any incorrect or misleading statement made to the company or for any fraudulent, unlawful or wrongful act or conduct or any likely act or conduct on his part;

(C)   To declare a resolution altering the memorandum or articles of the company as void if the resolution was passed by suppression of material facts or obtained by mis-statement to the members or depositors

(D)   To seek any other remedy as the Tribunal may deem fit.

CONSIDERATION BY TRIBUNAL

Section 245(4) provides that in considering an application under sub-section (1), the Tribunal shall take into account, in particular—

(a)   whether the member or depositor is acting in good faith in making the application for seeking an order;

(b)   any evidence before it as to the involvement of any person other than directors or officers of the company on any of the matters provided in this section;

(c)   whether the cause of action is one which the member or depositor could pursue in his own right rather than through an order under this section;

(d)   any evidence before it as to the views of the members or depositors of the company who have no personal interest, direct or indirect, in the matter being proceeded under this section;

(e)   where the cause of action is an act or omission that is yet to occur, whether the act or omission could be, and in the circumstances would be likely to be – authorised by the company before it occurs or ratified by the company after it occurs;

(f)   where the cause of action is an act or omission that has already occurred, whether the act or omission could be, and in the circumstances would be likely to be, ratified by the company.

PUNISHMENT FOR NON-COMPLIANCE OF TRIBUNAL'S ORDERS

Any Order passed by the Tribunal shall be binding on the Company, Members, Depositors, Directors, Auditors, Experts, Consultant, Advisors or any other person. [Section 245(6)]. In case the company or any officer who is in default does a non-compliance of any order passed by the Tribunal under section 245, then the fine/ punishment is as follows [Section 245(7)]:

➢   Company: Fine ` 5,00,000 to ` 25,00,000

➢   Officer in Default: Imprisonment up to 3 years and fine ` 25,000 to ` 1,00,000

REQUIRED MEMBERS FOR APPLYING ACTION CLASS SUITS

(A)   Members:

➢   Company having Share Capital: at least 5% of total number of members or 100 members whichever is less. (Listed or Unlisted)

➢   Unlisted Company: member or members holding not less than five per cent (5%) of the issued share capital.

➢   Listed Company: member or members holding not less than two per cent (2%) of the issued share capital.

➢   Company having not Share Capital: at least 1/5th of total number of members.

(B)   Depositors:

At least five per cent (5%) of the total number of depositors of the company or one hundred

(100) depositors of the company.

Depositor or depositors to whom the company owes five per cent of total deposits of the company.

PROCEDURE AFTER THE ADMISSION OF APPLICATION U/S 245(5)

In case of admission of Application [Section 245(5)]

- ➢ public notice shall be served on admission of the application to all the members or depositors
- ➢ all similar applications prevalent in any jurisdiction should be consolidated into a single application
- ➢ the class members or depositors should be allowed to choose the lead applicant
- ➢ the Tribunal shall have the power to appoint a lead applicant, who shall be in charge of the proceedings (If members/ depositors can't decide)
- ➢ two class action applications for the same cause of action shall not be allowed
- ➢ the cost or expenses connected with the application for class action shall be defrayed by the company or any other person responsible for any oppressive act.

"Activism" represents a range of activities by one or more of a publicly traded corporation's shareholders that are intended to result in some change in the corporation. The activities fall along a spectrum based on the significance of the desired change and the assertiveness of the investors' activities. On the more aggressive end of the spectrum is hedge fund activism that seeks a significant change to the company's strategy, financial structure, management, or board.

USE OF SHAREHOLDER ACTIVISM

Shareholder activism involves the efforts of the shareholders to bring about a desired change in the operations of the company or to influence the management in governing the company to protect the interest of the shareholders.

1. In India, the Companies Act 2013 is the main source of law relating to shareholder activism. In addition to the Act, regulations framed by the Securities and Exchange Board of India (SEBI) also provide rights and remedies to the shareholders of listed companies. With the enactment of the Companies Act and subsequent developments, the law has been updated to further facilitate shareholder activism.

2. Under the Companies Act 2013, shareholders' approval is required for dealing in certain matters. Shareholders can bring a

class action suit against the company, its directors and third-party advisers. They can sue against oppression and mismanagement, and to exit in certain specified circumstances.

3. The regulations framed by SEBI provide many additional rights and remedies to shareholders of listed companies to make their views known and to protect their interests more actively. Listed companies must constitute a stakeholders' relationship committee to provide a mechanism for redressal of shareholder grievances and to provide electronic voting facilities.

4. Proxy Advisory Firms (PAFs) regulated by Securities and Exchange Board of India (Research Analysts) Regulations 2014 have massively contributed to shareholder activism. A proxy advisor is any person who provides advice through any means to an institutional investor or shareholder of a company on how to exercise their rights in the company (including recommendations on a public offer or voting recommendations on agenda items). Recommendations by PAFs have proved to be influential in determining the voting pattern of shareholders.

5. The recent developments in Indian law have led to (among other things) increased corporate governance standards, creation of new shareholder remedies and improvement in shareholders' rights. Due to the ease of exercising, and enforcement of shareholders' rights, shareholders are now more willing to voice their opinion, resulting in increased shareholder activism.

6. Regulation of Shareholder Activism

7. The following rights (among others) are relevant to shareholder activism under the laws of India:

8. Right to receive information. Shareholders are entitled to receive information and documents such as:

9. annual return extracts;

10. audited financial statements along with an auditor's report; and

11. statutory registers maintained by the company (such as the register of members, debenture-holders, directors and key managerial personnel).

12. Right to give approval. A company is managed by the board, but the Companies Act 2013 restricts the powers of the board to an extent and certain important matters require the consent of the shareholders. Their approval can be obtained either by a simple majority or special majority, as prescribed under the Companies Act 2013. These include amending the company's memorandum of association or articles of association, appointing and removing directors, and obtaining loans and sale of undertakings above

certain thresholds. Shareholders have used this voting right as a tool to defeat resolutions they want to oppose.

13. The requirement of shareholder approval ensures active shareholder involvement in matters that are critical to the company. In public companies, shareholder approval is required by a special majority for matters or transactions, including:

14. Sale or lease of a company's whole or substantially whole undertakings;

15. Investment of compensation received as a result of any merger or amalgamation; and

16. Entering into related party transactions (RPT) over a certain threshold.

In some situations, the minority shareholders are strongly placed. In 2018, a public listed company proposed three RPT for shareholder consideration at its annual general meeting. All resolutions were defeated with a minor percentage of total shareholding opposing it, as interested shareholders of a public company are not permitted to vote on RPT resolutions. Material RPT's require shareholder approval and a related party cannot vote to approve these resolutions whether the entity is a related party to the particular transaction or not (*Securities and Exchange Board of India (Listing Obligations and Disclosure Requirements) Regulations 2015*).

1. **Right to appoint and remove directors.** The directors of a company are appointed by its shareholders. Independent directors appointed by listed companies and specific public companies are required to be approved by shareholders in a general meeting before they are appointed. In addition, small shareholders holding shares of not more than INR20,000 in value can propose the appointment of a director on the board of a listed company subject to certain terms and conditions. This way small shareholders can seek board representation.

In August 2017, a long standing pharmaceutical company received a proposal from over 1,000 small shareholders under a portfolio manager. They sought the appointment of a small shareholder director. However, the board successfully resisted the appointment of the director due to a conflict of interest.

Shareholders can remove a director before his/her term has expired by a simple majority in the manner prescribed under the Companies Act 2013. However, such a right will not be available in cases where the director has been appointed by the National Company Law Tribunal (Tribunal) or the company has opted for appointment of director basis proportional representation. Further, an independent director re-appointed for a second term can be removed by the company only by passing a special resolution and after giving him or her a reasonable opportunity of being heard.

In May 2018, the shareholders of a leading healthcare company voted by a majority to oust the director of that company.

2. **Right to appoint auditor.** The auditor is appointed by the shareholders in an annual general meeting at the recommendation of the board or the audit committee. This appointment is for a five-year period.

3. **Right to requisition a meeting.** Shareholders can requisition the directors to convene an extraordinary general meeting for consideration of company matters and for voicing their opinion. If the directors fail to convene an extraordinary general meeting, the requisitions shareholders can call a meeting on their own. The minimum threshold for calling such a meeting is 10% of the shareholders with voting rights in the company.

4. **Right to electronic voting.** Shareholders can benefit from the electronic voting facility as every listed company or a company having at least 1,000 members must have an electronic voting facility at general meetings. Electronic voting has increased shareholder participation and eased the process of voting.

REMEDIES TO THE SHAREHOLDERS

Shareholders that have been wronged can use the following when seeking a remedy:

1. **Grievance redressal mechanisms.** A listed company or a company with more than 1,000 shareholders, debenture holders, deposit holders and any other security holders at any time during a financial year must have a Stakeholders Relationship Committee to resolve security holder grievances. Listed companies must also be registered on the SCORES platform (operated by the Securities and Exchange Board of India). SCORES enables investors to file complaints and track the status or redressal of these complaints. This is an example of the shareholders' right to have their grievances and concerns heard.

2. **Oppression and mismanagement proceedings.** A minimum of 100 or 10% of the total number of members (whichever is less), or any member or members holding at least 10% of the issued share capital of the company, can approach the Tribunal to initiate proceedings for oppression and/or mismanagement on

the ground that the company's affairs are being conducted in a manner prejudicial to the interest of the company or its members.

3. **Class action suits.** If the rights of any of the members are infringed or the conduct of the management is prejudicial to the interest of the company or its shareholders, the following can bring a class action suit against the company, its directors and third-party advisers:

- a minimum of 100 members or at least 5% of the total number of members (whichever is less); or
- any member or members holding at least 5% of the issued share capital in an unlisted company or at least 2% of the issued share capital in a listed company.

4. **Derivative actions.** A single shareholder, irrespective of his/her shareholding in the company, can also bring a derivative suit on behalf of the company challenging a board resolution if it was detrimental to the interest of the company. However, the shareholder must approach the court with "clean hands". The derivative action procedure is set out in the Code of Civil Procedure 1908.

5. **Application to the Serious Fraud Investigation Office (SFIO).** The shareholders by passing a special resolution can intimate to the Central Government that the affairs of the company are required to be investigated. The Central Government, on receiving such a request, can order the SFIO to investigate the affairs of the company.

GOALS OF SHAREHOLDER ACTIVISM

1. Financial reasons

a. Activist shareholders exercise their rights to improve and increase shareholder value. Through such activism, shareholders' activists aim to create value by acting as a positive catalyst in the growth of the company.

b. Such creation of value by shareholder activists was seen when a listed arm of a global conglomerate proposed to sell one business unit to another subsidiary of its parent. Since it was a related party transaction, the proposal required special majority of the shareholders of the parent and the subsidiaries. However, the proposal was rejected due to a low valuation. The revised proposal increased the valuation, to the benefit of the shareholders.

c. A shareholder can hold shares in the company for several years to ensure long term return from the investment made in the company. This can be achieved by ensuring that the focus of the management is to balance and maximise long term returns on the investment made by such shareholders. Activist shareholders aim to improve the performance of the company to maximise the return on their investment. This also encourages proper and efficient management to increase the company's value in the long term.

d. Activist shareholders encourage cost cutting to maximise profits by ensuring the resources of the company are being utilised in a just and prudent manner.

e. Shareholder's voice their opinions and concerns more often. For example, nearly, a quarter of the shareholders of a financial conglomerate voted against the continuance of its chairman. A proxy advisory firm advised investors to vote against the resolution to reappoint the non-executive chairman of the company, as that person was on the boards of eight other companies (which could prevent him from discharging his duties effectively).

f. Shareholder activism occurred in a large automobile company in India where some shareholders raised concerns about the purchase of automobiles by the company from a related party. Strong opposition by the activist shareholders forced the company to modify the terms of the contract to secure approval.

Also, in 2014, a proposal for payment of extraordinary remuneration to top executives of a listed Indian automobile manufacturer did not get majority approval of shareholders, forcing the company to continue its earlier remuneration structure and reduce costs.

2.   Non-financial reasons

Activist shareholder ensures a high level of shareholder participation in the decision-making of the company and direct engagement of the shareholders with the management. This has a positive impact on the outcome of corporate decisions of the company and therefore improves corporate governance.

Activist shareholders aim to enhance strategic and operational decisions of the company to improve business operations and to align the policies of the company with policies prevalent in the market.

STRATEGIES USED BY ACTIVIST SHAREHOLDERS

The strategies used by activist shareholders include the following:

1. Shareholders purchase shares with voting rights in the company to influence the decisions taken by the management and to

ensure active participation in the affairs of the company to the extent permitted under the Companies Act 2013.

2. The shareholders adopt the strategy of interacting with the board on a regular basis and providing strategic advice to the board which is for the benefit of the company and its members. Consistent interaction with the board creates awareness of shareholder concerns and helps the board to take well informed decisions board.

3. In companies which are required to have a Stakeholders Relationship Committee, the shareholders actively participate in such committee to voice their concerns and grievances.

4. If companies are not proactively addressing shareholder concerns, the shareholders make public announcements to voice their opinions.

5. Shareholders can requisition the directors to convene a meeting to consider company matters and to effect a particular change.

6. Approaching the National Company Law Tribunal to initiate proceedings for oppression and/or mismanagement on the ground that the company's affairs are being conducted in a manner prejudicial to the interest of the company or its members.

7. Class action suits.

8. Application to the Serious Fraud Investigation Office (SFIO).

9. The Securities and Exchange Board of India (SEBI) can initiate action *suo moto* or after a complaint by an aggrieved shareholder if governance norms for listed entities (prescribed by the SEBI) are breached.

SHAREHOLDER DISCLOSURES
Disclosure requirements

The Companies Act 2013 provides that if a person's name is entered in the register of members of a company as the shareholder in that company, but that individual does not hold the beneficial interest in those shares, that individual is required to declare certain information to the company specifying (among other things) the name and particulars of the person who holds the beneficial interest in those shares. Further, every person who holds or acquires a beneficial interest in share of a company is also required to make a declaration to the company specifying (among other things) the nature of his/her interest and the particulars of the person in whose name the shares stand registered in the books of the company. In the event of a change in the beneficial interest in such shares, the persons mentioned above are required to make certain declarations to the company within a period of 30 days.

Following such declarations, the company is required to take note in its register and file a return with the Registrar of Companies (ROC). The Companies Act 2013 and the rules made under that Act provide for reporting by significant beneficial owners to the Registrar of Companies (ROC). This is in addition to the aforementioned requirements. The shareholding of the company filed with the ROC is available on the website of the Ministry of Corporate Affairs.

Penalties for non-compliance

If any person fails to make the declarations required as outlined above, without any reasonable cause, he/she can be subject to a fine which may extend to INR50,000. Where the failure is a continuing one, that person can also be subject to a further fine which may extend to INR200 for every day after the first day during which the failure continues, subject to a maximum of INR50,000.

TOOLS AVAILABLE TO ACTIVIST SHAREHOLDERS

Shareholder activists have the following legal and regulatory tools available to them. In outline, these are the:

1. Right to receive information.
2. Right to give approval.
3. Right to appoint and remove directors.
4. Right to appoint an auditor.
5. Right to requisition a meeting.
6. Right to electronic voting. This is available only in listed companies or companies with more than 1,000 shareholders.
7. Grievance redressal mechanisms. Listed companies or companies with more than 1,000 shareholders debenture holders, deposit holders and any other security holders at any time during a financial year must have a Stakeholders Relationship Committee. Further, listed companies must be registered on SCORES platform (operated by the Securities and Exchange Board of India). Both of these provide mechanisms to resolve shareholder grievances.
8. Oppression and mismanagement proceedings. If at least 100 members or 10% of the total number of the members (whichever is less), or members holding at least 10% of the issued share capital of the company can approach the National Company Law Tribunal to initiate oppression or mismanagement proceedings.
9. Class action suits.
10. Derivative actions.

11.   Application to the Serious Fraud Investigation Office.

PREVENTION OF SHAREHOLDER ACTIVISM

The red flags that may indicate that a company is (or is about to be) targeted by shareholder activists include the following:

- Substantial increase in the shareholding of a few shareholders, leading to control of the company by them.
- A director failing to fulfil their duties under the Companies Act 2013.
- Controversy regarding the financial transactions or ethically questionable behaviour of one or more board members.
- Frequent changes in management leading to issues in addressing the concerns of the shareholders and formulating the strategies to be adopted by the company.
- Lack of communication with shareholders.
- Disregarding shareholder concerns regarding major dealings of the company.
- Inability or unwillingness of the management to resolve the concerns of its shareholders.
- Poor financial performance together with low market performance compared to its peers in the industry.

Certain declarations concerning the beneficial ownership of the shares of a company are required to be disclosed by the relevant shareholder and the beneficial owner to the company.

STEPS TO TAKE WHEN FACED WITH SHAREHOLDER ACTIVISM

1.   Responding before a general meeting

The steps that a company can take when faced with shareholder activism before responding to concerns at a general meeting include:

- Proactively and directly dealing with the concerns of the shareholder activist.
- Assuring the shareholder activist that the issues raised will be considered seriously by the management.
- Objectively considering the ideas of the shareholder activist.
- Evaluating and communicating the risk factors relating to the proposal of the shareholder activist.
- Formulating an arrangement that is aligned to the interest of the shareholders and concerns of the company.

2.   Responding at a general meeting

At a general meeting, the company can take the following steps (among others):

- Elaborating on the proposed strategy to be implemented.
- Convincing the shareholder activists because the proposed strategy is in the best long- term interests of the company and its members.

3.   Responding after a general meeting

After a general meeting, the company can take the following steps:

- Continuous review of the governance policies of the company and the strategy implemented.
- Engaging in interactive dialogues with the shareholders concerned.

Risks and benefits of company responses

Promptly responding to the concerns of activist shareholders offers the directors an opportunity to embrace stakeholder interests and support the company's governance profile and long-term strategic plan. In addition to focusing on the financial performance of the company, focusing on a strategic plan will help the board of directors to ensure that it has adequate policy space to implement that plan and garner the support of shareholders.

Although there is a substantial risk that the company may fail to satisfy all of the concerns raised by activists despite its best efforts, demonstrating a proactive approach to the problem helps the management and the board of directors gain the confidence of a greater number of shareholders. Conversely, ineffective communication can create a multitude of activist shareholders' concerns.

CURRENT TRENDS AND DEVELOPMENTS

With the rise of shareholder activism in India, companies are required to maintain good corporate governance standards and ensure a high level of shareholder engagement. Greater participation of shareholders in companies and implementation of best practices adopted by companies will assist in maintaining shareholder credibility.

The legal and regulatory dynamics have enhanced protection of shareholders' interests. The Companies Act 2013 and the rules and regulations by Securities and Exchange Board of India (SEBI) have protected the rights of shareholders, especially minority shareholders.

From the recent developments in India, it appears that proxy advisory firms have played a significant role in the Indian market. The recommendations provided by proxy advisory firms

to shareholders include appointment of directors (especially independent directors) of companies, corporate transactions, appointment auditors and so on.

Regulators other than SEBI are also encouraging increased shareholder participation. This can be observed from the guidelines issued by the Insurance Regulatory and Development Authority of India on stewardship code for insurers. The code includes requirements for insurers to have a policy regarding their conduct in general meetings of companies they have invested in and related disclosures. This is to ensure more engagement of insurers with management, therefore improving governance and informed decisions by parties, and to improve the return on investments of insurers.

SEBI formed a committee on corporate governance to further consider corporate governance issues. A number of the Kotak Committee recommendations on corporate governance have been implemented.

The recommendations include (among others) the following:

- Board of directors:
- no person can hold directorship in more seven listed companies from 1 April 2020;
- the corporate governance report must include the expertise/skill-sets matrix of the board of directors;
- there must be a minimum of six directors in the top 2,000 listed entities by 1 April 2020; and
- there must be at least one female independent director in the top 1,000 listed entities 1 by April 2020.
- Improving safeguards and disclosures in relation to:
- related party transactions;
- utilisation of funds from QIP/preferential issue in the relevant financial year until those funds are fully utilised; and
- consolidated quarterly results.
- Addressing issues faced by investors on voting and participation in general meetings. Top 100 listed entities by market capitalisation must provide a one-way live webcast of the proceedings of the annual general meetings.
- Quorum for every meeting of the directors of the top 2,000 listed entities with effect from 1 April 2020 must be one-third of its total strength or three directors, whichever is higher, including at least one independent director.

- With the recent developments in the space of corporate governance, entities in India need to adapt to the changing policies and get involve in more shareholder engagement.

Key trends in shareholder activism

These are still very early days for shareholder activism in India but some initial trends are summarised below.

1. **Fissures in corporate India:** The rise of shareholder activism in India has coincided with

    succession issues, over-leveraged balance sheets and other issues that have made promoters and professional management of listed companies vulnerable. These have even affected companies with a better governance history.

    For instance, in late 2016 and 2017, Infosys, a US and Indian listed IT company with a good governance reputation, faced a period of sustained pressure from its original founder shareholders, which ultimately contributed to the resignation of its CEO. The founders criticised the level of severance payments paid to certain departing executives and the US$200 million Panaya acquisition, which led to an investigation by an international law firm (which reportedly exonerated the management team). Following this, in July 2017, the board of Infosys indicated its willingness to work with its founders. However, on 18 August 2017, Vishal Sikka, the incumbent CEO, resigned. Without naming the founders, he indicated that the criticism he faced made his role untenable.

    The Tata conglomerate was also subject to a battle for control in late 2016 and early 2017. Following differences between Cyrus Mistry, then chair of Tata Sons, and Ratan Tata, the former chair, on 24 October 2016, Cyrus Mistry was removed from his position as chair through a board resolution. This was followed by allegations and counter-allegations between the two individuals. Cyrus Mistry was removed as director from the various Tata Group companies between November and December 2016 and, ultimately, was removed as a director of Tata Sons pursuant to an EGM held on 6 February 2017, although this removal is still being litigated.

2. **Litigation v. other strategies:** Historically, litigation strategies have proved to be less effective. For instance, the litigation strategy employed by the Children's Investment Fund (TCI) against the directors of Coal India for breach of fiduciary duties between 2012 and 2014 did not meet with success. In 2014, TCI

withdrew its court claims and sold its Indian holdings. Equally, recent attempts by Cyrus Mistry, the deposed chair of Tata Sons, to seek relief under Sections 241 and 244 of CA 2013 (for oppression and mismanagement) were dismissed by the NCLT, and the Bombay High Court refused to entertain a separate representative suit against Ratan Tata (Cyrus Mistry's predecessor) for damages. Similarly, litigation by minority shareholders of Cadbury in relation to the valuation in a minority squeeze-out scheme failed as the court ruled against the minority shareholder group. A more effective technique that certain shareholders have used is to register complaints with regulatory authorities. For instance, in July 2019, the shareholders of Bharat Nidhi Limited objected to a share buy-back scheme and asked SEBI to investigate.

Given that promoters still remain powerful, the more effective strategies are likely to be those that involve investors working with the promoters or seeking to curb obvious abuses, for which there is likely to be greater institutional investor and regulatory support.

3. **Proxy firms:** Several proxy advisory firms are now active in India and are regulated by SEBI under the SEBI (Research Analysts) Regulation 2014.

   Proxy advisory firms recommended that shareholders vote against the Tata Motors executive remuneration resolutions in 2014 and claimed credit for the outcome. They have also been vocal on governance matters; for instance, in commenting on the leave of absence taken by the CEO of ICICI Bank (while allegations of impropriety are investigated). More recently, in 2019, proxy firms challenged the management of Sterling Wilson over the failure to repay debt out of its IPO proceeds.

   They do not have the same level of influence as in the United States but proxy firms are emerging as important market participants. However, these firms have also faced criticism around perceptions of their own conflicts of interest and, in 2019, SEBI recommended safeguards in this regard.

4. **Role of the media:** Although public campaigns by shareholders seeking strategic changes are uncommon, the media has emerged as a key player, for instance, in the engagement that Narayana Murthy, a founder of Infosys, had with its board in 2016 and 2017

5. **Greater investor participation:** In the past, collective action issues held back shareholder activism, with investors preferring

to simply exit their investments. However, mutual funds and other long-term investors in the Indian market now more actively engage with promoters (see Section IV). Part of this has been driven by regulation. Indian regulated mutual funds are now required by SEBI to vote on resolutions involving their portfolio companies and provide voting reports on a quarterly and annual basis. Efforts by India's insurance regulator to encourage market engagement by insurance companies are likely to continue this trend.

In addition to long-only investors, certain funds have sought to take activist positions in various listed companies, seeking board appointments (albeit unsuccessfully) and successfully removing a director (in the case of Fortis Healthcare). In 2019, the asset sale of the Leela Hotels to Brookfield was challenged by ITC, a non-financial investor, and Life Insurance Corporation, a state owned insurer, on the grounds that certain deal participants were related parties and hence could not vote in favour of the sale. This challenge and its subsequent appeal were dismissed, but it does illustrate that the extent of shareholders asserting their rights has now expanded.

RECENT SHAREHOLDER ACTIVISM CAMPAIGNS

1. **Blocking transactions:** There have been a number of instances where shareholders have been able to block transactions adverse to the shareholders' interests.

    Since shareholders with an interest in related party transactions cannot vote to approve them, minority shareholders can sometimes be strongly placed. For instance, in 2018, shareholders of Tata Sponge Iron Limited, holding just 3.77 per cent of the votes, were able to defeat the related party approval resolutions for this reason. Also, in July 2017, the shareholders opposed a related party transaction between Raymond Limited and its promoters (involving the sale of an asset at a significant undervalue). More than 97 per cent of the votes cast were against the transaction.

    Similarly, in November 2015, after pressure from its shareholders, Sun Pharma withdrew from a potential US$225 million investment in the United States.

    Finally, in 2016, HDFC Standard Life Insurance Company Limited and Max Life Insurance Company Limited announced a merger to create a new insurer and the deal terms included the payment of a 8.5 billion rupee non-compete fee to one of the promoters. Ultimately, the deal did not complete owing to regulatory concerns, but various proxy firms had strongly opposed the payment of this fee.

2. **Forcing renegotiation of terms:** In certain cases, shareholders have been able to force a renegotiation of terms in large transactions.

In 2014, Maruti Suzuki's proposed manufacturing contract with a shareholder, Suzuki, was criticised for failing to seek shareholder approval for the transaction. Some of the largest funds in India wrote a letter to Maruti Suzuki challenging the proposed transaction. Even Life Insurance Corporation of India, a state-owned insurer, not known for activism, reportedly engaged with the company. The transaction terms were modified, and the company ultimately did obtain shareholder approval as a related party transaction matter, in 2015.

In the public M&A context, minority shareholders threatened to challenge a mandatory share swap scheme (announced in December 2019) between Reliance Industries Limited (RIL) and Reliance Retail Limited, on the basis that they had not been provided an exit option. In January 2020, as a result of this shareholder opposition, RIL made this scheme optional.

3. **Changes to board composition:** Investors have had one notable success in removing a director of Fortis Healthcare in May 2018. This was in the context of investor concerns as to the board assessment of certain bids for the company, so this is a significant shareholder activism landmark in India. Also, in 2019, the board of CG Power and Industrial Solutions removed its promoter from his role as chairman (although this was not the removal of a directorship) in the wake of allegations of certain irregularities.

However, the question is whether attempts to change the composition of the board outside the particular circumstances set out above will work. In the past, this has not proved easy in practice. For instance, the attempt of a 20 per cent investor to seek board representation in relation to MRO-TEK and the attempt by Florintree Advisors to seek a seat on the board of PTC India did not succeed. Some investors have persisted in unusual ways, such as the provisions for a 'small shareholder' director by Unifi Capital s

In certain cases, shareholders have opposed the reappointment of senior incumbent management as directors. For instance, in July 2018, 22.64 per cent of the shareholders of HDFC Limited voted against the reappointment of Deepak Parekh, the group chair, as a director. Similarly, in September 2018, a significant number of investors opposed the re- election of Kumar Mangalam Birla (head of Aditya Birla Group) to the board of UltraTech Cement. Although both reappointments were ultimately approved, this scale of opposition in relation to such senior figures in corporate India is noteworthy.

Litigation has also occasionally been attempted as a strategy to force a change in board composition, although these are harder to achieve.

MODULE - 5
MAJOR CORPORATE GOVERNANCE FAILURES

BCCI SCANDAL: THE EARLY YEARS

The bank was established in 1972 by Agha Hassan Abedi, a Pakistani banker who envisaged a bank focused on the third world, and was incorporated in Luxembourg, with headquarters in London. Abedi had financial help in setting up the bank from Abu Dhabi, which became

BCCI's major shareholder

In the late 1970s, the Gulf shipping group owned by Abbas Gokal (who was BCCI's main borrower) was close to bankruptcy. BCCI secretly threw money at Gulf to keep it going and falsified the books at the same time. This carried on for the next 15 years, with BCCI creating fictional transactions to cover up other non-performing loans and by the end, the bank was consistently using customer deposits to paint a picture of financial health.

In 1980, the Bank of England (BoE) granted BCCI a licence to trade in the UK; a move which was regarded as a mistake by BCCI's creditors. They subsequently claimed that the BoE received alarming reports about BCCI but because it was the BoE that had granted a licence, it refused to admit its mistake. One BoE memo in 1982 actually described BCCI as *'on its way to becoming the financial equivalent of The Titanic'*.

During 1987, the BoE, along with others, formed a group of regulators to supervise BCCI. BCCI was then investigated for allegations of money laundering by a US Senate sub- committee, as well as links to the Panamanian dictator Manual Noriega. BCCI has also been linked to many other unsavory customers, for example, Colombian drug baron sand the Abu Nidal terrorist organization, while the CIA admitted in August 1991 that it used BCCI 'as a way to move money'.

The beginning of the end

Robert Mazur (we will come back to him later) was a federal agent who went undercover in the mid-'80s in an operation named C-Chase, and was able to infiltrate the Colombian Medellin Cartel by posing as a well-connected businessman. He then used this to infiltrate the private client division of BCCI and uncovered how it was able to manipulate complex international finance systems to help drug lords, tax cheats and corrupt politicians launder money. In 1988, he created a fake wedding in Tampa, Florida, to which he invited BCCI executives and drug dealers he had befriended while undercover. This was actually a dramatic takedown operation and led to more than 80 men and women being charged worldwide and BCCI pleading guilty to money laundering in a case that lasted six months Four bank officers were convicted and the bank had to pay a $14.8 million fine.

In 1990, auditors Price Waterhouse alleged that some transactions on BCCI's 1989 accounts were 'false or deceitful' and Swaleh Naqvi (the BCCI chief) resigned. Abedi, who had already retired following a heart attack, severed ties with the bank.

Exposed

Finally, in March 1991, the BoE ordered an investigation by Price Waterhouse, which found that there was 'evidence of massive and widespread fraud'. This investigation caused the BoE to announce that BCCI might never have been profitable and to close it down in

July 1991, with liabilities of $14 billion, later reduced to $10 billion. Its collapse caused over 6,500 depositors to lose their money, including the Emirate of Abu Dhabi, which is believed to have lost $2 billion.

Later in July the same year, Robin Leigh-Pemberton, the BoE Governor, told a parliamentary committee that fraud at BCCI involved current and former management and the culture was 'criminal'. The US Federal Reserve then fined BCCI $200 million for violation of ownership laws involving three American banks. Abedi and Naqvi were indicted by New York District Attorney Robert Morgenthau, who called the case the 'largest bank fraud in world financial history'.

Abedi, however, was in Pakistan, where officials refused to give him up; he died in 1995, never having been brought to justice. Meanwhile BCCI's liquidator, Deloitte Touche Tohmatsu, started trying to recover money on behalf of the creditors.

Official reports

In the wake of BCCI's closure, a report was published by Lord Bingham in 1992, which stated that the BoE failed to spot widespread fraud in BCCI. However, the conclusion was that the BoE was responsible for mistakes, rather than a conspiracy or deliberate negligence. In response to this, the BoE created a special investigations team to identify and prevent further fraud.

Later that year, the Americans published their own report entitled The BCCI Affair, written by Senators John Kerry and Hank Brown. This report was very scathing about BCCI and the BoE, which subsequently caused the BoE to describe Kerry's conclusions as 'extraordinary' and having 'no factual basis'. The report was, however, equally critical of the CIA, the Justice Department and of US regulators, saying they had information on BCCI and didn't use it and made flawed decisions which 'allowed BCCI to secretly acquire US banks'

The report claimed that BCCI had bribed world leaders and political figures as well as befriending them, discredited people who were telling the truth, 'Engaged in billions of dollars of largely anonymous trading in the US which included a very substantial level of money laundering' and didn't protect innocent depositors from the aftermath of the bank's poor practices, which were something the auditors knew about for years.

Justice

Deloitte began litigation in 1993 against the BoE, accusing the bank of 'malicious recklessness'. Then, after two years, the Luxembourg court granted a compensation deal which started the ball rolling on the first major payout since the bank collapsed. In 1997, Abbas Gokal was found guilty of conspiracy to defraud and account falsely and sentenced to 14 years in prison. As well as this, he was fined £2.9 million to be paid in two years or have an extra three years added to his sentence. He appealed this in 1999 and lost. He was then released in 2003 by the Home Office, even though he didn't meet the terms of his fine.

In the same year, Gordon Brown, when he became the UK's Chancellor of the Exchequer, transferred banking supervision from the BoE to the Financial Services Authority. The BCCI case is thought to have played a part in this.

The trial

Deloitte managed to recover billions of pounds for the creditors but only recovered 75% of losses via various legal actions. High Court action by Deloitte against the BoE started in January 2004. In this, the liquidators alleged that the BoE ignored fraud, money laundering and bribes at BCCI and as it was BCCI's regulator at the time, Deloitte claimed up to £1 billion in damages. The liquidators also claimed that the BoE was guilty of wilful misconduct.

The BoE declared it would fight till the end, even though the case could end up costing £100 million just in legal fees, and allegedly accused Deloitte of fighting a 'flimsy legal claim' and wasting the creditors' money in doing so.

The barrister for Deloitte, Gordon Pollack, claimed that the BoE 'shut their eyes' to the fraud happening at BCCI so it couldn't be blamed. He also described Mr Abedi as corrupt and had designed the structure of the bank to dodge controls, while advising he saw no corruption from BoE officials. He also stated that by granting BCCI a license to trade in the UK, it had a duty to supervise it.

The only thing the BoE admitted was that it could have done more to uncover the fraud. It fiercely denied that it was involved or purposely failed to intervene. It stated that it would have been futile to cover something up, as it was sure to surface after BCCI collapsed.

Over a year later, the trial was still going and then BoE Governor Mervyn King declared that the claim 'never should have been brought'. He also stated that the trial could cost the BoE and therefore the taxpayer, £100 million if it wasn't finished by the end of that year.

Finally, on 2 November 2005, a month after the BoE rejected an offer to settle the case, Deloitte dropped the case against the BoE after the High Court said it wasn't in their best interests to continue. Later the presiding judge called the failed lawsuit a 'farce'.

Mervyn King spoke out and said: 'There has never been a shred of evidence to support these disgraceful allegations, and the case has collapsed as we always expected it would'. He also stated that the BoE would be seeking compensation for the costs incurred during the trial.

The Aftermath

Fast forward to 30 January 2006 and the BoE made one of the biggest claims for costs in English legal history, when it called for £80 million from Deloitte. A day later, a judge agreed that costs should be awarded on an indemnity basis but would rule on the amount at a later date. Five months later, £73 million was awarded to the BoE, which called this 'an excellent result' and that it would be able to 'draw a final line under the case'.

The files were finally closed in 2012 when a final meeting was held in Westminster's Central Hall with 150 creditors, lawyers for the creditors and Deloitte where it was explained that the battle for recoveries was immense and worldwide. Deloitte told the meeting that its team had visited desert warehouses and they were only allowed to inspect some papers under armed guard.

Ordinarily, this would be the end of it but it seems as though the after- effects of the BCCI case were still being felt up until very recently. When the files were closed in 2012, the decision was made to abandon a case against Saudi Arabian business man Abdel Raouf Hassan Khalil which the liquidators had been pursuing since the early '90s. They had tried to enforce a payment order for $326 million, however they weren't able to get past several political and procedural obstacles.

When this action was finally closed in July 2013 by the Luxembourg Commercial Court, it prompted several creditors of BCCI, including Dr Adil Elias (who was a member of the BCCI creditors' committee in Luxembourg for 22 years), to criticize this decision. They asked the court to reopen the proceedings to recover the funds from Khalil.

However, in March 2016, the Court of Appeal in Luxembourg ruled against Elias, stating that he had 'no standing to bring a third-party opposition, because in such capacity, he was a party to the 5 July 2013 closure order'. They also ruled against the other creditors because although they were creditors of BCCI, especially in the UK, they weren't creditors in the Luxembourg liquidations and therefore they had no authority to oppose the closure order in Luxembourg.

MAXWELL

Robert Maxwell was born Jan Ludvik Hoch in modern day Ukraine (then part of Czechoslovakia) in 1923. He escaped to France during World War II and made his way to Britain, where he joined the British Army. After buying the rights to distribute German academic papers, he took over a small academic publisher, which later became Pergamon Press. During the 1980s he aggressively expanded his business empire, with the result that, by the end of the decade, he owned a string of companies, including Macmillan Publishers, the Daily Mirror and New York Daily News.

What was the scam?

Having taken on large amounts of debt, and following the launch of a string of expensive failures, Maxwell was reduced to shunting money between his companies to give the impression they were profitable, repeatedly changing the dates on which they reported earnings, in order to fool auditors. When this wasn't enough to keep his empire going, he looted money from the pension fund of the Mirror Group in an attempt to prop up its share price.

What happened next?

With his businesses on the brink of collapse, Maxwell was reported missing from his yacht on 5 November 1991. His body was later discovered in the Atlantic Ocean, an apparent suicide (officially considered an accidental drowning). His bankers called in their loans, and his looting of the pension fund was discovered. By 1992 his sons Kevin and Ian were forced to declare bankruptcy.

In the end, Maxwell's firms were liquidated and his sons were put on trial for fraud (they were ultimately acquitted).

Lessons for investors

While Mirror Group shareholders were wiped out, arguably the biggest losers were the pensioners whohad £460m looted from their fund. Despite a partial government bailout, as wellas money from the investment bankers who advised Maxwell, most pensioners had toaccept a 50% cut in the value of their pensions. Perhaps all this mess could have been avoided had the people dealing with Maxwell heeded the words of the government investigation of the shadowy dealings at Pergamon in the 1970s, which concluded that "he is not in our opinion.

ENRON

Enron scandal, series of events that resulted in the bankruptcy of the U.S. energy, commodities, and services company Enron Corporation and the dissolution of Arthur Andersen LLP, which had been one of the largest auditing and accounting companies in the world. The collapse of Enron, which held more than $60 billion in assets, involved one of the biggest bankruptcy filings in the history of the United States, and it generated much debate as well as legislation designed to improve accounting standards and practices, with long-lasting repercussions in the financial world. Below are some reasons, as per experts, for scandals :

The Love for Money

Needless to say, this is perhaps the oldest temptation that can be associated with humans. We already mentioned these people are financially secure and hence the primary motive is not more money to buy more stuff but to bolster one's self-image.

Going to the Extremes

In most cases, any company's management focus and goal are to ensure they maximize shareholder value by doing just about whatever it takes to boost a company's stock price. This mindset led many to take extreme steps.

The Ethics

Compliance approach is just one step above the notion that 'following laws and regulations is all that an employee or a manager needs to do to be considered ethical but with this approach, you deal with problems that are old, not new; you're fighting the last battle. The classic example of this is the Enron Scandal and that is what we are going to talk about in this article.

The Beginning

Enron was founded by Kenneth Lay in the merger of two natural gas transmission companies, Inter North Inc. and Houston Natural Gas Corporation in 1985. After a year the merged company was renamed Enron in 1986 from the initial HNG Inter North.

What Exactly did Enron do?

The company lost its exclusive right to operate its pipelines in the early 1900s after the U.S. Congress brought in a series of laws to deregulate the sale of natural gas. Enron later transformed itself into a trader of energy derivative contracts, acting as an intermediary between their customer and natural-gas producers. Enron soon dominated the market for natural-gas contracts, and the company started to generate huge profits on its trades under Jeffrey Skilling's (CEO) leadership.

Over the next few years, the company hired top MBA candidates and emphasized aggressive trading. One worth mentioning recruit was Andrew Fastow, who quickly rose through the ranks to become Enron's chief financial officer. The bull market of the 1990s fueled Enron's ambitions and contributed to its rapid growth for many quarters. The company started trading derivative contracts for a wide variety of commodities—including coal, paper, electricity, coal, and steel—and even for the weather.

In October 1999, Enron created Enron Online (EOL) which was an electronic trading platform that focused on commodities. In every transaction, Enron was involved – it was either the buyer or the seller. To get more people on the trading platform, Enron offered its reputation, credit, and expertise in the energy sector.

Earning through Investment made in Global Market

The peak – awards and share price

The company was named "America's Most Innovative Company" by Fortune magazine for 6 consecutive years starting from 1996. Enron's stock price reached an all-time high of US$90.75 per share in mid-2000.

What caused Enron to collapse? Mark to Marketing Accounting

Before we go further, it is important to understand how the company managed its accounts. The company incorporated mark-to-market accounting for the energy trading business in 1992 and used it on an unprecedented scale for its trading transactions. Under this rule, when companies have outstanding energy-related or other derivative contracts (either liabilities or assets) on their balance sheet at the end of a particular quarter, then they must adjust them to fair market value, booking unrealized losses or gains to the income statement of the period. The major issue with the application of these rules in accounting for long-term futures contracts in commodities such as gas is that there are often no quoted prices upon which to base valuations. Companies that have these types of derivative instruments are free to develop and use discretionary valuation models based on their methods and assumptions. Now getting to the reason as to why such a big company which was working in so many verticals collapsed:

Blockbuster Video

Blockbuster was the former juggernaut video rental chain. In July 2000, Blockbuster and Enron Broadband Services entered a partnership and decided to enter the burgeoning VOD market. As per the industry expert, VOD was a good and sensible pick but Enron started logging expected earnings based on the expected growth of the VOD market which inflated its numbers. In mid-2000, EOL was executing about $350 billion in trades and when the dot- com bubble began to burst, the company decided to build high-speed broadband telecom networks. They spent hundreds of millions of dollars on the project but had no returns. When the recession hit in 2000, Enron crumbled since it had the exposure mostly in the volatile parts of the market.

Its own weight

By the fall of 2000, the company started going down. Jeffrey Skilling was able to hide the financial losses of the trading business and other operations of the company since the company used mark-to-market accounting. Enron would build a project such as an energy plant and immediately put the profits on its financial books, even though the company had not made a single penny from the asset. In the next quarter, when the revenue from the energy plant came less than the projected amount, the company transferred the asset to an off- the-books corporation where the loss would go unreported. They never took the losses on the books.

Who took down Enron?

Though it is difficult to point fingers to a single person but amid what all was happening in the company which was taking it to south, Andrew Fastow, who was the chief financial officer since 1998 came up with a plan to project the company in sound financial shape despite the fact that many of its subsidiaries were losing money.

He along with others formulated a scheme to use off-balance-sheet special purpose vehicles(SPVs) which is also known as special purposes entities, to hide their high debts and toxic assets from creditors and investors. The standard Enron-to-SPV transaction was performed like this: Enron transferred some of its rapidly rising stock to the SPV in exchange for notes or cash. The SPV would subsequently use the stock to hedge an asset that is listed on Enron's balance sheet. In turn, Enron would guarantee the SPV's value to reduce apparent counterparty risk and hence turn the table on its side.

If Enron's share prices fell, this directly compromised the ability of the SPVs to hedge. It was a very dangerous difference – Enron's failure to disclose conflicts of interest.

Arthur Anderson was another major player in the Enron Scandal. He was running the accounting firm Arthur Andersen LLP who oversaw Enron's accounts. The firm was one of the five largest accounting firms in the US at that time and Andersen had a reputation for quality risk and high standards management.

How was Enron caught?

Despite Enron's poor accounting practices over the years, Arthur offered its stamp of approval and signing off on the corporate reports for years. Many analysts started to question Enron's earnings and the company's transparency by April 2001,

What year did Enron collapse?

Enron was in freefall by the summer of 2001. Skilling resigned as CEO due to personal reasons in August 2001. Around the same time, analysts started to downgrade their rating for Enron's stock and the stock came down to 52 week low of $39.95. The company reported its first quarterly loss on October 16. The earning was further reduced when it closed its Raptor SPV so that it would not have to distribute 58 million shares of stock. This looked fishy and caught the attention of the SEC.

If this was not all, Enron changed pension plan administrators which forbid employees from selling their shares for the next 30 days. When the news came out that the SEC was investigating Enron and

SPV, Fastow was fired from the company. The company also restated earnings going back to 1997.

By the end of 2000, Enron had losses of $591 million and had $628 million in debt. The final nail in the coffin was put by Dynegy, which had previously announced it would merge with Enron but backed the deal on 28 November 2001. Enron filed for bankruptcy on 2 December 2001 amid all crises.

Who all were punished in the Enron Scandal?

Arthur Andersen was one of the first people against whom charges were laid. Arthur's firm was found guilty of obstructing justice for shredding Enron's financial documents to obscure them from the SEC in June 2002. On appeal, the conviction was overturned in a few months, however, the firm was deeply disgraced by the scandal and dwindled into a holding company.

Several of Enron's top executives were charged with insider trading, conspiracy, and securities fraud. Enron's founder and former CEO Kenneth Lay were convicted on six counts of conspiracy and fraud and four counts of bank fraud. He died of a heart attack in Colorado prior to sentencing.

For facilitating Enron's corrupt business practices Enron's former CFO Andrew Fastow pled guilty to two counts of frauds – securities fraud and wire fraud. He served more than five years in prison by cooperating with federal authorities. He was set free from prison in 2011.

Former Enron CEO Jeffrey Skilling received the harshest sentence of all the people involved in the Enron scandal. Skilling was convicted of scam and insider trading. He originally received a 24-year sentence, but it was reduced by 10 years in 2013.

How many Enron employees lost their jobs?

The shareholders lost $74 billion in the four years leading up to Enron's bankruptcy. From 2004 to 2011, the company paid its creditors more than $21.7 billion.

The day after Enron filed for bankruptcy, it fired 5000 workers which were approximately 25% of its total strength of 21,000 employees. The layoffs at Enron's headquarters (Houston) were especially brutal, where 4,500 of the 7,500 workers were asked to leave. Laid-off workers received a mere $4,500 severance payment, the company did not take into account how many years they had worked for the company. Enron also canceled all medical and health insurance for the 5,000 laid-off workers.

What happened after the Enron collapse?

At that time, the Enron scandal was the greatest financial scandal in the history of the US economy. Post the scandal, increased oversight and regulation have been enacted to help prevent the corporate scandal of Enron's magnitude.

Many companies reeled the damage caused by Enron for many years post 2001. The most recent incident happened in March 2017, when a judge granted a Toronto-based investment firm the right to sue former Enron CEO Jeffrey Skilling, Credit Suisse Group AG, Deutsche Bank AG, and Bank of America's Merrill Lynch unit over losses incurred by purchasing Enron shares.

Downfall and bankruptcy

As the boom years came to an end and as Enron faced increased competition in the energy- trading business, the company's profits shrank rapidly. Under pressure from shareholders, company executives began to rely on dubious accounting practices, including a technique known as "mark-to-market accounting," to hide the troubles. Mark-to-market accounting allowed the company to write unrealized future gains from some trading contracts into current income statements, thus giving the illusion of higher current profits. Furthermore, the troubled operations of the company were transferred to so-called special purpose entities (SPEs), which are essentially limited partnerships created with outside parties. Although many companies distributed assets to SPEs, Enron abused the practice by using SPEs as dump sites for its troubled assets. Transferring those assets to SPEs meant that they were kept off Enron's books, making its losses look less severe than they really were. Ironically, some of those SPEs were run by Fastow himself. Throughout these years, Arthur Andersen served not only as Enron's auditor but also as a consultant for the company.

In February 2001 Skilling took over as Enron's chief executive officer, while Lay stayed on as chairman. In August, however, Skilling abruptly resigned, and Lay resumed the CEO role. By this point Lay had received an anonymous memo from Sherron Watkins, an Enron vice president who had become worried about the Fastow partnerships and who warned of possible accounting scandals.

The severity of the situation began to become apparent in mid-2001 as a number of analysts began to dig into the details of Enron's publicly released financial statements. In October Enron shocked investors when it announced that it was going to post a $638 million loss for the third quarter and take a $1.2 billion reduction in shareholder equity owing in part to Fastow's partnerships. Shortly thereafter the Securities and Exchange Commission (SEC) began investigating the transactions between Enron and Fastow's SPEs. Some officials at Arthur Andersen then began shredding documents related to Enron audits.

As the details of the accounting frauds emerged, Enron went into free fall. Fastow was fired, and the company's stock price plummeted from a high of $90 per share in mid-2000 to less than $12 by the beginning of November 2001. That month Enron attempted to avoid disaster by agreeing to be acquired by Dynegy. However, weeks later Dynegy backed out of the deal. The news caused Enron's stock to drop to under $1 per share, taking with it the value of Enron employees' 401(k) pensions, which were mainly tied to the company stock. On December 2, 2001, Enron filed for Chapter 11 bankruptcy protection.

Lawsuits and legislation

Many Enron executives were indicted on a variety of charges and were later sentenced to prison. Notably, in 2006 both Skilling and Lay were convicted on various charges of conspiracy and fraud. Skilling was initially sentenced to more than 24 years but ultimately served only 12. Lay, who was facing more than 45 years in prison, died before he was sentenced. In addition, Fastow pleaded guilty in 2006 and was sentenced to six years in prison; he was released in 2011.

Arthur Andersen also came under intense scrutiny, and in March 2002 the U.S. Department of Justice indicted the firm for obstruction of justice. Clients wanting to assure investors that their financial statements could meet the highest accounting standards abandoned Andersen for its competitors. They were soon followed by Andersen employees and entire offices. In addition, thousands of employees were laid off. On June 15, 2002, Arthur Andersen was found guilty of shredding evidence and lost its license to engage in public accounting. Three years later, Andersen lawyers successfully persuaded the U.S. Supreme Court to unanimously overturn the obstruction of justice verdict on the basis of faulty jury instructions. But by then there was nothing left of the firm beyond 200 employees managing its lawsuits.

In addition, hundreds of civil suits were filed by shareholders against both Enron and Andersen. While a number of suits were successful, most investors did not recoup their money, and employees received only a fraction of their 401(k)s.

The scandal resulted in a wave of new regulations and legislation designed to increase the accuracy of financial reporting for publicly traded companies. The most important of those measures, the Sarbanes-Oxley Act (2002), imposed harsh penalties for destroying, altering, or fabricating financial records. The act also prohibited auditing firms from doing any concurrent consulting business for the same clients.

Arthur Andersen, Arthur Andersen LLP was one of the largest public accounting firms in the 1990s, with more than 85,000 employees operating in 84 countries. During the last decade of the partnership's life, auditors at several regional offices failed to detect, ignored, or approved accounting frauds for large clients paying lucrative consulting fees, including Enron Corp. and WorldCom Inc. In 2002 the partnership was found guilty of obstruction of justice for destroying documents related to the Enron audit, a decision later unanimously overturned by the United States Supreme Court.

Consulting Schemes

For more than a half century, Arthur Andersen—cofounded as Andersen, DeLany & Co. in 1913 by Arthur E. Andersen, a young accounting professor who had a reputation for acting with integrity— was primarily an auditing firm focused on providing high-quality standardized audits. But a shift in emphasis during the 1970s pitted a new generation of auditors advocating for clients and consulting fees against traditional auditors demanding more complex auditing techniques. The problem worsened when the company's consulting division began generating significantly higher profits per employee than the auditing division. Auditing revenues had flattened, and growth came primarily through consulting fees. Consulting schemes encouraged by Andersen partners included the following:

- Using highly qualified consultants from other regional offices to market their services during client presentations and then not including them on the project team after the contract was obtained
- Determining the client's budget for consulting services and then selling as many consulting services as possible up to that budget limit, even if the services were unnecessary
- Charging clients a partner's high billable-hour rate and then assigning most of the work to lower-paid and less-qualified staff

The Enron Audit

The combination of more complex financial statements, more aggressive accounting techniques, greater concern for customer satisfaction, greater dependence on consulting fees, and smaller cost-effective sampling techniques created many problems for auditing firms. Arthur Andersen's Houston office was billing Enron $1 million per week for auditing and consulting services, and David Duncan, the lead auditor, had an annual performance goal of 20% increase in sales. Duncan favorably reviewed the work of Rick Causey, Enron's chief accounting officer and Duncan's former colleague at Andersen. Duncan let Enron employees intimidate Andersen auditors, such as locking an Andersen auditor in a room until he produced a letter supporting a $270 million tax credit.

The Indictment

In June 2001 the Securities and Exchange Commission (SEC) issued a cease-and-desist order against Andersen regarding any securities violations for its role in a $1.43 billion accounting fraud at Waste Management Inc. The cease-and-desist arrived after Andersen had already reached a civil settlement and agreed to pay a $7 million fine for malfeasance with regard to the Waste Management case. Andersen partners were warned that any future violation would result in an extreme penalty from the Justice Department.

By late September 2001, Enron insiders knew the firm would publicly announce on October 16 a third quarter operating loss, along with an after-tax nonrecurring charge of more than $1 billion. Both Enron and Arthur Andersen went into a crisis management mode to prepare for an anticipated SEC investigation. On October 12, Andersen's in-house lawyer requested that the director of Andersen's Houston office comply with the company's documentation retention policy—all extraneous documents should be destroyed.

As expected, the SEC requested Enron audit information on October 17. Six days later, Duncan ordered his audit team to destroy documents at a pace quicker than required by the documentation retention policy. Within 3 days, an unprecedented amount of material had been shredded, and e-mails and computer files deleted, in Houston and several other regional offices. The SEC formally subpoenaed Andersen for Enron-related material on November 8, though the shredding came to a stop only the following day.

CEO Joseph Berardino immediately notified the SEC on finding out about the excessive document shredding, and he fired Duncan following the public uproar. Andersen's response was considered inadequate given that three other major corporations for whom Andersen recently issued unqualified or clean audit opinions—Global Crossing, WorldCom, and Qwest—were either being investigated by the SEC, drastically restating previous financial statements, or abruptly declaring bankruptcy.

On March 14, 2002, the Justice Department indicted Andersen for obstruction of justice. Clients wanting to assure investors that their financial statements could meet the highest accounting standards abandoned Andersen for its competitors. They were soon followed by Andersen employees and entire offices. Berardino was forced to resign, and thousands of employees were laid off.

In early April, Duncan pleaded guilty to one felony count of obstruction of justice. Andersen requested and received a speedy trial because of the mass client defection. On June 15, 2002, Arthur Andersen was found guilty of shredding evidence and lost its license to engage in public accounting. Three years later, Andersen lawyers successfully persuaded the United States Supreme Court to unanimously overturn the obstruction of justice verdict on the basis of faulty jury instructions. But by then there was nothing left of the firm beyond 200 employees managing its lawsuits.

VIVENDI (FRANCE)

A water company called *Compagnie Generale edes Eaux (CGE)* was created on December 14, 1853 by an Imperial decree of Napoleon III. Later on the company was named Vivendi which diversified into media and telecommunication industry. Lot of acquisitions and massive expansion during eighties and nineties turned the French water utility into the World's second largest media company. In 2000, Vivendi

Universal Entertainment was created with the merger of the Vivendi media empire with Canal+ television networks and the acquisition of Universal Studios from Canadian Company Seagram.

In July 2002, Vivendi reported that it had a liquidity crises and disclosed a loss of Euro 23.3 billion. The group collapsed due to the following flaws in governance.

1. **Overexpansion:** Jean-Marie Messier led the company to make costly acquisitions and expand too fast. These jeopardized the company's financial structure. It overpaid for the acquisitions and funded them with debt. The company irrationally diversified into unrelated and risky areas and lacked strategic focus.

2. **Ineffective Board:** The board consisted of directors who were CEO friendly. They failed to question management strategy and heavy debt. Board lacked independence and objectivity as the CEO dominated it.

3. **Accounting Manipulations:** The CEO and the CFO (Guillanme Hannezo) improperly adjusted various reserve accounts and prematurely recognized income violating GAAP of the US to

boost Vivendi's earnings. The company did not disclose the Cegetel. Current account and Maroc Telecom side agreement. Off-balance sheet commitments played a major role in the company's failure. Operating earnings of minority owned subsidiaries were included to mislead investors. "Gain on sale" of a subsidiary were accounted for in contravention of the established rules.

4.   **Audit Failure:** The audit committee failed to warn the board about the risks associated with the deceptive accounting practices and liquidity problems in its reports.

5.   **Excessive Compensation:** The CEO was paid unreasonably high compensation. The company was forced to write off large amounts. Pay was not aligned with performance.

6.   **Insider Trading:** Senior executives exercised options for personal gains ahead of sensitive news.

Jean-Marie-Messier was forced to resign and was found guilty of embezzlement in 2011. The company began to reorganize to stave off bankruptcy. It announced a strategy to sell non -strategic assets and reduced its stake in Vivendi Environment to 40% and sold its stake in Vinci Construction.

WORLDCOM

Founded initially as a small company named Long Distance Discount Services in 1983, it merged with Advantage Companies Inc to eventually become WorldCom Inc, naming its CEO as Bernard Ebbers. WorldCom achieved its position as a significant player in the telecommunications industry through the successful completion of 65 acquisitions spending almost $60 billion between 1991 and 1997, whilst also accumulating $41 billion in debt. During the Internet boom WorldCom's stock rose from pennies per share to over $60 a share as 'Wall Street investment banks, analysts and brokers began to discover WorldCom's value and made "strong buy recommendations" to investors.' During the 1990's WorldCom evolved into the 'second-largest long distance phone company in the US' mainly due to its aggressive acquisition strategy.

A cycle became apparent in the marketplace where an acquisition was seen as a positive move by the analysts leading to higher stock prices of WorldCom. Consequently, this allowed WorldCom to gain greater financing and backing for further acquisitions repeating the cycle. One of the most significant and largest acquisitions was that of MCI Communications Inc in 1998, becoming the largest merger in US history at that time. British

Telecommunications were also in the running for the takeover of MCI Communications making a $19 billion bid, when Bernard Ebbers the CEO of WorldCom decided to place a counter bid 1.8 times higher than that of what BT had placed, at $35 billion. Evidently this takeover was agreed and the merger between the two brought MCI WorldCom into second position behind that of AT&T in the telecommunications market.

However, from 1999 to early 2002, CEO of the company, Bernard Ebbers along with other senior management used fraudulent and improper accounting methods to mislead investors and other directors. Their fraudulent accounting method had mainly two approaches: 'The reduction of reported line costs' and the 'exaggeration of reported revenue'. These practices were to ignore the generally accepted accounting principles (GAAP) in addition to not informing the users of the financial statements of the changes to the previously used accounting practices. This was done to reduce their E/R ratio, the main key performance indicator used to measure the performance of telecommunications companies. It is the relationship between their main expenses; line costs (the rental of telephone lines) to its revenues and the lower figures consequently produced more recommendations by analysts increasing stock prices.

The eventual failure of WorldCom was caused by the disruption of the cycle, as discussed before, when the planned acquisition of Sprint Corporation in 1999-2000 was stopped by pressures from the US Department of Justice and the European Union over concerns of it creating a monopoly. As a result, WorldCom lost its main growth strategy and left Bernard Ebbers few options to enhance the business further. Either they had to consolidate all the previous acquisitions into one efficient business, which they had failed to do so far, as they had only concentrated on the takeovers or to find other creative ways to sustain and increase the share price.

The CEO chose the latter and in July 2002 WorldCom filed for Chapter 11 bankruptcy after disclosures were made about the improper accounting methods used to inflate revenue's and reduce expenses. By the end of 2003, it was estimated that the company's total assets had been inflated by around $11 billion.

The Fraud

The members of senior management were engaged in a continuing series of improper accounting manipulations to try and achieve market expectations on growth, making the financial reports more appealing. This was achieved through basic fraudulent methods, including changes to financial estimates, early revenue recognition, erroneously capitalisation of the long-term assets, as well as alteration of the reserves in order to improve the earnings picture.

WorldCom's managers modified their assumptions on accounts receivables, by adjusting the amount of uncollectible bills owed to the company and as a result increased the total amount of accounts receivable. Managerial assumptions played two important roles here; firstly, they determine the amount of funds reserved to cover bad debts, as the lower the perceived need of non-collectable bills, the smaller the reserve required. This resulted in manipulation of the reserves, reducing them when needed to increase earnings. Secondly, when selling receivables to third parties the assumptions are used to identify the quantity available for sale, which WorldCom utilized. This manipulation was easily achieved as many of the WorldCom's customers were small, start-up telecommunication businesses with little data and history of repayment likelihood, leaving a large degree of judgement from management to set these figures.

Line cost accruals were exploited in a similar way to that of the bad debt reserves, due to the judgement needed in deciding upon figures. Line cost accruals estimates are extremely difficult to make with precision, being best practice to adjust them frequently. This, of course, provides further opportunities for falsification. With the importance of line costs to the company's bottom line and with Ebbers promise to reduce expenses; the accruals were adjusted on a regular basis to improve the company's overall margins, maintaining the high growth rate now expected by the market. WorldCom's finance chief, Sullivan later admitted to the court that he falsified financial statements of the company and in particular ordered the General Accounting department to reduce Wireless' Division's expenses by US$150 million.

In fact, during the second quarter of 2000, the total accounts receivables at WorldCom Inc rose 12.6% to US$926 million, but the allowance only increased by US$443 million, or 3.5%, leading to higher earnings of $69 million.

The large acquisition of MCI gave WorldCom another opportunity to fiddle its books as it could now apply its dubious methods to all the new assets and expenses of MCI. Therefore they started reducing the book value of some MCI assets whilst also increasing the value of goodwill by the same balancing amount. This gave greater flexibility for achieving their targets as smaller amounts of expenses were taken against earnings by spreading the charges over decades rather than the year it was incurred. 'The net result was

WorldCom's ability to cut annual expenses, acknowledge all MCI revenues and boost profits from the acquisition.'

Next, there was the existence of a 'Corporate Unallocated Revenue Account', which included entries of corporate level adjustments. This was to assist Ebbers in adjusting the performance of WorldCom by profit smoothing, such that the predicted 15 percent year on year growth could be achieved. The access to the "Corporate Unallocated Schedule", which was an attachment to the Monthly Revenue Schedule, was only available to the senior management.

This schedule included the journal entries to the revenue account that erroneously increased the revenue of the company.

According to US GAAP Code 605, the account of such sort is fictitious, as it does not satisfy the criteria, and thus could not be treated as a legal form of revenue. The management, knowing this fact, restricted the number of people who had access to the monthly revenue, so that the fraud in revenue recognition would not be discovered. In addition to that, WorldCom tended to recognise the revenue, which was yet to be received from long term contracts, even before the actual service was provided. This, of course, was another violation of the US GAAP.

Furthermore, in a bid to reduce line costs, WorldCom capitalised the excess capacity expenses that were not generating revenue. The reason given was that these lines are costs which should have been incurred after the related benefits were generated. Although this arrangement does not oppose the classification of asset in FASB Concept Statement No 6, 'Assets are probable future economic benefits obtained or controlled by a particular entity as a result of past transactions or events,' there was no proper business or accounting rationale for these procedures. The latter include journal entries of $798 million and $560 million, made to capitalise 'line costs' during 2001. Indeed, according to FRS 16, costs that are related to day-to-day servicing, or wear and tear repairs of Property Plant and Equipment (PPE) would be expensed, unless the PPE is enhanced as a result of the expenditure. Consequently, we can see that WorldCom has wrongly classified its expenses as an asset account despite the PPE not being enhanced at any state. This would lead to the reduction of expenses, increment in total assets, and ultimate increase in profits as well as a stronger balance sheet.

Lastly, other reserves were also manipulated to manage earnings. The reserves, which were often set aside by WorldCom to cover foreseeable costs and losses, were inflated to create 'hefty slush funds' that could be used to increase profits.

Auditing Issues

Actions of the company's management yielded an environment where fraud activities were easily accomplished. For this reason, the internal audit function, designed to supervise and hold employees accountable, was suppressed by a few senior members in an attempt to limit their exposure to the sensitive information. This was achieved by senior management keeping the internal audit department understaffed, generally under qualified and busy with other projects as well as retaining information from them. They also hampered efforts from internal auditors to find information once they became wary of the accounting processes used. The effort to delve into the financials was brought by Cynthia Cooper the Vice President of internal audit who did eventually help uncover the truth by gathering information after-hours to avoid suspicion and supervision by her repressive bosses. Cynthia questioned external auditors Arthur Anderson over some of the methods and they refused to respond initially eventually stating that they had approved the methods and that she should leave it at that. The internal controls meant to help supervise were controlled by the directors so proved useless as information could be changed, stopped or edited.

Arthur Andersen's involvement being the Auditors of WorldCom would have been to find the irregularities in the company's accounts. The level of complexity of the fraud found in WorldCom were more of judgement as opposed to those complex issues raised through Enron (who Arthur Anderson also audited), yet they were still missed. However, following their failure at Enron, WorldCom switched to KPMG as their auditing firm. The resulting implication for Arthur Andersen is that it lost public trust and was implicated in the frauds of both Enron and WorldCom due to not fulfilling their duties.

Corporate Governance and Accountability Issues

WorldCom's failure was down to a multitude of underlying issues and shortcomings. Firstly, one might have to blame the system of the market for their method of assessing the value of a company solely on its share value. This created situations where a company could behave in an unsolicited manner. The pressure of achieving targets led to the company creatively constructing some of its financials to meet expectations laid down by the market, which might have been over-optimistic.

The aggressive acquisition strategy used by Ebbers was brought through from his previous ventures where he found himself adept at raising money, mainly due to his likeable personality. The appointment of a CEO that had little knowledge and no background in the phone technology market led to Ebbers doing what he knew; raising funds and this was used on these acquisitions. However, in his quests he failed to consolidate these companies into one efficient business leaving only one route to improve stock values; more acquisitions. The failure to consolidate the firms was also assisted by his remuneration package being to myopic only focussing on quick profits as opposed to measurement over a period of years focussing on sustainable growth. Subsequently this focussed his attention on increasing share prices now as he received large amounts of his remuneration in shares, and an increase in share price increased his wealth, in the short run anyway.

Infectious greed was apparent among the investors and market, expecting and demanding maintained high returns. Ebbers owning many shares in WorldCom may have also been overtaken by this, however as a CEO he must also promote and act in the best interests of the company and this is where he failed his fiduciary duty to all shareholders and stakeholders. This meant the continuance of the fast growth acquisition strategy which was detrimental to the company's long-term success.

The culture of WorldCom was another problem that was among the underlying causes of its downfall, being apparent in all aspects of the company, but mostly passed down the ranks from top management starting with Ebbers. A downfall of the firm was the absence of accountability from some of the top management. Ebbers tried to argue in his defence that he was a hands-off director who wasn't involved in the detailed aspects of the firm and hence not involved in the fraud, however he had the authority and forced others to comply. There was no direct accountability on him to align his and the firm's objectives of providing true and fair accounts, as there were little repercussions for his actions. He was able to gamble with other people's money whilst either increasing his value of shares and remuneration when successful or having a severance payment if the company starts failing.

The audit committee and the rest of the board not only failed to oppose Ebbers and his CFO, Scott Sullivan, but even financed Ebbers and others with large loans. Consequently, Ebbers was allowed to continue with other pursuits setting up and running other companies utilising loans from WorldCom. The latter, of course, has created several conflicts of interest and independence issues, as well as allowing the attention of the CEO to divert from his core responsibilities.

Effects on WorldCom

The bankruptcy case of WorldCom was considered to be unprecedented in terms of its scale until the breakdown of Lehman Brothers in 2008. While the debtors of WorldCom were protected from some losses, WorldCom's shareholders received nothing. Within days, the stock of not so long ago major player in the telecommunication industry fell well under $1. By the same token, 17,000 WorldCom employees lost their jobs together with insurance and pensions, which have collapsed along with the share price. Three years after the fraud was revealed, Bernard Ebbers, who had already left the company's CEO position, was found guilty and sentenced to 25 years of prison for the charges of fraud, conspiracy and filing false documents. On April 2004 WorldCom emerged from Chapter 11 under the name of MCI with Michael Capellas as new CEO and CFO Robert Blakely. Supported by 200 employees of the company's external auditor KPMG and an additional 600 people workforce from Deloitte & Touch they then had the task of settling the company's remaining debt of $35 billion. Eventually, in February 2005, MCI ceased to exist as an independent company when it was bought by Verizon Communications for $8.4 billion.

WorldCom's fraudulent activities gradually took its toll on the entire U.S. telecommunications industry. Equipment manufacturers such as Lucent Technologies, Nortell Networks, and Corning which have initially been benefitting from WorldCom's fictitious profitability and projections ultimately suffered with depressed stock prices and were forced to lay off work forces, too. WorldCom's then larger rival, the telecommunication company AT&T (American Telephone & Telegraph) had been laying off tens of thousands in the late 90's as it was trying to match WorldCom's phantom profits which eventually led to its acquisition by Baby Bell SBC Communications in December 2005.

Legislative Consequences

The WorldCom scandal could potentially have discredited US GAAP standard setting provoking the assumption that the fraud could only have occurred due to deficient accounting principles. However, there is a broad consensus that the WorldCom disaster was rather a failure of corporate governance. Following the downfall of Enron, the Securities and Exchange Commission had not yet enacted any new laws. However, after the senior management of WorldCom was charged with fraud, the Congress was pushed to answer the critics through legislative actions. Thus, a new US federal law, the Sarbanes-

Oxley Act (SOX) emerged in 2002. It now applies to any company registered with the SEC and contains eleven sections that specify duties concerning the issues of corporate governance, compliance and disclosure.

In answer to the fact that at Worldcom, members of the senior management have been involved in the fraud, CEOs and CFOs can now be directly and individually be held responsible for the accuracy of financial statements. Moreover, it is no longer allowed to give credit to their directors or officers as WorldCom did to Ebbers. Concerning the relationship to the auditing company it includes guidelines stipulating that audit firms cannot provide any additional services that may compromise their independence and auditors can not in any way be involved in management decisions. Moreover, a new auditor rotation system that requires audit partners to change every five years and audit firms every seven years respectively has been imposed.

In Europe, the reactions to the Worldcom accounting scandal of the U.S. included the implementation of the mandatory 'Annual Corporate Governance Statement'. The Company

Act 2006 has replaced the Memorandum and Articles of Association with a single document followed by the attempt to shorten the time limit on information delivery for small companies from ten to seven months after the financial year end. Alteration of the statement of duties of directors also took place together with the Operating & Financial Review being introduced for large firms. All of these changes were to try and bring shareholders and other stakeholders closer to their investments to supervise them more closely.

ARTHUR ANDERSEN

At "Andersen U.," the lush, 150-acre campus where Arthur Andersen LLP has trained tens of thousands of new recruits, there's a shrine to ethical accounting.

A display in the Andersen Heritage Center is devoted to yellowing press clippings of a long- ago campaign to clean up the accounting industry by Leonard Spacek, who led the firm from 1947 to 1963. In one, he accused Bethlehem Steel of overstating its profits in 1964 by more than 60%. In another, he bashed the Securities and Exchange Commission for failing to crack down on companies that cooked their books, saying that at best the regulatory agency has been "a brake on the rate of retrogression in the quality of accounting."

Now, it's the quality of Andersen's accounting that has set off an ethical crisis. Since 1993, the firm has been embroiled in a series of major accounting scandals -- from Sunbeam Corp. to Waste

Management Inc. to Enron Corp. Facing an obstruction-of-justice charge in a Houston federal court, Andersen itself is disintegrating and will likely be gone in a matter of months regardless of the verdict -- a humiliating end to a company that once stood as the world's largest professional-services firm and whose 85,000 employees last year generated $9.3 billion in revenue.

Andersen's descent from conscience of the accounting industry to accused felon didn't happen overnight. Rather, it stemmed from a series of management miscues and compromises over the decades. As the firm grew from a close-knit partnership to a globe- spanning behemoth, pressure to boost profits became intense. Andersen leaders responded by pushing partners to become salesmen -- upsetting the delicate balancing act any auditor must perform between pleasing a client and looking out for the public investor.

This shift saw the rise of a new breed of accountant -- such as the senior executive who punctuated his speeches with violin music and exhorted his troops to "empathize" with the companies whose books they checked.

Andersen spokesman Patrick Dorton acknowledges that the firm has made some mistakes in the past, but says it was undertaking reforms. He adds: *The issues and concerns raised affect the entire profession and not only Andersen.*

Arthur Andersen himself originally built his business by putting reputation over profit. In 1914, months after the 28-year-old North western University accounting professor founded his tiny company, the president of a local railroad demanded that he approve a peculiar transaction that would have lowered the company's expenses and boosted earnings. Mr. Andersen, who at the time was worried about meeting his next payroll, told the president that there was *not enough money in the city of Chicago* to make him do it, according to a book published by the firm in 1988. The client promptly fired the accountant, but Mr. Andersen was vindicated months later when the company filed for bankruptcy.

Mr. Andersen lived in a bygone era. Back then, competition among accounting firms was muted. The closest auditors came to selling was gentle networking on the boards of local charities. What the business lacked in excitement, it made up in reliability: Under federal laws enacted in the 1930s, public companies had to submit their financial statements to independent auditing every year. Partners at the firms earned enough to drive a Cadillac and join the local country club, but no one got rich being an auditor. In the late 1960s, a mid-level Andersen partner made about $30,000, or $160,000 in today's dollars.

Daniel Malachuk joined Arthur Andersen in 1970, fresh out of the Navy with a master's degree in finance. Flying to Chicago for his orientation, he remembers being met by a driver holding a cryptic "Arthur An" sign -- a nod to federal rules at the time that barred advertising. He was driven to the campus of the newly opened Andersen U., officially known as the Center for Professional Education, located on the Fox River about 40 miles from the firm's Chicago headquarters. The former college campus had a one-hole golf course, running trails and gourmet food prepared by the same company that cooked for the Chicago Bears.

Over the ensuing 30 years, Mr. Malachuk saw the firm change to the point that making profits eventually dwarfed all else. He and other partners joked that the four cornerstones were really "three pebbles and a boulder."

Seeds for Demise

Although nobody knew it at the time, the seeds for Arthur Andersen's eventual demise were sown in 1950, when the firm introduced the "Glickiac" to the world. Named after its inventor, an Andersen engineer named Joseph Glickauf, the clunky device created a sensation by demonstrating that computers weren't just for scientists: Companies could use them to automate their bookkeeping. This ushered in an entirely new business. Rather than just audit the books, Andersen would set up the computers clients needed to keep the books. It wasn't long before Andersen boasted by far the largest technology practice of any accounting firm, raking in huge profits.

The flood of money introduced a new element of tension into the partnership. Under rules set by the auditors who ran the firm, all of the profits from all the practice areas had to go into one big pot to be divided among partners. But since the average consultant brought in more money than the average auditor, the consulting side complained the arrangement was unfair.

The week after New Year's Day in 1989, at a world-wide meeting of the firm in Dallas, the consultants finally made their break. They won an agreement to separate into two units -- Arthur Andersen and Andersen Consulting -- under a Geneva-based parent company known as Andersen Worldwide SC. But most importantly, the accounting side agreed to make the profit-sharing more equitable. Under a complex formula, the less profitable of the two firms would get a check for a small portion of the profits of the more profitable one.

The implications for the auditors were grim: Growth in the traditional accounting business was slowing because of competition, and audit fees were in a tailspin. Despite grueling hours, accountants' salaries were lagging behind those of other professionals such as lawyers and investment bankers. And they bridled at the thought of being eclipsed by the swashbuckling consultants. Under the accounting side's top partner, Richard Measelle, Arthur Andersen fought back. "It was a matter of pride," Mr. Measelle says.

To make sure auditors weren't just auditing, they began to be judged on how much new business they brought in. A superb auditor "who could not get a lick of business" was secure in the 1970s, says Mr. Measelle, who held the top post until 1997. But now, "their job security was a lot less."

Mr. Measelle believed he could boost sales while maintaining high auditing standards. But, he isn't sure both parts of his message got through. "I have to admit that there was this feeling that the No. 1 thing was to make your numbers and to make money," Mr. Measelle said, but "that wasn't what we were trying to do."

To cap costs, Andersen began requiring partners to retire at 56 years of age, enforcing a policy that was long overlooked. This made way for less-expensive -- and less-experienced -- partners. It created more revenue per partner -- in recent years, average partners made around $600,000 -- but left fewer partners overseeing audits.

"Though most auditors at Arthur Andersen are competent and honest," a longtime audit partner says, "a whole new breed was not steeped in new training and was far more focused on selling."

The auditors and the consultants competed fiercely, turning the annual race for profits into a devilish sport. In 1993, Arthur Andersen's cost-cutting efforts and some sales success combined with a weak market for the consultants to make the race even closer than usual. With just a few months left in the firm's fiscal year, the warring sides were neck and neck. So each swept around the office for expenses they could cut, revenue they could post. The auditors won -- and to commemorate drew up a poster that showed Mr. Measelle driving a car that was leaving Andersen Consulting in its dust.

In this competitive environment, Steve Samek emerged as a force within Andersen. A product of the gritty Chicago suburb of Cicero, Mr. Samek graduated from Southern Illinois University with an accounting degree and made partner at 32. Like most Andersen partners, he was clean-cut with a haircut looking as if it hadn't changed since he was six years old. But unlike many, Mr. Samek had a flair for the dramatic and loved the public stage. By the end of the decade, he would be running Andersen's entire U.S. operation and giving as many as 100 speeches a year.

As an auditor, he sometimes approved aggressive accounting tactics. In the early 1990s, Mr. Samek picked up a potentially lucrative client, a fast-growing restaurant chain called Boston Chicken. In auditing its books, he allowed the chain to keep details of losses at its struggling franchisees off its own financial statements as it groomed for a public offering. The IPO was a resounding success, soaring 143% in its first day of trading, and, for a time, Boston Chicken was a marquee client. Mr. Samek was rewarded for his work, getting praised in an internal performance review for turning "a $50,000 audit fee into a $3 million full-service engagement."

The system eventually collapsed and the company, by then called Boston Market Corp., filed for bankruptcy protection in 1998. Andersen had helped create a "facade of corporate solvency," according to a pending lawsuit filed last year in Phoenix federal district court by the company's bankruptcy trustee.

Mr. Samek, who left the account before the 1993 IPO, points out that the SEC approved of the accounting before the company went public. Mr. Dorton, the Andersen spokesman, says the lawsuit has no merit and that Boston Chicken's risky business plan was widely discussed in part because the company's financial statements had the appropriate disclosures.

Mr. Samek, now 49, rose quickly. In 1989, five years after he made partner, he was named to run a large portion of the firm's Chicago auditing practice overseeing about 350 people. In 1996, he became the firm's world-wide head of auditing, with indirect responsibility for 40,000 people. In the spring of 1998, he was put in charge of all of Andersen's U.S. operations, which account for about half of the firm's revenue.

Even as Mr. Samek tried to inspire the troops, problems with Andersen's audits began to mount. Andersen paid investors $110 million for its botched audits of Sunbeam, the home appliance maker that was caught artificially boosting revenues by offering retailers incentives to accept more product than they could sell. And in 1997, client Waste Management Inc. had the largest earnings restatement to date, wiping out $1.7 billion in profits that it pulled in through the 1990s.

'Rainmaker'

The lead auditor on Waste Management was Robert Allgyer, who was known inside the firm as "the Rainmaker" for his success in cross-selling extra services to auditing clients. He was clearly successful at selling to Waste Management, which paid $17.8 million in fees unrelated to the audit between 1991 and 1997, against audit fees of $7.5 million. But he was also signing off on drastically inaccurate books. Among other things, the fast-growing trash hauler wasn't properly writing off the value of assets such as garbage trucks as they aged, a ruse that pumped up reported profits.

The SEC's acting commissioner, Laura Unger, concluded that the agency had the "smoking gun" it was looking for to prove that the lure of consulting fees compromised auditor independence. The SEC filed suit in March 2002, accusing six former Waste Management executives of fraud. It alleges that Mr. Allgyer's judgment was skewed by consulting fees, in particular a $3.7 million "strategic overview" of Waste Management operations. The project lasted for 11 months, but the client didn't adopt the recommendations. One former Waste Management board member later described the project as a "boondoggle."

Soon enough, Andersen executives had another crisis to take their minds off Waste Management. Efforts to expand the accounting side of the business were petering out. By 1997, auditing and tax work brought in $1.8 billion, up just 12.5% from 1993, according to Bowman's Accounting Report, an industry newsletter.

Andersen Consulting, meanwhile, had rebounded strongly, more than doubling revenue to $3.1 billion during the period as companies around the world went on a spending spree to upgrade their computer systems. The consultants were now bringing in 58% of the overall firm's revenues, and subsidizing the accountants to the tune of about $150 million a year -- and complaining bitterly about it.

After a showdown in San Francisco in December 1997, Andersen Consulting partners voted unanimously to split off entirely. They filed an arbitration claim with the International Chamber of Commerce. The old Andersen had been building its own consulting practice, but it couldn't make up for the revenue it was about to lose.

Andersen by now was implementing a strategy to sell more audit work by handling far more than the traditional, once-a-year external audit of the public books. Now, it was pitching clients to outsource their internal bookkeeping operations.

Andersen's laboratory was Enron, an audit client since 1986. Andersen in the mid-1990s hired Enron's entire team of 40 internal auditors, added its own people and opened an office in Enron's Houston headquarters that was as big as some regional Arthur Andersen offices. With more than 150 people on-site, Andersen staff attended Enron meetings and helped shape new businesses, according to current and former Andersen and Enron employees.

The experiment came at a time when Andersen was becoming increasingly decentralized, with more and more power residing with local "office managing partners," each with their own revenue targets and balance sheets. At the same time, several members of the "Professional Standards Group" -- a panel of internal experts who handled tricky accounting questions -- had been moved from the Chicago headquarters to local offices to give clients quicker answers.

The thrust of both moves was to make it harder for auditors to fight back against clients who wanted to test the limits of accepted accounting standards. Enron, for example, represented just a small fraction of Andersen's revenues. But to David Duncan, who served as the lead auditor to the energy company, it was his livelihood.

Enron became so powerful that one Houston-based member of the Professional Standards Group complained that his advice against certain accounting practices was being ignored. The audit partner, Carl Bass, told Mr. Duncan that Enron should take a $30 million to $50 million accounting charge for a specific transaction. "The team apparently does not want to go back to the client on this," Mr. Bass said in a December 1999 e-mail to a colleague in Chicago that was obtained by congressional investigators. Four months later, Mr. Bass was removed from his Enron oversight role in response to complaints by Enron's chief accounting officer at the time, Richard A. Causey, about Mr. Bass's resistance to the company's financial-reporting practices. Mr. Causey's attorney didn't return calls seeking comment.

The Enron audit was part of a broader move by Andersen to reshape itself into a "New Economy" powerhouse offering a wide array of auditing services that their fast-growing clients needed.

A month after Mr. Samek's testimony, Arthur Andersen was crushed when an arbitrator ruled that the firm wouldn't receive a $14 billion payment it had been hoping for from the departing partners at Andersen Consulting, now known as Accenture Ltd. Arthur Andersen's CEO, Jim Wadia, resigned immediately.

SATYAM SCAM

When the 2008 recession hit the world, India was not only going through a financial crisis but also an ethical crisis. Imagine a hypothetical scenario in the stock market where the very basic financials provided to you by a company are manipulated. This was what happened with Satyam Computer Services. The Satyam scam was finally exposed early in 2009. Analysts dubbed the scam as India's own Enron.

The Flawless Public Façade

Satyam Computer Services Ltd was founded in 1987 in Hyderabad by brothers, Rama Raju and Ramalinga Raju (henceforth Raju). The name in the ancient Indian language Sanskrit meant 'Truth'. The firm began with 20 employees offering IT and BPO services across various sectors.

The initial success of the company soon led to it getting listed and opting for an IPO in the BSE in 1991. Post this the company soon got its first Fortune 500 client- Deere and Co. This further allowed the business to grow rapidly into becoming one of the top players in the market. Satyam soon became the fourth largest IT software exporter in the industry after TCS, Wipro, and Infosys.

At the peak of its success, Satyam employed more than 50,000 employees and operated in 60+ countries. Satyam was now seen as the prime example of an Indian Success story. Its financials too were perfect. The firm was worth $1billion in 2003. Satyam soon went on to cross the $2billion mark in 2008.

During this period the company had a CAGR of 40%, operating profits averaging 21% with a 300% increase in its stock price. Satyam was now an example to other companies as well. It was showered with accolades from MZ Consult for being a 'leader in Indian Corporate Governance and accountability, the 'Golden Peacock Award' for Corporate Accountability in 2008.

Mr Raju too was revered in the industry for his business acumen and was awarded the Ernest and Young Entrepreneur of the Year Award in 2008.

Late in 2008, the board of Satyam decided to takeover Maytas a real estate company owned by Mr Raju. This did not sit well with the shareholders which led to the decision being reversed in 12 hours, impacting the stock price. On December 23rd the World Bank barred Satyam from doing business with any of the banks' direct contacts for a period of 8 years.

This was one of the most severe penalties imposed by the World Bank against an Indian outsourcing company. The World Bank had alleged that Satyam had failed to maintain documentation to support fees charged to its subcontractors and the company also provided improper benefits to the banks' staff.

But were these allegations true? At this point, Satyam was India's crown jewel! Just 2 days later Satyam replied demanded the World Bank to explain itself and also apologize as its actions had damaged Satyam's investor confidence.

Satyam Scam: What was behind the Curtains?

As the investors were still coping up with the failed acquisition of Maytas and the allegations by the World Bank on January 7th, 2009 the markets received the resignation by Mr Raju and along with it a confession that he had manipulated accounts of Rs. 7000 crores. Investors and clients all around the World were left shocked. This just couldn't be happening!

In order to understand the scam, we would have to go back to 1999. Mr Raju had begun inflating the quarterly profits in order to meet the analyst expectations. For eg the results announced on October 17, 2009, overstated quarterly revenues by 75% and profits by 97%. Raju had done this along with the company's global head for internal audit.

Mr Raju used his personal computer to create a number of bank statements in order to inflate the balance sheet with cash that simply did not exist. The company's global head for internal audit created fake customer identities and fake invoices in order to inflate the revenue.

This, in turn, would allow the company easy access to loans and the impression of its success led to an increase in the share price. Also, the cash that the company had raised from the markets in the US never even made it to the balance sheets. But this was not sufficient for Raju, he went on to create records for fake employees and would withdraw salaries on their behalf.

The increased share price drove Raju to get rid of as many shares as possible and maintain just enough to be a part of the company. This allowed Raju to make profits from their sales at high prices. He also withdrew $3 million every month as salaries on behalf of employees that did not exist.

It was also rumoured that Raju knew the plan(route) for a metro that was to be built in Hyderabad. The foundation of the metro plans was laid in the year 2003. Raju soon diverted all the money into real estate with hopes to make a good profit once the metro was functional. He also set up a real estate company called Maytas.

But unfortunately, just like every other sector the real estate sector too was hit badly during the recession of 2008. By then almost a decade of manipulation of the financial statements had led to the hugely overstated assets and underreported liabilities. Nearly $1.04billion in bank loans and cash that the books showed was non-existent. The gap was simply too big to fill!

By now whistle blowing attempts were also starting to arise. Company director Krishna Palepu received anonymous emails from the alias Joseph Abraham. The mail exposed the fraud. Palepu forwarded it to another director and to S. Gopal krishnan a partner at PwC – their auditor.

Gopal krishnan assured Palepu that there were no truths in the mail and a presentation would be held before the audit committee in order to assure him on 29th December. The date was later revised to 10th January 2009.

Despite this Raju had a last resort. The plan included a takeover of Maytas by Satyam which would bridge the gap that had accumulated over the years. The new financials would justify that the cash had been used to purchase Maytas. But this plan was foiled after shareholder opposition.

This forced Raju to put himself at the mercy of the law. Raju later mentioned It was like riding a tiger, not knowing how to get off without being eaten.

Satyam Scam: How Raju was able to get away with the Scandal?

The next big question while studying this big scandal is how was Ramalinga Raju able to get away with the Satyam Scam in a company of over 50,000 employees?

The answer to this lies in the miserable failure of PriceWaterhouseCoopers(PwC) their auditor. PwC was the external auditors to the company and it was their duty to examine the financial records and ensure that they are accurate. It is surprising how they did not notice 7561 fake bills after auditing Satyam for almost 9 years. There were multiple red flags that the auditors could have caught upon. Firstly a simple check with the banks would have revealed that the bills were not valid and the cash balances were overstated. Secondly, any company with that big of cash reserves as Satyam would at least invest them in an interest yielding account. But that was not the case here. Despite these obvious signs, PwC seemed to be looking the other way. Suspicion towards PwC was later increased when it was found out that they were paid twice the fees for their services. PwC was not able to detect the fraud for almost 9 years but Merrill Lynch discovered the fraud as part of their due diligence in merely 10 days.

The Aftermath of Satyam Scam Exposure

Two days after the confession was made Raju was arrested and charged with criminal conspiracy, breach of trust, and forgery. The shares fell to Rs.11.50 on that day compared to heights of Rs.544 in 2008. The CBI raided the house of the youngest Raju sibling where 112 sales deeds to different land purchases were found. The CBI also found 13,000 fake employee records created in Satyam and claimed that the scam amounted to over Rs. 7000 crores.

PwC initially claimed that their failure to catch the fraud was due to the reliance placed by them on information provided by the management. PwC was found guilty and its license was temporarily revoked for 2 years. Investors too became vary of other companies audited by PwC. This resulted in the share prices of these companies falling by 5-15%. The news of the scam led to the Sensex falling by 7.3%

The Indian stock markets were now in turmoil. The Indian government realizing the impact this could have on the stock markets and future FDIs immediately spurted to action. They began investigating and quickly appointed a new board to Satyam. The board's goal was to sell the company within the next 100 days.

With this aim, the board appointed Goldman Sachs and Avendus Capital to help fast track the sale. SEBI appointed retired SC justice Barucha to oversee the transaction in order to instil trust. Several companies bid on April 13, 2009. The winning bid was placed by Tech Mahindra who went on to buy Satyam for 1/3rd of its value before the fraud was revealed.

On 4th November 2011, bail was granted to Raju and two others accused. In 2015 Raju, his 2 brothers, and 7 others were sentenced to 7 years in prison.

Closing Thoughts

There has been no scam that affected the CA and audit firms like the Satyam Scam. The increasing nature of these scams has made dependence on such professionals much more crucial highlighting the importance of ethics and CG in their roles.

White-collared crimes like these do not only make the company look bad but also the industry and the country

LEHMAN BROTHERS

Lehman Brothers filed for bankruptcy on September 15, 2008. Hundreds of employees, mostly dressed in business suits, left the bank's offices one by one with boxes in their hands. It was a sombre reminder that nothing is forever—even in the richness of the financial and investment world.

At the time of its collapse, Lehman was the fourth-largest investment bank in the United States with 25,000 employees worldwide. It had $639 billion in assets and $613 billion in liabilities. The bank became a symbol of the excesses of the 2007-08 Financial Crisis, engulfed by the subprime meltdown that swept through financial markets and cost an estimated $10 trillion in lost economic output.

Lehman Brothers History

Lehman Brothers had humble origins, tracing its roots to a general store founded by German brothers Henry, Emanuel and Mayer Lehman in Montgomery, Alabama, in 1844. Farmers paid for their goods with cotton, which led the company into the cotton trade. After Henry died, the other Lehman brothers expanded the scope of the business into commodities trading and brokerage services.[2]

The firm prospered over the following decades as the U.S. economy grew into an international powerhouse. But Lehman face plenty of challenges over the years. The company survived the railroad bankruptcies of the 1800s, the Great Depression, two world wars, a capital shortage when it was spun off by American Express (AXP) in 1994 in an initial public offering, and the Long Term Capital Management collapse and Russian debt default of 1998.[3]

Despite its ability to survive past disasters, the collapse of the U.S. housing market ultimately brought Lehman to its knees, as its headlong rush into the subprime mortgage market proved to be a disastrous step.

The Prime Culprit

The company, along with many other financial firms, branched into mortgage-backed securities and collateral debt obligations. In 2003 and 2004, with the U.S. housing bubble well under way, Lehman acquired five mortgage lenders along with BNC Mortgage and Aurora Loan Services, which specialized in Alt-A loans. These loans were made to borrowers without full documentation.[4]

At first, Lehman's acquisitions seemed prescient. Lehman's real estate business enabled revenues in the capital markets unit to surge 56% from 2004 to 2006. The firm securitized $146 billion of mortgages in 2006—a 10% increase from 2005. Lehman reported record profits every year from 2005 to 2007. In 2007, it announced $4.2 billion in net income on $19.3 billion in revenue.[4]

The Colossal Miscalculation

In February 2007, Lehman's stock price reached a record $86.18 per share, giving it a market capitalization of nearly $60 billion. But by the first quarter of 2007, cracks in the U.S. housing market were already becoming apparent. Defaults on subprime mortgages began to rise to a seven-year high. On March 14, 2007, a day after the stock had its biggest one-day drop in five years on concerns that rising defaults would affect Lehman's profitability, the firm reported record revenues and profit for its fiscal first quarter. Following the earnings report, Lehman said the risks posed by rising home delinquencies were well contained and would have little impact on the firm's earnings.

The Beginning of the End

Lehman's stock fell sharply as the credit crisis erupted in August 2007 with the failure of two Bear Stearns hedge funds. During that month, the company eliminated 1,200 mortgage- related jobs and shut down its BNC unit. It also closed offices of Alt-A lender Aurora in three states. Even as the correction in the U.S. housing market gained momentum, Lehman continued to be a major player in the mortgage market.

In 2007, Lehman underwrote more mortgage-backed securities than any other firm, accumulating an $85 billion portfolio, or four times its shareholders' equity. In the fourth quarter of 2007, Lehman's stock rebounded, as global equity markets reached new highs and prices for fixed-income assets staged a temporary rebound. However, the firm did not take the opportunity to trim its massive mortgage portfolio, which in retrospect, would turn out to be its last chance.[5]

Hurling Toward Failure

In 2007, Lehman's high degree of leverage was 31, while its large mortgage securities portfolio made it highly susceptible to the deteriorating market conditions. On March 17, 2008, due to concerns that Lehman would be the next Wall Street firm to fail following Bear Stearns' near-collapse, its shares plummeted nearly 48%.

By April, after an issue of preferred stock—which was convertible into Lehman shares at a 32% premium to its concurrent price—yielded $4 billion, confidence in the firm returned somewhat.[7] However, the stock resumed its decline as hedge fund managers began to question the valuation of Lehman's mortgage portfolio.

On June 7, 2008, Lehman announced a second-quarter loss of $2.8 billion, its first loss since it was spun off by American Express, and reported that it raised another $6 billion from investors by June 12.[5] According to David P. Belmont, "The firm also said it boosted its liquidity pool to an estimated $45 billion, decreased gross assets by $147 billion, reduced its exposure to residential and commercial mortgages by 20%, and cut down leverage from a factor of 32 to about 25."

Too Little, Too Late

These measures were perceived as being too little, too late. Over the summer, Lehman's management made unsuccessful overtures to a number of potential partners. The stock plunged 77% in the first week of September 2008, amid plummeting equity markets worldwide, as investors questioned CEO Richard Fuld's plan to keep the firm independent by selling part of its asset management unit and spinning off commercial real estate assets. Hopes that the Korea Development Bank would take a stake in Lehman were dashed on September 9, as the state-owned South Korean bank put talks on hold.

The devastating news lead to a 45% drop in Lehman's stock, along with the firm's debt suffering a 66% increase in credit-default swaps. Hedge fund clients began abandoning the company, with short-term creditors following suit. Lehman's fragile financial position was best emphasized by the pitiful results of its September 10 fiscal third-quarter report.

Facing a $3.9 billion loss, which included a $5.6 billion write-down, the firm announced an extensive strategic corporate restructuring effort. Moody's Investor Service also announced that it was reviewing Lehman's credit ratings, and it found that the only way for Lehman to avoid a rating downgrade would be to sell a majority stake to a strategic partner. By September 11, the stock had suffered another massive plunge (42%) due to these developments.

With only $1 billion left in cash by the end of that week, Lehman was quickly running out of time. Over the weekend of September 13, Lehman, Barclays, and Bank of America (BAC) made a last-ditch effort to facilitate a takeover of the former, but they were ultimately unsuccessful.[7] On Monday, September 15, Lehman declared bankruptcy, resulting in the stock plunging 93% from its previous close on September 12.

Lehman stock plunged 93% between the close of trading on September 12, 2008, and the day it declared bankruptcy.

Where are They Now?

Former chair and CEO Richard Fuld runs Matrix Private Capital Group, which he founded in 2016. The company manages assets for high-net worth individuals, family offices and institutions.[9] He reportedly sold an apartment in New York City for $25.9 million as well as a collection of drawings for $13.5 million.

In years following the collapse, Fuld acknowledged the mistakes the bank made though he remained critical of the government for mandating that Lehman Brothers file for bankruptcy while bailing out others. In 2010, he told the Financial Crisis Inquiry Commission the bank had adequate capital reserves and a solid business at the time of its bankruptcy.

Erin Callan (now Erin Montella) became chief financial officer at the age of 41 and resigned in June 2008 following suspicions she had leaked information to the press. Her LinkedIN profile lists her as an advisor at Matrix Investment Holdings. Other stints include six months serving as head of hedge fund coverage for Credit Suisse and co-founding a non-profit that provides paid maternity leave to mothers. In 2016, Montella published an autobiography, *Full Circle: A Memoir of Leaning in Too Far and the Journey Back*, about her experiences in the financial world.

The Bottom Line

Lehman's collapse roiled global financial markets for weeks, given its size and status in the U.S. and globally. At its peak, Lehman had a market value of nearly $46 billion, which was wiped out in the months leading up to its bankruptcy.[1]

Many questioned the decision to allow Lehman to fail, compared with the government's tacit support for Bear Stearns, which was acquired by JPMorgan Chase (JPM) in March 2008. Bank of America had been in talks to buy Lehman, but backed away after the government refused to help with Lehman's most troubled assets. Instead, Bank of America announced it would buy Merrill Lynch on the same.

KINGFISHER AIRLINES

Vijay Vittal Mallya was born in Bantwal, Karnataka, on 18th December 1955 to Vittal Mallya, who was a successful businessman and chairman of the United Breweries (UB) Group, and Lalitha Ramaiah Mallya. He graduated from St. Xavier's College, Kolkata, with a B.com degree in 1976. At the age of 27, he became the chairman of UB Group, which is a conglomerate company most famous for its selling of beer and liquor, after his father's death. While he was very young and inexperienced for the position, the employees, who were working from his father's time and were much experienced than him, believed from the beginning that he is not an ordinary young man and would take the company to the next level of success, which later became true. Initially, the turnover of the company was at Rs. 350 crores at the time of his father. With his consistent hard work and determination, the company's valuation rose from Rs. 40 crores to Rs. 6,000 crores. In 2007, Forbes magazine declared him as the 40th richest man in India. It was the golden moment for him.

He, further, tried to expand his business by investing in different sectors such as the newspaper, chemical industry, and the engineering sector. However, he learned that the most profiting business was the selling of beer and liquor; hence, he only focused on it. He ambitioned to expand his business globally. Consequently, his company spread over 57 countries, and in 2015, it became the second-largest selling of beer and liquor brand in the world and received a doctorate in 'Business Administration' from the University of Southern California.

Strategy for promotion

The Indian Ministry of Health (IMH) conducted research and found that the consumption of cigarettes, liquor, and beer is extensively harmful to health. Therefore, it imposed a complete ban on advertisement and branding for its promotion. On 8th September 2008, Cable Television Network (Regulation) Amendment Bill was passed by the parliament, which prohibits the advertisement of beer and liquor in India.

However, India, which is the second-largest populous country in the world with approximately 1.3 billion people, is a good source of money for the business of selling alcoholic beverages. So, the companies use the surrogate methods for its advertisement and branding such as displaying it in movie scenes and T.V. shows in the name of soda. Similarly, Vijay Mallya used different ways to promote his brand, named Kingfisher. He kept the name of his residence as the 'Kingfisher Villa,' hence, whenever his house was shown on the news, ultimately, the brand was promoted. Moreover, he started sponsoring events and bought one of the IPL teams named 'Royal Challengers Bangalore,' to promote the Kingfisher liquor brand. This enabled him to become the second-largest brand in the world.

Establishment of Airline

On 9th May 2005, Vijay Mallya launched the Kingfisher Airlines (KFA). It was a completely new experience for him to have a business in the aviation industry. He had the same ambition of expanding KFA to a global level as his initial business. For this, he ensured luxurious facilities for flight passengers. According to him, the passengers should be treated like his guests, and nobody should go with a disappointed after using their flight.[5]Gradually, it became the most luxurious and the second-largest domestic flight in India, having one-fourth share of domestic travellers of India.

As soon as he received success in domestic airline services, he aspired to achieve the same for the international flights. According to the then 5/20 rule by the Indian Ministry of Civil Aviation, the criteria for having a business of international flights was a minimum requirement of five-year experience in domestic service and twenty airplanes for international flights.[6]To expand KFA at a global level, he had to wait for another three years for eligibility.

Adverse decisions

However, he did not want to wait for that long. He became impatient and hence, decided to buy an airline company that is already eligible for international service. Accordingly, he bought Air Deccan, which was known for its low-cost airline service in India. Both KFA and Air Deccan were very distinct airlines and had no link with each other, as one was the most luxurious, the other was the cheapest. This created a pressure on him to manage the services at low budget. His vision for the business was, "Only Expansion, No Profitability."

The name of Air Deccan was changed to'King fisher Red.' He categorised the two airlines based on facilities provided. The passengers who desired to travel in a luxurious flight would opt for Kingfisher Airlines, whereas those who wanted to travel at low fares would opt for Kingfisher Red Airlines. However, the facilities of Kingfisher Red were no less to KFA. As compared to the other low fare airlines, Kingfisher Red had many lavish facilities. The passengers became happier with Kingfisher Red than KFA due to good facilities at a lower cost.

Soon, the market stake of KFA started declining, and the operative cost began turning into debts. To balance the situation, he increased the fare cost of Kingfisher Red. It resulted in passengers to leave even that airline, and they diverted towards other cheaper airline services. Consequently, Vijay Mallya started experiencing a great deal of loss in his airline business. There were three main reasons for the failure;

1. due to an increase in ticket prices,
2. inflation of fuel in the market, and
3. due to economic slowdown, also known as a recession, in 2008.

Impact of downfall

His airline business was in downfall. Due to the non-recovery of landing charges, some of the airport hubs such as Bangalore and Hyderabad International airports changed specific policies for KFA and Kingfisher Red airlines that they have to pay first and then only they could land their flights on their airports.

Moreover, he was also banned from buying fuel from two prominent Indian oil and natural gas companies, namely, Hindustan Petroleum (HP) and Bharat Petroleum, due to his already existing vast due charges. Besides, the Indian Oil company did agree to provide fuel but on a cash basis, which means after the full payment of fuel in advance.[7]This was because they all lost faith from Vijay Mallya that he would pay on time.

Foreign Direct Investment

Since it became challenging to manage the business, he decided to contact foreign companies for their investment in his business. This seemed a possible solution for his financial crisis. Accordingly, he managed to convince one foreign airline company named Etihad Airways to invest in Kingfisher Airline. However, until 2012, it was not allowed in India to have a Foreign Direct Investment (FDI) in airlines sector. The airline industry was 100% domestically owned business during that time.

This became another obstacle for Vijay Mallya. He then decided to convince the government of India to alter specific policies as he was facing financial distress. He eventually applied for an application. Nevertheless, since it was entirely a government work, it took much time for its approval. Meanwhile, he got himself engaged in the work of making Kingfisher Calendars and focused on taking auditions of the models for the same.

Consequently, he could not pay the salaries to his airline employees due to his downfall and busy schedule. After several months of the strike, the employees started leaving the job and joined other airline companies as it was not digestible for them to know that despite saying that it is a bad phase, Vijay Mallya was busy taking the auditions of the models. Following that, the Kingfisher airlines got closed. In December 2012, the government also cancelled its license.

Support from banks

The last possible option which he was left with was taking the loan from the banks. He specifically targeted Public Sector Undertaking (PSU) Banks, which are government-owned banks. He ended up taking a loan from seventeen different banks, out of which the majority were PSU banks. Private banks were reluctant to give him a loan. However, the two banks, namely, HDFC and ICICI banks, gave the loan to the UB Group against the securities of United Spirits Limited, and later they recovered their money by selling the shares.

Debt restructuring fraud

After receiving loans in dense masses, he applied for a scheme called 'debt restructuring,' which is a process where the debts of a financially distressed company, who are incapable of repaying, are renegotiated and reduced to restore bank liquidity. In this case, the debt was converted into equity, which means to wave off the debt, and instead, the company would give its shares to the bank upto the value of debt. The shares of KFA was valued at Rs. 64.49,whereas it was trading at Rs. 39.90 in the market. The justification given by Vijay Mallya was that since they have a bad phase in their business, the market trading value is decreased to Rs. 40, otherwise the real valuation was of Rs. 65. However, it was later found that their all-time high value of the share was Rs. 48. Indirectly, he was trying to wave off his debts.

Political Connection

The reason behind the PSU banks giving loans to Vijay Mallya, despite his dooming business and low credibility, was because he was a member of Rajya Sabha (Upper House) and had good political connections.[8]It resulted in banks officials to get involved in the landmark kingfisher scam. The banks were pressurized by the government officials to grant him the loan. Due to this reason, SBI Bangalore granted a loan of about Rs. 1,600 crores to him.

Moreover, according to the banking norms, when a certain amount of loan is given to a person, and if he wantsfunds beyond thatlimit, then a 'No Objection Certificate' (NOC) is required. Initially, SBI bank was not ready to grant him this certificate as there were already existing debts against him. However, it was exposed that P. Chidambaram, the then Finance Minister of India, helped him in getting the loans. Hence, SBI did a meeting, loosened their policies and granted him NOC under pressure.

Left India

On 2nd March 2016, Vijay Mallya got into many negotiations with banks. When the debt amount rose to Rs. 9,000 crores including interest rate, he asserted that he is ready to pay Rs. 6,000 crores, which was just the principal amount. He demanded to wave off all the interest amount. However, the banks wanted the full recovery of debt. In the meantime, he escaped from India and got settled in Britain. Today, he is in the 'Wanted List of India' for his wilful default, and since he is residing in a foreign country, he could not be presented before the court.

Allegations

The section 82(1) of Criminal Procedure Code, 1973 (CrPC) providesthat if any person prevents himself from the execution of a warrant, the court may write a proclamation requiring him to be present at the mentioned place within thirty days of that proclamation. Further, section 82(4) of CrPC provides that if the person does not comply with section 82(1), he would be classified as a 'proclaimed offender.'

On 18th April 2016, a non-bailable warrant was issued against Vijay Mallya by the Enforcement Directorate (ED), as he was accused of not recovering bank debts. He was required to appear at a specified location, but he never came. Despite calling him several times by the ED, he avoided to appear and instead asserted that all the allegation against him are made-up. Due to this kind of behaviour, he was categorised as a 'proclaimed offender.'

1. to have good faith and to act in the best interest in terms of obtaining business outcomes and employees respectively,
2. to exercise his duties with reasonable care, skill and diligence, and to use his judgements independently,
3. to avoid circumstances which may conflict with the interest of the company, and
4. to avoid any unjustified gains, the breach of it would amount to a fine equal to that gain.

Vijay Mallya was also charged under section 166 of the said act due to the following reasons;
1. he failed to exercise his fiduciary duties to his employees, shareholders and investors,
2. he compromised corporate ethics while buying the Deccan Airlines,
3. he paid Rs 30 crores to the owner of Deccan Airline named G.R. Gopinath, without letting his shareholders know, which showed how little he cared for his shareholders and created suspicion of dishonesty, and
4. he misused his power and connections to get a loan from banks.

Changes after the Kingfisher Scam

Following the Kingfisher scam, the Central Vigilance Commission (CVC) directed the PSU banks to make the loan verification more robust and stricter by hiring consultancies or by setting up a new division for the second time verification of the documents based on which the loans are granted by the banks. Moreover, SBI affirmed to protect the bank's interest and public money after the lessons learned from the kingfisher scam.

The aftermath of Kingfisher Scam

Since Vijay Mallya is one the persons in the 'wanted list of India,' he had tried to convince government officials, presently Bhartiya Janta Party (BJP) is the ruling political party. However, he is not able to. Recently, on the social media (twitter) platform, he offered to pay the 100% debt to the banks. All his attempts to persuade the government have been in vain.

Ultimately, the general public is the one who suffers from the loss caused by the kingfisher scam since it was their hard-earned money collected by the government as tax for the welfare of everyone. Hence, instead of tying-up with the business tycoons in financial frauds, government officials must prevent it by saying 'no' to corruption.

Satyam Computer Services Ltd was founded in 1987 in Hyderabad by brothers, Rama Raju and Ramalinga Raju (henceforth Raju). As the investors were still coping up with the failed acquisition of Maytas and the allegations by the World Bank on January 7th, 2009 the markets received the resignation by Mr Raju and along with it a confession that he had manipulated accounts of Rs. 7000 crores. Mr Raju used his personal computer to create a number of bank statements in order to inflate the balance sheet with cash that simply did not exist. There has been no scam that affected the CA and audit firms like the Satyam Scam. The increasing nature of these scams has made dependence on such professionals much more crucial highlighting the importance of ethics and CG in their roles.

Ultimately, the general public is the one who suffers from the loss caused by the kingfisher scam since it was their hard-earned money collected by the government as tax for the welfare of everyone. Hence, instead of tying-up with the business tycoons in financial frauds, government officials must prevent it by saying 'no' to corruption.

REFERENCE

1. COSO. (2017). Internal Control-Integrated Framework. John Wiley & Sons.
2. Gao, J., & Yuan, Y. (2018). Auditing and corporate governance. Springer.
3. Knechel, W. R., & Salterio, S. E. (2018). Auditing: assurance and risk. Routledge.
4. Simnett, R., & Carcello, J. V. (2019). Auditing and assurance services: an integrated approach. Cengage Learning.
5. Smith, K. L., & Smith, K. (2018). Corporate governance and accountability. John Wiley & Sons.
6. Solomon, J., & Turner, J. (2018). Corporate governance and accountability. John Wiley & Sons.
7. Beasley, M. S., Buckless, F. A., Glover, S. M., & Prawitt, D. F. (2018). Auditing & assurance services: a systematic approach. McGraw-Hill Education.
8. Carcello, J. V., & Neal, T. L. (2019). Auditing and assurance services: an integrated approach. Cengage Learning.
9. COSO. (2013). Enterprise Risk Management-Integrated Framework. John Wiley & Sons.
10. DeFond, M. L., & Subramanyam, K. R. (2018). Auditing: a business risk approach. John Wiley & Sons.
11. Gao, J., & Yuan, Y. (2018). Auditing and corporate governance. Springer.
12. Knechel, W. R., & Salterio, S. E. (2018). Auditing: assurance and risk. Routledge.
13. Simnett, R., & Carcello, J. V. (2019). Auditing and assurance services: an integrated approach. Cengage Learning.
14. Smith, K. L., & Smith, K. (2018). Corporate governance and accountability. John Wiley & Sons.
15. Solomon, J., & Turner, J. (2018). Corporate governance and accountability. John Wiley & Sons.
16. Beasley, M. S., Buckless, F. A., Glover, S. M., & Prawitt, D. F. (2018). Auditing & assurance services: a systematic approach. McGraw-Hill Education.
17. Carcello, J. V., & Neal, T. L. (2019). Auditing and assurance services: an integrated approach. Cengage Learning.
18. COSO. (2013). Enterprise Risk Management-Integrated Framework. John Wiley & Sons.
19. DeFond, M. L., & Subramanyam, K. R. (2018). Auditing: a business risk approach. John Wiley & Sons.

20. Gao, J., & Yuan, Y. (2018). Auditing and corporate governance. Springer.
21. Knechel, W. R., & Salterio, S. E. (2018). Auditing: assurance and risk. Routledge.
22. Simnett, R., & Carcello, J. V. (2019). Auditing and assurance services: an integrated approach. Cengage Learning.
23. Smith, K. L., & Smith, K. (2018). Corporate governance and accountability. John Wiley & Sons.
24. Solomon, J., & Turner, J. (2018). Corporate governance and accountability
25. Solomon, J., & Turner, J. (2020). Corporate governance text and cases

9 788819 606342 9